Ballot Box to Jury Box

The Life and Times of an English Crown Court Judge

Ballot Box to Jury Box
The Life and Times of an English Crown Court Judge

Published 2006 by
WATERSIDE PRESS
Domum Road
Winchester SO23 9NN
Telephone 01962 855567 UK Local-call 0845 2300 733
Fax 01962 855567
E-mail enquiries@watersidepress.co.uk

ISBN 1 904 380 19 0

Catalogue-in-Publication Data A catalogue record for this book can be obtained from the British Library

Cover design Waterside Press. Main cover photograph by Zachari Macaulay

Printing and binding Antony Rowe Ltd, Chippenham and Eastbourne

North American distributors Sole agents: International Specialised Book Services (ISBS), 920 NE 58th Ave, Suite 300, Portland, Oregon, 97213-3786, USA
Telephone 1 800 944 6190 Fax 1 503 280 8832 orders@isbs.com www.isbs.com

Ballot Box to Jury Box

The Life and Times of an English Crown Court Judge

John Baker

To Sybil.

With every good wish

from

John Baker

WATERSIDE PRESS

Acknowledgements

Much of the source material for this book comes from press cuttings collected by my late mother, Dora Rolston. The dates of political activities and legal cases were all recorded and the material itself was of the greatest help to me. I knew nothing about this until shortly before she died.

I am also grateful to Francis Bennett, author and publisher, who gave me much useful advice on how to write a book and read a number of my early drafts.

Then, Ray Foster, who was with me at Kingston Crown Court for over twenty years ending up as Chief Clerk (now called 'Court Manager'!), gave me great help over cases there and the building of the new Crown Court.

I am also indebted to Bryan Gibson of Waterside Press and his assistant, Jane Green, who took great trouble to edit and re-edit my typescript, making many helpful suggestions about phrasing and style.

My wife, Joy, read with great patience all that I had written, making many helpful criticisms and corrections, but any errors that remain are solely my responsibility.

Then my English master at Wellington School, Somerset and a former Leicester, Cambridge and England scrum-half, Jim Parsons, who was has given me firmer encouragement each time we have met at Lords to complete the book before he gets much older. I have a feeling he wants to mark it out of ten and make a comment which I hope will be generous!

Finally, as I have looked back, I have realised that there are many people with whom I have lost contact and I have wondered what has happened to them. If any of these would like to get in touch with me, would they please do so through the National Liberal Club, Whitehall Place, London SW1 2HE - and I will do my best to reply quickly.

John Baker

October 2005

Ballot Box to Jury Box
The Life and Times of an English Crown Court Judge

CONTENTS

Acknowledgements *iv*

CHAPTER

About the author

His Honour John Baker was born in Calcutta and educated at Plymouth College, Wellington School, Somerset and Wadham College, University of Oxford where he was Treasurer of the Oxford Union in 1948.

He was admitted as a solicitor in 1951 and became a partner with Amery Parkes and Co where he worked on the pioneering scheme to provide legal advice to members of the Automobile Association. He then became a partner in Goodman Derrick and Co specialising in libel, copyright and franchising of the early independent television stations, before switching to the Bar in 1960 – where he joined the chambers of the Sir Dingle Foot QC, MP. He became a Crown Court Recorder in 1972 and a circuit judge in 1973, being appointed resident judge at Kingston-upon-Thames Crown Court (1982-1998), Liaison Judge for Magistrates and the Probation Service and chair of the Lord Chancellor's Advisory Committee on the appointment of Justices of the Peace for South West London. He also sat as a Deputy High Court Judge.

Beyond these roles, John Baker was a regular broadcaster on radio and television including on legal matters and televised debates. An active member of the Liberal party from his student days, he stood three times for Parliament in the General Elections of 1959, 1964 and 1970 and was chair of the Liberal Party Committees on Co-partnership in Industry and Broadcasting as well as a Trustee of the National Liberal Club for three years from 2000.

Having now left both the ballot box and jury box behind, John Baker lives in Richmond, south-west London with his wife Joy.

CHAPTER 1

From Calcutta to Oxford

At first, I did not like the expression "mission statement". I thought it was rather grandiose and pretentious. Then, as I came across it more often, I realized that it was not only useful but summed up rather well an aim or object in doing something. So I thought I would invoke it now because I want to give some reasons for writing this book. They go beyond just something to occupy my time and keep my mind ticking over during my retirement.

The main reason is that I have become increasingly annoyed at the derisory way that Judges are portrayed and referred to in the press. They are considered to be a bunch of Oxbridge graduates who come from privileged backgrounds, who have never known hardship, live narrow lives frequenting London clubs, know little about how the majority of people are brought up and live, and are quoted as making rather ignorant and stupid remarks. Of course, some of these criticisms contain grains of truth but one criticism has changed over the years. Judges used to be drawn as short tempered old sadists who relished ordering men to be flogged and boys to be caned and put the black cap on their wigs with enthusiasm when about to pass the death sentence. Nowadays, they are drawn as liberal softies who let the public down and fail to send criminals to prison for lengthy periods. Hence such headlines as, "Rapist Walks Free from Court".

I shall try and show where I think the truth of all this lies and I shall do this from my own experience because I have had a fortunate but in some ways, unusual life before I was appointed to be a Circuit Judge. I am going to spend some time dealing with my early life when the unusual side played a big part.

•   •   •

I have always taken a keen interest in the press and cannot remember when I did not try and read a newspaper so I have been interested to find out, when looking for material about my beginnings, that two newspaper notices about my birth are contradictory concerning the date!

According to a Calcutta paper, I was born on 5th November, 1925 but according to the *Western Morning News* — who stated they had the information by cable — I was born on the 6th. My mother, who should know, used to say that I was born at 5.30 a.m. local time on the 5th. So I always have been a Guy Fawkes. This is a useless day on which to have a birthday, especially in the early years, as a good proportion of my presents literally went up in smoke!

My mother had gone to India in 1924 after her marriage in Stoke Damerell Church, Devonport in Plymouth. I know very little about my father except that he was born in India as was his father who was an engineer who helped build the Bengal Railway. These Indian births were to cause me some problems after Independence in 1947. My father was a broker in the jute business which existed between Dundee, Scotland and Calcutta. Apparently, he was good at memorising figures but much liked the social life and sport, especially cricket. He got into debt and received a warning from his firm who paid off his debts,

Mine was a difficult birth and my mother came back to Devonport when I was six months old. When the *SS Mantola* arrived, we were the first off and I went into the arms of my maternal grandfather, Henry Herbert Swiss, who was to play a very important part in my life.

My father did not join us for some time and my only memory of him is playing with a Hornby train with my cousin Stuart Earl, later a dentist and exactly four years older than me, at the end of the lounge in my grandparents' house at 7 Somerset Place, Devonport which fortunately survived the bombing during the Second World War. I was either three or four years old.

The world economic depression had begun and my father was out of work. He went to Canada to find employment. Shortly afterwards, he sent a bombshell letter to my mother saying that they had never really got on and they should get divorced. My mother wrote to him and thought he had gone out of his mind but the situation did not change. I never saw him again and I do not think that my mother ever recovered from the shock despite her re-marriage in October 1940. She wanted to expunge the memory of my father from her life and was always reluctant to talk about him to me. She once said, "The mention of his name gives me a nasty jolt", but a curious incident was to follow in the summer of 1940. 1 picked up a few snippets, for example, about his Military Cross in the First World War when he was an officer in the Ghurkas. He never made any financial provision for me. My grandfather did not think it would be worthwhile to pursue him in Canada. He never wrote me a letter or remembered my birthday.

My grandfather took on the responsibility for my education which he faithfully discharged until I was admitted as a solicitor in October 1951 – when he came with my mother to the ceremony at the Law Society in Chancery Lane. He was not a man of great wealth, a master printer who had a printing works, a retail shop and the bookstall at the Royal Naval Barracks in Devonport. He believed in education and paid the fees and expenses for his two sons, Rodney and Kenneth, both of whom became Presidents of the British Dental Association, as did Kenneth's son Peter in 2001, thus setting a record for one family. I was never pressurised to follow them and felt quite free to choose my own career which as you can see I did.

My mother went to good schools in Devonport and then boarded in Bournemouth. She was going to Louvain in Belgium but this was prevented by the outbreak of the First World War. She was always aggrieved that she was turned down for one school in Devonport because her father was not a professional man but "in trade". Her friend was accepted though, as her father ran a shop that sold *pianos and music*. Class distinction sometimes has fine boundaries!

My mother divorced my father and had to go to London for the hearing by a High Court judge even though the suit was undefended. In those days, divorce carried a social stigma even for the so-called innocent party and, having a young son, she led a rather isolated life. She had few friends of either sex. Her position was made much worse because at this time my grandfather left my grandmother – I believe for another woman. They were never divorced and he supported her generously for some thirty years. The family home in Devonport was sold and I left with my mother and my grandmother to go to a flat right next to Plymouth Hoe in Leigham Street. About fifty years later, when I was a Circuit Judge and asked to sit in the Crown Court at Plymouth, I stayed at what was then the Mayflower Hotel and the car park was on the site of the flat which had been demolished in the Second World War.

Being about five years old, I started going to the Hoe Grammar School which was within walking distance. Boys could go there until school leaving age which was then fourteen, and beyond. The school buildings were a series of converted houses in Lockyer Street together with some houses in adjoining streets. The school was founded in 1867 in a house in Lockyer Street and twenty years later it was acquired by Mr G. P. Dymond, then aged 23. He remained the headmaster until he died in September, 1939. It was carried on by his family but only until March, 1941 when it was severely damaged in two air raids. It was never rebuilt and did not start up anywhere else. Yet the Old Boys, known as Old Drakonians after Sir Francis Drake, remained in existence holding regular functions in Plymouth and London until a final lunch at the Grand Hotel, Plymouth in September 2000 which my wife and I attended. There were about seventy-five present including some half-a-dozen members of the Dymond family.

G. P. Dymond was more than a successful schoolmaster. He was a Liberal and a Methodist who was fully active in civic life becoming an alderman and then mayor of Plymouth. His school was there to teach the basics: reading, writing and arithmetic were prominent with great attention to detail especially in English grammar and spelling, helped by such jingles as: "i before e, except after c". I was anxious to do well. I had to tell my grandfather how I was getting on and though I did not fear him, I was anxious not to upset him. As a businessman, he would not like to feel that his money was being wasted.

My mother did not overprotect me. I was never conscious of the lack of a male influence at home. When people, including other boys, asked where my father was, I just used to say that he had "gone away". This was not unusual on a temporary basis in Plymouth where there were many service families who had separations.

From early times, I was no good at sport. This would have been an enormous disappointment to my father. I could never run and was nearly always last in every race. To my mother's annoyance, I was Christened John Arnold after a double international who played both football and cricket for England. I used to read avidly about his career, summarised on the back of a cigarette card.

Perhaps it was because of my lack of success that I followed sport with enthusiasm, particularly the local soccer club, Plymouth Argyle. I seldom saw them but I read as much as I could in the newspapers and kept a scrap book. I knew the names of all the players and recall them from 1935. Players did not change clubs as much as they do now. The defenders remained the same, except for injuries, for several seasons. They were: Cann (goalkeeper); Roberts and Rae (full backs); Gorman, McNeill, Black (T) (half backs). The forwards chopped and changed except for the most outstanding player, the outside left, Sammy Black who scored many goals from acute angles. The local papers, year after year, talked about him playing for Scotland but he never even had a trial. Plymouth is a long way from Scotland though two trains left North Road Station every day at 8. 35 a.m. and 8. 40 a.m.: one for Glasgow and the other for Edinburgh.

First team Argyle footballers got £8, £9 or £10 per week during the season according to the match result, while the reserves got less, I think from £4 to £6. It has always surprised and disappointed me that a city the size of Plymouth never had First Division football in the old days let alone the Premiership today. Much football is played in Devon and Cornwall but local talent has seldom blossomed. When it has, the player moves to a more prestigious club and I think Argyle must get nearly all the money which they need to keep going from fees paid for transfers—at least in the past. Raymond Bowden went to Arsenal and Paul Marriner to Ipswich. Both played for England.

Football had more class divisions than today. Soccer was the national game that attracted the big crowds of "ordinary people". The crowds were bigger than today except for the great clubs like Manchester United and Liverpool who have supporters' clubs all over the world. In Plymouth, the pre-war average gate would be about fifteen thousand. I recall them playing Southampton in the old Division Two in the late nineteen-thirties when nothing was at stake for either club, and the crowd of 8,000 was considered to be disappointing.

Rugby Union football, in contrast to soccer, was an amateur game basically played and followed by middle class and upper class people, though not in Wales or in Cornwall. This has been summarised by the jingle: "Soccer is a gents' game played by roughs; rugger is a rough game played by gents". Compared with soccer, there were fewer spectators and the gates were generally smaller than in the lower divisions of league football. There were no leagues or points systems in rugger. Most public schools played rugger though there were some exceptions such as Harrow and Repton.

The two local rugger clubs were Plymouth Albion and Devonport Services. They both had first class fixtures though they seldom beat top class clubs like Cardiff and Leicester who liked to visit the Westcountry on Easter tours. Sometimes my mother used to take me to watch Devonport Services who were predominantly a Naval side. I do not know why she went except to get me interested in something manly. She did not have any friend she wanted to see and I do not remember going with anybody else, even another boy. She did once comment to her own mother that she could tell the officers from the "men" by their features! I remember two "men" who were outstanding. Able Seaman Knapman, the full back, and Marine Webb, a second row forward who was capped for England—which was quite a feat and showed that the Westcountry was not entirely overlooked as the press often claimed. They played for several years and were clearly not sent to sea during the winter months!

The outstanding match I saw in Devonport was in 1935 between the New Zealand All Blacks and a combined Devon and Cornwall side. The visitors won easily. Their captain was called Joe Manchester, whose hair was parted in the middle, which I imitated when I got home but only for one day! Both Services and Hospital rugby have declined and this took place before professionalism came to Rugby Union in the nineteen-nineties. There may be a number of reasons such as the increase of other leisure attractions and increased pressure on studies and getting qualifications and promotion.

Hoe Grammar School had a gym but no other outdoor facilities nearby. I do not remember playing any organised games there though I did join the Cubs and had some outdoor activities from that.

For reasons that I never knew, we changed flats with some frequency. It is certainly not that my grandfather quibbled at paying the rent. Looking back on it, I think that both my mother and grandmother were most unsettled after the failure of their marriages. They did not take any embitteredness out on me but, if my father was mentioned, it was with scorn and derision. I must have been curious about him and whether I was going to see him again.

Psychology and psychiatry were in their infancy and somewhat derided so there was never any suggestion of having what today is called counselling. Anyway, I doubt if I needed it as I was always a busy, active child and eager to learn all sorts of things.

We moved from Leigham Street to Osborne Place where there were houses on only one side of the road. It faced East and looked across the famous bowling green on Plymouth Hoe. I always thought that if Francis Drake did ever play bowls, it could not have been there as he would never have been able to see the Spanish Armada! Some people say he was probably never on the Hoe at all but with his ships at Stonehouse Harbour. I hope there is no further evidence that will destroy the legend—which does make some sense because if the Spaniards were coming up the Channel with a westerly wind behind them, Drake with his smaller ships would have wanted to wait and get astern of them.

Beyond the Hoe, our flat looked over to the Citadel and the old Aquarium where my great aunt's sister worked. This was useful as when I went there I used to say that I wanted to see her and got in free! She was called Amy Clark and lived with her sister, Ada, and a cousin called Ethel Byford. All three were regular chapel goers and never a drop of alcohol passed their lips—or so they thought! For a number of years we used to go to their house for Christmas. Apart from myself, Uncle Arthur, Ada's husband, was the only male present. When we arrived, it was always explained that they were teetotal. We appreciated that and then, during the day, they would further explain that they had been out and collected elderberries. They were great walkers on Dartmoor. From the elderberries they had made wine. It would have been stored for about three months and was clearly pretty potent but we never told them so!

One incident I shall always remember whilst living at Osborne Place was that one evening I was playing a scratch game of cricket on the Hoe when my mother came along and said that I was playing with the wrong set of boys and that the Grammar School boys were further along. As I had provided the stumps, bails and bat, the game had to stop. I am pretty sure I went home with my mother totally mystified. I did not understand about the class system and how this was reflected in the education system. This was particularly unfair to Hoe Grammar School where the fees were very small and in the late nineteen-thirties, it began to run at a loss. The pupils were drawn from many walks of life and it certainly was not geared to the so-called "officer class".

In 1935, I went to London for the first time. I stayed with my Uncle Rodney and Auntie Muriel in Eastcote where he practised as a dentist and she was the receptionist. He enjoyed the compliments that were passed about her by some of the men patients. She was and always remained extremely attractive and had modelled clothes.

I was taken to Lords by a family called Ayre to see Middlesex play Somerset. I was enthralled though not allowed to go into the Long Room. That did not come until until I became a member of the MCC over forty years later. I was determined to watch every ball but all I remember of the scores, I hope accurately, is that Harold Gimblett, a hard hitting, left handed opening batsman for Somerset made 69. Later, he played in three matches for England but without great success.

I also remember 1935 being the year of the Silver Jubilee of King George V and Queen Mary. I saw the street decorations in London as well as Plymouth. Being a Naval port, Plymouth was especially loyal to the Sailor King as he was known. In the country generally, there was great loyalty and deference to the monarchy. Everybody stood still whenever the National Anthem was played. The men removed their hats or, if in uniform, they saluted. It was played at the end of every film show and every concert on Plymouth Hoe and elsewhere. I never heard of Republicanism except in Ireland and by the latter nineteen-thirties bombs in post boxes were quite prevalent, the work of the IRA.

In 1935, we again moved flats. This time to Elliott Street which ran between Leigham Street and Osborne Place. I was unconcerned about it. I always had a small but comfortable room and I know that my mother did her best for me in this and every other respect. She was going through a very difficult time and had suffered a great loss of pride. When it was clear that my father was not returning from Canada, she had no income. Very few middle-class women worked after they were married. Their place was running the home and looking after the children, but with domestic help. Unmarried daughters often remained at home to look after elderly parents. It was every woman's aim to make a successful match and not be left "on the shelf".

My mother really had no alternative but to accept the offer to work for her father. Though not trained, she could cope with the books and what today, we would call the "admin". She worked every day except Saturdays and was paid twenty five shillings per week. She once told me that on the first day she cried all the way to the office. Her devotion to me never faltered and I always seemed to be properly clothed for school with cap and blazer and have the necessary writing and other materials and money for the occasional outing—but who paid for what, I never knew.

About this time, when I was ten, I was conscious of the man who in 1940 was to become my stepfather and whom I then called "Pater". He was Arthur Comyn Rolston, an only child who lived with his parents in one of the most elegant streets in the Hoe district of Plymouth called The Crescent. He was fifteen years older than my mother and the indications are from photographs and letters I have seen that he was in love with her from an early age but he was a shy and somewhat reserved man. She was more extrovert and a positive personality. He must have been very cut up when she married my father. To modern eyes, it is very curious that he never did any work.

He was good at games from the time he went to Kelly College, Tavistock. He did not get any blues at Cambridge but he played hockey and tennis for Devon. He got a pass degree at Caius College, Cambridge and was going to study medicine. He served in the First World War and went on a curious expedition to Murmansk at the time of the Russian revolution. Returning to civilian life, he was not in good health and caught pneumonia. He stayed at home but recovered sufficiently to play hockey and tennis, join the Territorial Army and become the honorary secretary of the Plymouth Orchestral Society for some twenty-five years.

He played the tympani and became knowledgeable about classical music to the extent that he wrote very detailed notes about the works played by the orchestra It was a full orchestra, mainly amateurs but stiffened by professionals in the woodwind and brass sections especially from the Royal Marines whose director of music became a friend. He was Major F. J. Ricketts who under the name of Kenneth Alford, was a most distinguished composer of military marches, the best known being "Colonel Bogey". Pater once told me that he wrote it while a young bandsman with the Argyll and Sutherland Highlanders. He sold it to Boosey and Hawkes for, I think, £10. It was popular for many years and used as the theme music for the film, "The Bridge Over the River Kwai". When King George V was introduced to him, he said that he understood that there were some rather rude words that were sung to the tune of Colonel Bogey, which was true. Major Ricketts explained that he did not write them!

Boosey and Hawkes behaved very honourably and in view of the continued popularity of "Colonel Bogey", from which they must have derived a considerable sum, they sent Major Ricketts what Pater told me was a "generous cheque". I was glad to have met him.

Pater interested me in military music and took me to hear bands playing on Plymouth Hoe. I got to know the various instruments and listen to the parts they were playing. He was an authority on British military uniforms and used to paint lead soldiers with meticulous accuracy. All this was very worthy but it produced no money.

My mother and I used to go to the Rolstons' house for tea, usually on Sundays. Mrs Rolston was a bent, shrivelled up person who seldom went out. She used to make up little presents for people and was known, somewhat oddly, as Fairy Godmother or F. G. Her husband was an eye surgeon who practised from his house and had appointments to hospitals in Plymouth and London. I always understood him to be successful and well-regarded. I do not think he took any part in public life, He used to come in for tea which was a sit down meal around a table. Every one had the same type of rather small cane chair and, somewhat surprisingly, they were painted red. One had to start with a piece of bread and butter or a sandwich if there was one, before passing to the cake or a bun.

Mr Rolston, senior was always friendly in a formal way. He used to ask my mother where we had been and what we had been doing but said very little about himself. In his presence, Pater said very little. There must have been an arrangement between them about the payment of some sort of allowance.

Mother and Pater began to have a social life together, going to various functions and dances. It was, therefore, a surprise when my mother, grandmother and I had another move. This time it was away from the Hoe district and the Rolston house to a part of Plymouth called Mutley. We went to a flat in Gordon Terrace which was beside and above the railway line, not far from the mainline Great Western Station known as North Road. It is now just called Plymouth Station. I was no longer seeing the ships from the Hoe but I got to know quite a lot about trains and especially the classes of engine. I used to make a list of what I had seen. The line was used by both the Great Western and Southern Railways. The trains were frequent and as far as I could tell they kept to time! The highlight of the day was the Cornish Riviera. The claim used to be: "Paddington to Plymouth in under four hours". The train was due to leave Paddington at 10. 30 a.m. and arrive, non-stop, at Plymouth at 2. 29 p.m. It nearly always did from what I saw. The engine would be a GWR King Class. I always knew whether it was "King George V" because, as he was the reigning monarch, it had a silver bell on the front. I used to count the coaches or trucks on goods trains which were sometimes very long indeed, especially when bringing broccoli from Cornwall. I have counted more than one hundred trucks, generally pulled by two engines. Goodness knows where they all ended up. Perhaps not all at the same place.

The Southern Railway ran commuter trains from Plymouth to either Callington or Gunnislake which were much used by dockyard workers. As far as I know, the dockyard was always the largest employer in Plymouth even in times of recession, high unemployment and, between the wars, naval disarmament. This railway line still runs despite a number of efforts to close it. Many other small lines in the Westcountry were closed as a result of the reorganisation following the report chaired by Dr Beeching. Communications are more than what the accountants see when they open the books.

The purpose of moving to Gordon Terrace was to provide a home for me that was convenient for Plymouth College. This was a purpose built school, though it has never been completed and has always looked lop-sided. It had facilities on the campus—to use the American word. There were eight acres of playing fields, a swimming pool, fives courts and a gym as well as science laboratories. It had a staff of specialists and a good reputation as a predominantly day school which got good examination results and scholarships to universities. I had to take an entrance examination and passed well enough to be put in the A stream. Though at times erratic, I was usually in the top half of the class. I knew my grandfather was still paying. The fees were more than Hoe Grammar School but still modest.

I was still no good at games though I did try especially at cricket but my reactions were slow. Everybody was expected to join the Officers' Training Corps, I think when we were 14 or 15, and put on army uniform. We marched, drilled, and learned about small arms weapons and rifle shooting. Some of the masters were the officers and we had training exercises on Dartmoor. It turned out to be a useful preparation when one joined up for the Second World War.

I think that the school was a happy one overall and there were certainly some unexpected incidents that I remember very clearly. We were taught Latin by the Headmaster, H. W. Ralph, always known as either the Head or Mr Ralph. I did not know his first name until I went to an Old Boys' Dinner some thirty years later. He was a serious stern looking man but he did just about smile once. For his class and some others, we had to sit alphabetically. Perhaps the master had a crib on his desk for easier recognition. I can remember that the front row was: Atkins, Badcock, Baker, Bailey, Brown G. G. W. , Cox A. R. C. , Ford and the boy at the end by the door, Hussell who was known as "Doormouse". He was most inappropriately named for he was large and very slow in his movements, worse at gym than I was. One afternoon the Head came in a bit late and looking flustered as if he had been detained by a tiresome parent. He walked up to his desk and said, "Oh dear! Hussell, go and see if I have left my *Latin for Today* in my study". Slowly, Hussell got up, opened and shut the classroom door with great deliberation and disappeared. He would have had to pass the school tuck shop on his way which was his favourite place. Eventually, he came back empty handed and having closed the door, he stood there and said, "Yes, sir, you have". Never had the whole class laughed so loudly and the Head, after a little hesitation, was able to raise a smile.

Hussell went unpunished. Punishment was one matter I disliked about Plymouth College. The cane was used very frequently by some masters; others who could command interest and attention by the force of their personalities, did not have the need for it.

One master called W. G. M. Jones who played rugger as a second row forward. for Plymouth Albion and Devon, and was a big and powerful man, used to set tests which he would mark and then beat those who fell below a certain mark. The same boys got beaten week after week. What this was meant to achieve, I never understood.

Every morning there was the school assembly in the so called "Big School". The whole school was there arranged in classes, the juniors at the front and the prefects around the side. The attendance of the staff varied. The school stood up when they entered walking down from their common room in order of seniority and in their gowns, led by the Headmaster. A hymn was sung to piano accompaniment. There were some prayers and then the school notices. The Head would then read out a list of boys who had been reported to him and this resulted in a beating in his study. I used to wonder how a man could do this after singing a hymn about Christian love and forgiveness. I wonder nowadays how the regime would have altered if there had been girls at the school.

As far as I know, there were never any meetings with parents or a Parents Association. The school was founded in 1877 and in 1896 was amalgamated with Mannamead School. The Old Boys are still known as Old Plymouth Mannameadians or OPMs. There was a Preparatory Department. The main school had ten yearly forms in two streams thus covering five years. The sixth form was divided into three: Classical, Modern and Science. The brightest boys learned Greek from their third year. They were destined for the Classical Sixth which had a very good record of getting scholarships to Oxford and Cambridge under an inspired teacher called L. C. Lord. Again, I never knew his full names.

When I was allocated to the Greek class, my mother, showing some courage, rebelled and asked that I should learn German. How this was done I do not know but she succeeded and I had a very good teacher called W. W. Woodcock who was known as "Timber". I still have my German Grammar and Vocabulary exercise books. In 1938 or 1939, the school decided to give a free place to an Austrian refugee called Auskerin. I was put in charge of him. We got on well and my German must have improved.

At this time, my mother joined the Auxiliary Territorial Service (ATS), later to become the Womens' Royal Army Corps (WRAC). Because of her commitment to me, she volunteered for local service only, so she could not be commissioned. She started as a sergeant and became a sergeant major which was the highest she could go. She often worked at Mutley Barracks which was the headquarters of the Devon and Cornwall (Fortress) Royal Engineers who were commanded by Pater! This was a Territorial Unit and therefore all were part-timers except the Adjutant Officer who was attached to them. I was always puzzled about how my stepfather came to be a Sapper. He was the least technical of men but the unit was concerned with coastal defence and manned the searchlights so I suppose that engineering qualifications were not needed. They had to cooperate and coordinate with the Artillery who, of course, manned the guns and, from what I was told, this was not always successful. It does seem a strange division of responsibilities and was ended in May 1940 after the fall of France when England faced invasion. I believe that there were also some social problems as my mother was not allowed in the officers' mess!

At the beginning of September 1939, my mother, grandmother and myself were on holiday staying at the Belmont Hotel, Looe which had a nice position above the bridge on the eastern side. The Second World War broke out on the third and I remember my mother telling me that she had heard the broadcast by Neville Chamberlain and that he sounded a broken man. She returned to Plymouth at once and I became a boarder at Plymouth College. There were only a few of us, perhaps ten, under a master called Holman. There was an occasional air raid but only by one or two planes.

When the French surrendered in 1940, Plymouth Sound was absolutely full of ships, the biggest of which was the old French battleship, Paris which dated, I think, from 1909. There were all sorts of boats and though I was only 14 I was taken up the River Dart looking for persons who had gone ashore from Belgian fishing boats. The possibility of spies and saboteurs being landed was obvious. My grandfather told me that the Royal Navy boarded Surcouf, the world's largest submarine to prevent her leaving and falling into German hands. The French were in the position that their lawful government had formally surrendered to the Germans. General de Gaulle had come to London and urged the French to fight on. He had no authority and the position in and around Plymouth was difficult and fluid. However, nothing serious happened as far as the French ships were concerned as it did in North Africa with sad and serious consequences for both sides. That the British and French, meant to be Allies, should fire on each other was appalling.

The air raids on Plymouth began to intensify and I got to know the whirring noise of the German planes, Heinkels and Dorniers, from the more even noise of the RAF engines. When the siren went, we had to go to air raid shelters, usually at night.

All seemed to be going reasonably well at Plymouth College but in the summer of 1940, came another bombshell in my life. My grandfather decided that my life in Plymouth with the air raids and my mother's increasing duties in the ATS , was not satisfactory and, as always, he wanted the best education for me. I was told that I was going to start next term at Wellington School, Somerset, a small public school near Taunton, not to be confused with the better known Wellington College in Berkshire which specialised in getting boys into the Army. I was extremely upset. One day in the summer holidays, I met "Timber" by chance, outside the gates of Plymouth College. I just said, "I've left" and he replied, "You've whatted?" When alone, I cried considerably. I do not recall ever doing this before or since.

My mother and I went to Wellington School to be shown around. The Headmaster was Aubrey Price, known as Aubrey, who had come about a year before from St. Peter's York. He was the new broom. For many years, the school, formerly, the West Somerset Grammar School, was run by the Corner family. It had got into the educational doldrums with declining numbers though the war was to change that.

Aubrey was an enthusiast, full of energy. He entered into everything, sometimes with a loss of dignity. The staff were clearly divided. Some, mainly the younger ones, were fiercely loyal, others were distinctly less keen. Aubrey had served in the First World War in the Royal Naval Air Service, the forerunner of the Fleet Air Arm. He enthused the Corps, now known as the Junior Training Corps which had a drum and bugle band and which led the parades with some panache. Aubrey would attend the school rugby matches and shout very loudly, keeping level with the play. He was an able science teacher and had a good sense of humour and the ridiculous which sometimes degenerated into sarcasm. I experinced this when I expressed a view about Germany with which he disagreed. He sneered, "I suppose next you will say that the Treaty of Versailles was unjust". I was perplexed and said nothing which was probably what he wanted to achieve. I never forgave him for deceiving my mother for whom he had a very high regard. He once told me that I had "a mother in a thousand". This was because of her determination to do the best for me after her divorce.

He deceived her on our visit to the school when he showed us around. My mother and I understood that I was going to be in Willows House where I knew a boy, David Pitts, who had come from Plymouth College and had lived near me. Aubrey took us there and then said, fiddling in his pockets, "Oh dear! I have forgotten the key". We then went elsewhere. When I was accepted for the school, I was told I was in the School House which was divided into Lights and Darks. I was in Lights. My mother found out from the Pitts family that Willows House had been vacated to accommodate a preparatory school from Eastbourne called Edinburgh House which had been going through a difficult time with air raids. Thus the visit and the forgetfulness about the key were all a charade. I did not tell anyone at school about it. I doubt if it would have done any good and I was kept very busy settling into a new life.

Fortunately, Plymouth College and Wellington School used the same examination board so that my studies were able to continue reasonably smoothly, but, of course, the teachers were different. They were a varied lot. Some were elderly, two of whom, "Dappy" Baker and Oscar Hughes had been awarded the Military Cross in the First World War. Others were either unfit for military service or were conscientious objectors. One who was unfit through poor eyesight, though he was later to join the RAF when standards were relaxed, was Jim Parsons. He was in his early twenties and played rugger as an unusually tall scrum half for Cambridge, Leicester and England. For this, he was something of a hero to the boys. He had an engaging personality with a delightful smile and taught English. My class had to study the English Romantic poets: Wordsworth, Shelley, Coleridge, Keats and Byron. He was a very good teacher who commanded respect and I do not recall him having to punish anybody. He was an Aubrey supporter and I was sorry that he left after my second year at the school.

He did not return to teaching after the war but had a very successful career in industry with Guest, Keen and Nettlefold. We met up again some thirty years later in 1954 when I married Joy Heward – about which, more later – and in about 1970, we went to a dinner at the Dorchester Hotel to celebrate the centenary of Roedean School. Jim Parsons was there as he had married Stephanie Tanner one of the nieces of the Headmistress and a contemporary of Joy's. We have kept in touch ever since and in recent years we have met by arrangement during the Test Match at Lords. I think we have done it five times.

Nineteen-forty was the year of a curious incident concerning my father. It happened in the summer after the fall of France when he walked unannounced into my grandfather's shop in Marlborough Street, Devonport. He was a sergeant in Princess Patricia's Canadian Light Infantry. He asked to see my mother and myself. Grandpa did not think he should see my mother. However, he raised no objections to him seeing me. Although some arrangements were made, nothing came of it as his unit was sent away from the Plymouth area rather suddenly.

I knew nothing about this, which is probably just as well as it saved speculation and, perhaps, anxiety. Some years later, my mother told me that she was in a tram in Union Street when she saw my father walking along. She immediately got out and chased after him but lost him in the crowd. I asked her why she had done this as it seemed so out of character. She really did not know. She must have acted on impulse.

The next thing I knew about my father during the War was that he was the last man to be rescued after the Germans invaded and overran Crete in 1941. By then, he had rejoined the Ghurkas and he reached the rank of Colonel. My mother said, more predictably, "The devil looks after his own". He returned to Canada after the war but he never tried to make contact with me again or, to be more charitable, he never succeeded.

1940 was a dramatic year for me in a number of ways. Not only did I go to Wellington School but there were two family weddings. As we are a small family, they do not happen very often. In the summer, my Uncle Kenneth married Jean Frecker at Epsom where she ran a dancing school. They had met during our holiday at Looe the previous September. Jean was very talented and trained successful dancers, two of whom got to Covent Garden. She later taught teachers of dancing. She adjudicated at many festivals and is a Patron of the Imperial Society of Teachers of Dancing. During the war, she drove an ambulance and danced in shows for the forces. She has always been a very correct, church going person and it caused considerable family laughter when her grandson, Nicholas Swiss, was asked at school what his grandparents did during the war and replied, "Grandpa was in the Royal Air Force and Grandma was a stripper". Apparently, that was the only type of dancing he had heard of!

The second wedding I could not attend. It was in October. The Headmaster sent for me and said that my mother had got married. It was a small wedding in Plymouth. From the photos, it seems there were only six people at the Registry Office including my grandfather who always referred to Pater as Arthur Rolston. I doubt whether they had ever met before but I know he told him, "You look after Dora and I will look after John".

Pater always remained a distant figure. I think we were incompatible and it was clear that marrying at the age of fifty-five and in the circumstances of the war, he was never going to have any children of his own. I had to adjust and settle in at Wellington. I was able to get a reasonable school certificate in July 1941 and in December, I took German as an additional subject. I think I was the only pupil! Fortunately, the very good French master, H. S. Evason, was glad to have me and keep his hand in.

However, before these examinations, on 21st March, 1941 a tragedy happened because Pater's family house was destroyed in an air raid. He was not there as he was then stationed at Barton Stacey in Hampshire with a chemical warfare unit. His father had died but my mother and "F. G. " were in the house. My mother heard "F. G." call out "Dora!" a number of times. She had been sitting in a big chair with a semi-circular back which fell forward and fortunately engulfed her. My mother got out of the house. The raid was still going on and she found a Lieutenant Nicholson and two midshipmen, one called Gabb, and asked them to come and help rescue the old lady which they succeeded in doing. She lived on for some four years in a nursing home in Tavistock and was well into her eighties. She retained a vivid and accurate recollection of what had happened. She used to write rather nice and kind letters to me and I visited her in the school holidays. Captain Nicholson, as he became, was awarded the MBE. but Pater always said, I think correctly, that my mother deserved something as well. The Blitz and especially this experience had a permanent effect on her. She was very sensitive to noise — particularly unexpected bangs, and she never liked the siren that ended every episode of the TV programme "Dad's Army"! She had lost her home after only five months of marriage. She had taken some belongings to The Crescent including her piano which she much valued as she was a talented pianist.

I was also homeless. In 1940, my grandfather thought that my grandmother as well as myself should leave Plymouth. She went to the Croft Hall Hotel and later the Monksilver at Torquay. I used to stay there during the holidays though once I went to the home of a friend at Wellington called Rowland whose father was the Church of England Minister at Egloshayle near Wadebridge, Cornwall. The family were very kind to me. This arrangement was instigated by Aubrey Price who was a devout Christian and could preach a very good sermon. I suppose he was the embodiment of "muscular Christianity".

I do not think that Aubrey could settle anywhere. He was one of those people who came into an institution, in his case a school, quickly saw what he thought need to be changed, set about to do it, made friends and enemies and then moved on. From Wellington, he went to a naval training school at Wymondham, Norfolk, then to Goldsmith's College, London where I once went to see him. After that he took Holy Orders and the Archdeacon of the Diocese to which he was appointed was the Chaplain at Wellington whom he had disposed of upon his arrival there! After that, I do not know how he fared.

I am grateful to Wellington School for a number of things. One is that it had a Debating Society called the Raban Society, after I think, the first headmaster. I found that I could speak and think on my feet. Fortunately, I had an audible voice and seemed to be able to hold the attention of the audience, a number of the masters used to attend and they were very encouraging. I gained in confidence.

The second plus was that hockey was introduced to the school by a new master called Tommy Lawson. I was persuaded to play in goal and although I was a bit slow I got into the school team. This was the only success I had in sport apart from table tennis which did not really count.

I went on to take my higher certificate. I enjoyed this as students were able to specialise in their best subjects instead of doing a lot of things across the board. I took English, French and German which I passed and got a school award in German. I was also taught Spanish by a master called Kay who had recently come to the school. He once told me that he had no ambition, which I found rather sad and I do not think that Aubrey would have approved either! Still, Mr Kay was a good teacher and we just did Spanish for the enjoyment of it without the strains of any examination. It was a useful foundation for getting by in Spain on holiday visits as I could pronounce it even though my vocabulary was limited.

Wellington School had a link with Wadham College, Oxford which had Somerset connections. It was founded by Nicholas and Dorothy Wadham at the beginning of the 1600s. They came from Merifield near Ilminster. Certainly at the beginning, most of its students came from the Westcountry. The Warden was a Governor of the School and Maurice Bowra (later to be knighted) came for Commemoration Day. I was impressed by his remarks. He became an instant hero figure and I remember that at the tea party afterwards I offered him a sandwich, which he accepted with enthusiasm!

I wanted to do my National Service in the Navy and also to go to Wadham. This was possible by being accepted for what was called a short course. I joined the Navy by passing a medical at Exeter. There was some doubt about my fitness owing to ear trouble. I had recently had a mastoid operation and the surgeon, in a letter to my mother, doubted whether I would be accepted for the services. I put Oxford first on the university application and, to my delight, I was selected for Wadham. My step-father never said anything about not choosing the Army or Cambridge. Jim Parsons told me he would have been very upset. In fact, by this time, Pater had been retired from the Army on age grounds. He was born in 1885. To his credit, he got a job as the area manager for Navy, Army and Air Force Institutes (NAAFI) around Salisbury Plain. It was a responsible job as there were many service camps and stations around there and they continuously increased in the build up to D-Day. His area extended to near Marlborough. He was given a small khaki painted Ford car and occasionally he allowed me to go with him. I doubt whether I was insured! We lived at The Grange, Idmiston, a hamlet between Salisbury and Tidworth—and later at Tidworth. In the summer of 1943, I helped the local farmer with the harvest and earned some pocket money before I arrived at Wadham in the October,

I was no longer a schoolboy but an ordinary seaman and an Oxford undergraduate. A new life, or rather, two new lives were about to begin.

CHAPTER 2

Oxford, the Navy and the Liberals

I think I played the two rôles of undergraduate and naval trainee successfully. As soon as I saw the front quadrangle of Wadham and discovered the Hall, the Chapel and the garden, I was entranced by it and knew it would play an important part in my life. I was spurred on by its tradition of teaching law and producing lawyers who had succeeded in the profession. It was so different from school. Attendance at lectures was not compulsory. There was no check on who went and the consumer really did rule. Years later, Paul Foot got into terrible trouble when he, no doubt with others, did an assessment of the performance of lecturers in a number of faculties. One sure clue was how many attended at the beginning of term and how many there were at the end. Maurice Bowra told me that he had to work very hard to prevent Foot from being sent down. This was particularly kind of Bowra because unlike Uncle Michael, Paul Foot was not a Wadham man.

There were some lecturers who attracted large audiences which went far beyond those who were reading their subjects. I know it can be invidious to name names but C. S. Lewis, A. L. Rowse and A. J. P. Taylor were undoubted crowd pullers. It is interesting how people were often not known by their first names. I am not going to name any of the worst lecturers as my knowledge is limited to the law faculty.

The academic highlight of the week was the tutorial, in Cambridge known as a "supervision". Ideally, it was one-to-one but Oxford after the war was very crowded and it had to be one-to-two or even three. During the war, Wadham had no law don and we were farmed out to tutors in other colleges. I was lucky in having C. H. S. Fifoot of Hertford College whose enthusiasm for legal history he imparted to me and which I have never lost. In the two terms I was there, I did criminal law and constitutional law. The tutor would set an essay to be done in a week. This was the new discipline, so different from school. With all the attractions of Oxford, it was so easy to procrastinate and leave things for a few days. One great refrain throughout my time at Oxford was to hear somebody say, "Sorry, I can't stop. I'm in a crisis! I've an essay to finish by tomorrow".

For the law student, the subject had to be researched by looking up textbooks and the leading cases and articles in learned legal periodicals such as the *Law Quarterly Review*, which was rather favoured as it was Oxford-orientated. For many years, it was edited by the Master of University College, Professor A. L. Goodhart, QC. One had to use one's nous on where to start but I soon got to know where to find the basic books and proceed from there. It could be quite a laborious process as there were no computers, web-sites, internet or sources of information other than books. There were no typing facilities so the essay had to be written in longhand.

Then, at the appointed time, one had to go and read the essay. I do not know whether it was meant to give one confidence but the ability to read one's own writing and to give sensible expression to it is a useful attribute. The tutor would have to listen, otherwise, he could not ask questions about it. Some would sit there looking wise and a pipe was a useful prop. I often wondered how many tutors could listen and at the same time think of other things. The experienced must have got to know what the key points were. I thought I got on reasonably well at this. The so-called "short course" was only two terms if you started as I did in October. Full term was only eight weeks so the time was soon over. At the end was an exam in both subjects. I was glad that I got reasonable marks, though nothing outstanding.

The other part of daily life was the University Naval Division. Members spent one half day and one full day in a boat house or on the River Isis, learning things about the Navy such as knots and splices, Morse, semaphore and boat drill. One could row in a whaler, sailing was very limited because of the narrowness of the river. The Division was commanded by A. B. Emden, the Principal of St. Edmund Hall (known as Teddy Hall) who had the rank of Lieutenant Commander. I seemed to cope reasonably well and most of what we were taught was quite useful.

After the course was over, there was a short wait until we had to report to *HMS Ganges*, a shore establishment for naval training at Shottley, near Harwich. I quite enjoyed this. We slept in huts and began to widen our knowledge about the navy and naval weapons. I was absolutely terrified of climbing the ship's mast and thankful we did not have to go right to the top. How the "button boy" can do that and then stand on his head, I do not know. There was more scope for sailing cutters and whalers which I enjoyed.

After some weeks there, we were divided into three to go to training cruisers. I joined *HMS Corinthian* at Rosyth. She was a converted merchant ship. The others were D Class light cruisers that had been pensioned off to the Reserve. *Corinthian* was quite comfortable considering the number aboard her. We slept in hammocks. We did not go far out to sea. We kept watch and had lifeboat drills and gun practice. I think it was the noise of the guns that started my ear trouble again—though it was not to show itself for some weeks. The nearest we got to any action or excitement was when we were nearly involved in a collision during a very dark night when we were out at sea. I just saw the other boat which was quite large and uncomfortably close. Nobody told us any details and we heard no more about it.

I did quite well on *Corinthian* and was one of the few cadets who were promoted from Ordinary Seaman to Able Seaman. I therefore arrived at *HMS King Alfred,* a shore establishment at Shoreham, with some confidence but somehow I began to lose it. The officer in charge was Commander Henry Barnes and it was soon clear that he took a dislike to me. There was often rivalry between the naval ports of Chatham, Portsmouth and Devonport and he was scathing about people from the Westcountry who he thought were thick and slow. It did not help that I was not good at sport. The most encouragement he gave me was that I was "borderline". However, in the end, along with some others, I was not recommended for a commission.

I was sent to Chatham Barracks. D-day had passed while I was in Scotland and the rôle for the Navy was increasingly focused on the Pacific.

Unexpectedly, I then started something interesting. I have always been interested in languages, although at this time, it was limited to a working knowledge of French and German and some basic Spanish. Somehow, I started a course in Japanese. What we did was to hear Naval expressions and conversations as if we were listening in on a wireless. This was not easy to do as there would be built in background noise. I seemed to cope though I was anxious that my hearing was not as acute as it might have been. Unfortunately – and I believe this was unrelated – my old ear trouble flared up again. I was put into the naval hospital and was then told that I would be discharged from the Navy as being below the required physical standard. I did not grieve over this though I was disappointed that my naval career had not been more successful.

I knew I wanted to be a lawyer and so set about enquiring how I could get back to Wadham and resume my studies. Fortunately, Maurice Bowra had an open policy. If you were on the books, you were a member of the College and could come back. Of course, when the demobilisation began in earnest, the College itself could not accommodate everybody and one had to look for digs. I was lucky because I was there a little before the great post-war expansion and was able to be "in college" for one year and then in digs for the following two.

The next problem was finance. I had no resources of my own and I applied for a grant. To my delight and surprise, I was given a grant for three years and one term which covered fees and a lot of the college bills. I could not quite understand it, because the Bachelor of Arts (BA) degree was for three years and I had already done two terms. However, I was not going to query the decision but be grateful for it. Apart from Wadham, I got in touch with my old tutor, C. H. S. Fifoot, who was very helpful in explaining the syllabus and suggesting what I might read before I returned to Oxford.

One of the staunchest beliefs that my grandfather had was that if you started something, you finished it – so he approved of my going back to Oxford to get my law degree. He continued to support me and give me a small allowance.

I returned to Oxford before VE Day on 8th May, 1945. There were many celebrations which have been written about by Margaret Thatcher (*née* Roberts) who was reading chemistry at Somerville. I remember at a dinner in Hall, Maurice Bowra booming away that "Wadham is untouched". He lived for the College and in time he was appointed Warden – in 1938 until he died in 1971.

In 1945, Wadham had still not got a law don and again we had to be farmed out to various tutors in different Colleges. This lasted until the following year when W. O. Hart returned from war service. Latterly, he had been concerned in Washington with the terms of lend-lease agreements between the UK and the USA. He certainly expected his pupils to work hard and I thought that the amount of reading he required us to do was at times, excessive. I would rather have been asked to read less and understand more. His wartime experience had obviously widened his horizons. Maurice Bowra kept his fellowship open during the war and never forgave him for leaving Wadham after about two years and taking the appointment of director or chief executive (I am not sure of the title) of the proposed new town of Stevenage. At a College gaudy – or reunion - Maurice Bowra could not contain his scorn and referred to him as having become a *Gauleiter* (the name that used to be given to the head of a Nazi administrative district). It must be appreciated that there was then much more anti-German feeling than there is now.

A university with its many activities does provide an opportunity of finding out what one's interests are and pursuing them. At Wadham, I continued to play hockey. There was not much competition in a small College to be a goalkeeper and I think I coped reasonably well without being outstanding. I did not seek a trial as I felt I had no chance of getting a blue. I could see the other college goalkeepers from the other end of the pitch. The University goalkeeper was Roderic Hewitt of Merton and very strangely in the late nineteen-sixties we came to live with our families in the same road in Richmond, Surrey. He had read forestry and was in the Headquarters of the Forestry Commission in Berkeley Square. He did not like this. He had not joined to be in London but in the country among and studying trees. His wish was granted when he was appointed to the New Forest. He had two boys and I had two girls. Friendships developed but nothing more. The families have kept in touch ever since. Sadly, Roderic has died but we still see his widow, Theo, on the edge of the New Forest.

The hockey goalkeeper for Trinity College, and another blue, was John Woodcock who for many years was the cricket correspondent of *The Times*.

I have kept various photographs of groups, committees and teams while at Oxford and have often wondered what has happened to a number of people in them. I have not followed the practice of my grandfather who kept a photo of the Board of Guardians who administered the poor law in Devonport. When any member died, he took out a pencil and drew a circle around his head! Once, he showed me the photo and proudly proclaimed that he was the last survivor. I was loathe to contradict him but I pointed out that Mr Albert Gard, a solicitor was still alive. Grandpa explained that Mr Gard was not a member of the Board but their clerk and did not count!

Our Wadham hockey team did produce one man of subsequent distinction, Sir Sydney Giffard, KCMG, who became Deputy Under Secretary of State at the Foreign and Commonwealth Office and Ambassador to Japan. He was made an honorary fellow of the College in 1991.

Apart from the hockey team, I tried to take part in various college and university activities. I felt I had a natural interest in politics. Before I arrived at Wadham, I was introduced by my Uncle Rodney, the dentist I mentioned in *Chapter 1*, to a man called Ivor Wilkinson, a scientist at Balliol. He was quite helpful about life at Oxford in wartime and advised me to join the Oxford University Conservative Association (OUCA). I knew very little about party politics. There had been a political truce during the War. The last general election had been in 1935 when I was ten. Ivor Wilkinson told me that OUCA had the best speakers which was probably true as they were the majority party in the coalition government led by Winston Churchill. So I joined. I still have the card for the Michaelmas term, 1943. It was an impressive programme. In the four weeks of November, the meetings were addressed by Cabinet Ministers, James Grigg, Duff-Cooper, Brendan Bracken and Oliver Lyttleton.

I listened and learned. The following term was almost as impressive. I went to the Annual Dinner at the Randolph Hotel, Oxford where the undergraduate speakers were Geoffrey Rippon and Adrian Head who became a Circuit Judge in Norfolk. I do not think I ever went to another Conservative Dinner! This was because when I returned to Oxford, the political mood had changed. I did formally join OUCA but I was attracted to the Liberals. Shortly after Victory in Europe Day, a General Election was called rather hastily, for Thursday 5th July. This was before the war against Japan had ended. There was a lot of feeling that Winston Churchill wanted to take maximum advantage of his highly successful wartime leadership and hoped this would spill over for him as leader of the Conservative Party. It was a gamble that completely failed for Labour was returned with a huge — unexpectedly — majority. It rose from 166 to 393 seats while the Conservatives fell from 361 to 189 and the Liberals from 20 to 12.

But I am jumping ahead. I put the results before the campaign! I was attracted to the Liberals because I felt it was time for a change from Conservative government and, indeed, I was not sympathetic to Conservative principles. I believed that there had to be a great leap forward in social welfare provisions that had been started by Asquith and Lloyd George only to flounder when the Liberal party became divided. One hoped that those divisions were over though there were still some so called Liberal Nationals left who had remained in coalition with the Conservatives but, by 1945, they were indistinguishable from them. They had no separate Whip in the House of Commons. It was a joint Whip.

The Liberals had a great boost when Sir William Beveridge joined them. He had been the Master of University College, Oxford and had produced a mammoth work called *Full employment in a Free Society*, which became the blueprint for the establishment of the post-war welfare state. He had a very able team of assistants including Harold Wilson and Frank Pakenham (later, Lord Longford) but he did not join them in the Labour Party. He was not a socialist. He hesitated for some time about whether he should remain independent but I think he realised he needed a party platform from which to operate. An opportunity came in a sad way as it does in wartime. In August, 1944, Captain George Grey the Liberal MP for Berwick was killed in action in Normandy. He was a great loss and Lady Violet Bonham Carter was certain that one day he would have been leader. So there had to be a by-election and Beveridge agreed to stand as the Liberal candidate. He was unopposed but lost the seat the following year at the General Election.

When party politics returned, I think that the name and reputation of Beveridge was the greatest asset of the Liberal party. His programmes for social reform were clear and could be put into a dynamic election manifesto. I thought that the Liberal programme of a constructive alternative to socialism was very persuasive; so did many other people but it was not translated into votes. The Conservatives played upon the fear of personal control under a socialist state. Labour had a programme of taking key industries under public control, called nationalisation. Winston Churchill spoke in dire tones of Britain becoming a police state. It did him little good but it did make it difficult for a third party to break through.

I attended with some enthusiasm the meetings and study groups of the University Liberal Club and a small group of us stayed behind after the end of term to help in the Oxford City constituency. The sitting member was Quintin Hogg who won the seat in 1938 in what was called the "Munich by-election". He was in favour of the agreement signed by Neville Chamberlain with Adilf Hit;ler. His only opponent in the by-election was A. D. Lindsay, the Master of Balliol who called himself "Progressive". It was furiously fought. Amongst those who spoke against Quintin Hogg was Edward Heath, a recent President of the Oxford Union. Flushed with this success, Quintin Hogg, after being wounded in the Western Desert while serving as a Captain in the Rifle Corps, re-entered the political fray with great gusto. Some Liberals, of whom I was one, used to follow him around during the General Election of 1945 and go to his meetings. He was always combative and good fun but he had a bit of a short fuse. We would goad him, ask awkward questions and when he lost his temper, we would cheer wildly!

Throughout the country, Conservative candidates were doing little more than attach themselves to the Churchill label. "Let him finish the job" was one slogan with a benign picture. Some Liberals painted on the railway bridge near Oxford station, "Love me, love my Hogg". For this exercise in parliamentary democracy, there were three candidates. I have mentioned Quintin Hogg, the Labour candidate was Frank Pakenham – later Lord Longford - and the Liberal was Antony Norman, an RAF Wing Commander and son of the Governor of the Bank of England. Apart from being candidates, they had one other thing in common, they were Old Etonians! There was never a joint meeting at which they could have worn the tie. Quintin Hogg won by about two thousand. Frank Pakenham was very disappointed. He thought he had won. Antony Norman was not a bad third, better than many Liberal candidates, who on the whole, were people of some quality. The future party leader Jo Grimond was one of the nearest misses. He lost by 329 votes in Orkney and Shetland. He was to get his revenge in 1950.

After the election, I went to my first Party Conference. It was in Friends' House, Euston Road. With a very few exceptions, it was a gathering of the defeated. The older delegates, especially those on the platform, were ones who had been in the party when it was either in government or a considerable force in Parliament. The younger delegates like myself, were radicals who were hoping for better things in the future. We had a long time to wait. Surprisingly I thought, Archie Sinclair was not there. I know it is a long way from Caithness to Euston but he had been the leader of the Party at the election. The speech I remember was from lady Violet Bonham Carter. It was, as always, well prepared and stirring stuff—calls to remain firm and carry on the Liberal campaign in the constituencies. In the evening, there was a general debate and I made a contribution about "ownership for all" as a distinctive alternative to socialism. I was glad to represent the Oxford University Liberal Club and I made contacts that were to provide useful future links. I remember speaking shortly after to Lady Violet and Lord Samuel when the *Oxford Guardian* was relaunched and they sent helpful messages.

The *Oxford Guardian* became a magazine of some influence in the university. One of its regular features was a commentary on the debates in the Union under the title of "Skunk". He was Anthony Walton who had been President of the Oxford Union. He was a physicist who became a QC at the patent Bar. A lover of repartee, he once followed a right wing, Tory Sir Herbert Williams, who was a visiting speaker at a debate in the Union. Sir Herbert launched into a wide ranging attack on the Liberal and Labour parties. He made no constructive suggestions of his own. Anthony who was and remained a Liberal, referred to the visitor coming to Oxford and raking up as much political mud as he could find and putting it in other parties' dustbins. "We know why he has to do that—" (dramatic pause), "his dustbin's full!"

I was not a member of the Union until I came back to Oxford. I enjoyed the cut and thrust of debate and the performances of the visiting speakers, some, like Anthony Eden and Harold Macmillan, very distinguished and very different in their styles. Eden, the debater, taking up points made by previous speakers and concluding with his own bit; Macmillan the prepared, polished, scholarly orator. I made my maiden speech. It was helpful to be active in the Liberal club which still had a good membership despite the general election catastrophe.

By 1946, a large number of ex-servicemen had returned to Oxford and the attendance at debates was often several hundred. Soon, some political figures emerged. Outside the Union, during the war, the Socialist Society had become very left wing, with many so-called "fellow travellers" with the Communist party. Tony Crosland, Tony Benn and Fred Mulley were prominent in forming a mainstream Labour Club. Tony Benn was already a good political tactician. The Union was then an all male Society. Occasionally, there were women speakers, nearly always guests. Tony wanted women to be admitted as members. He could move a motion to this effect, I think, once a year. However, once he whipped up his supporters and caught his opponents napping. The motion was carried. A retired clergyman who must have been a life member, stood up quivering with emotion, supported by his black furled umbrella. He shouted out, "Mr President, I demand a Poll of this Society", which he was entitled to do under the rules. Immediately, a man sitting opposite me called Selinski from Pembroke College, stood up and said, '"Mr President, I am a Pole of this Society". There was great laughter and cheering.

Both Tony Crosland and Tony Benn were elected to terms as president, as was Seymour Hills, another Labour supporter. The voting was not wholly party political. In the years after the war, all three parties had their successes. For the Liberals, in addition to Anthony Walton, there were John Long and Basil Wigoder QC (later the Lord Wigoder). For the Conservatives, there were Clive Wigram, Sir Edward Boyle, Peter Kirk and Roger Gray who have all, sadly, died. The survivor is Ronald Brown who became head of the RAF medical service. There was one independent, Peter Kroyer, who was awarded the Distinguished Flying Cross (DFC), in the RAF. A commanding figure with a powerful voice, I never heard anything about him after Oxford. I got as far as Treasurer, being heavily defeated for President by Edward Boyle.

One President, just before I joined was Rudi Weisweiller, with whom I have remained in contact. He kindly came from Austria with his English wife Pamela, to my seventieth birthday. They and others, were great surprises. It was all kept from me by Joy. I had to go and answer the door!

Rudi was a refugee who got to England in the nineteen-thirties. He and his family had a *Schloss* between Linz and Salzburg. They were forced to sell it to the Nazis at a derisory price. It is near where Hitler was born and the *Schloss* became a meeting place and social centre for top Nazis. For this and what follows, I am grateful to Rudi for telling me. When the war ended, the Americans arrived and did some damage, not least by driving a lorry through the front door! When they left, the *Schloss* fell into the hands of the newly created Austrian government. This must have been in 1954 as I visited Vienna at this time as part of a North Atlantic Treaty Organization (NATO) delegation of young politicians.

The Weisweiller family sued for the return of the *Schloss* on the ground that the sale to the Nazis was under duress. There was litigation at various levels by way of appeals but, in the highest Court, the Weisweillers won. The price they paid was the cost of the proceedings. The Austrian government was not a party to the sale so could not be blamed for what had happened. So the family went back and still live there. Rudi has always been most hospitable. At Oxford, he had 'open house' once a week in his digs in Hollywell Street. Joy and I have been to the *Schloss* twice and enjoyed its setting and the countryside.

Politics occupied much of my time in Oxford – in retrospect, perhaps too much, but it was what I enjoyed doing. In addition to University politics, I thought it right to try and help the Young Liberals get going. The main party had no future if it could not attract them. I remember the first meeting at the time of the 1946 Conference was in a top room of the *News Chronicle* office in Bouverie Street, off Fleet Street. I remember looking out on to the river. This part of London was to become familiar territory after I left Oxford.

I tried to keep my head above water with my work. I was more interested in the general subjects like legal history and jurisprudence than the subjects that required much memorising including the names of cases and what they had decided. If there had been more time, I would have liked to have read something other than law and broadened my knowledge and horizons, perhaps a modern European language and then travelled more.

I did not know how I would do in my Finals. I felt I was a bit patchy. In the end, to my disappointment, I got what was called, "by no means a bad third". In those days, there were no two: ones and two: twos, but logically there were firsts, seconds, thirds and fourths. The last of two of these have been abolished. The fourths were a small class each year but it has included one Prime Minister, two Lord Chancellors and one Lord Chief Justice. The jingle was:

The firsts are the friends of the examiners,
The seconds are the people who work,
The thirds are the people who do not work,
And,
The fourths are the friends of the examiners.

With that result, I did not know what to do. My grant went on for another three terms. I loved Oxford, Wadham in particular. If I had got a second, I would not have hesitated to have returned and tried to do the two year course for the Bachelor of Civil Law (BCL) in one year. I sought advice but nobody was really helpful, though not discouraging. I had nobody to turn to at home. It was down to me and I decided to continue at Oxford. I thought if I could even scrape a BCL in double time, it would be a useful qualification and so it has proved. The classes were small. There were about six or seven of us. Some were clearly academic stars in embryo and were going to get firsts. I suppose the most distinguished must have been the Rt. Hon. Sir Zelman Cowen, AK, GCMG, GCVO, who not only became Provost of Oriel College after a string of other appointments, but from 1977-82 was Governor-General of Australia! Then there was Tony Honoré, a Rhodes Scholar from South Africa who became Regius Professor of Civil Law at Oxford. The one I got to know best was Peter Carter who was appointed the law fellow at Wadham in 1949. I met him when I returned to Oxford from time-to-time. He filled the gap which had existed since the departure of W. O. Hart. In my BCL year, I was taught by Norman Francis of Lincoln College. He was a part-timer. I think, like a number of barristers who had done well at Oxford and were just starting at the Bar, he used to come to Oxford at weekends and earn some money. Still, he was a good teacher and did his best for me. He was appointed a County Court judge in 1969 and he was, I think, somewhat surprised when I introduced myself to him in 1973 at a judges' meeting. He sat mainly at Cardiff.

Of the others in our small group, I recall Hiram Powell with whom I completely lost touch and Michael Kempster who became a judge in Hong Kong and Bermuda. I slogged along especially with evidence, private international law and the Roman law of theft. I did mange to scrape through and got another third. This has now been abolished and Wadham got the last one! I was just glad to pass and only wish I had had more time to absorb the syllabus.

I have often wondered whether I did not make a mistake in doing this. By staying on at Oxford, I had lost the lead I had over very many contemporaries who were demobbed a year or so later. I really wanted to go to the Bar. I once mentioned this to my mother but really she did not see how I could do it. In fairness to my grandfather, it was asking too much for him to keep me in the early years when it would be too difficult to earn fees. If I qualified as a solicitor, I would be able to earn a salary after finishing the articles of clerkship as they were called. I had no contacts at the Bar at all. However, my last year at Oxford was a great experience. Not only was there the challenge to do the BCL but there were memorable debates in the Union. In addition to those I have already mentioned, William Rees-Mogg, Keith Kyle, Donald Southgate, Robin Day and Dick Taverne were emerging as formidable debaters while Gerry Noel, Kenneth Harris and Ken Tynan were guaranteed makers of laughter. Ken Tynan did much to revive the theatre at Oxford, both Oxford University Dramatic Society (OUDS) and the Experimental Theatre Club. Donald Swann was at the piano while Lindsay Anderson produced the Wadham play and others.

There was so much going on; great games of rugger at the Iffley Road ground and interesting cricket in the Parks led by Martin Donnelly who had already played for New Zealand.

Life is much more than work and on balance, I never regretted my extra year at Oxford.

CHAPTER 3

Starting Out in the Law

I had to set about becoming a solicitor. My great-uncle, Arthur Williams, was most useful. He introduced me to two of the partners in a firm in Devonport where he was the managing clerk. The firm was Gill, Akaster, Leest and Russell. So I met Alec Leest and R. C. Hunter Russell. My mother and step-father did not return to Plymouth after the war but bought a house in Sutton, Surrey. I was told how provincial firms had London agents. For Gill, Akaster, as the firm was usually called, they were Stafford Clark and Co. who had premises in the City at Laurence Pountney Hill off Cannon Street.

Dr. Stafford Clark had recently died and I was given an introduction to the new senior partner, Alec Jennings. He was a man proud of himself — and with some justification because he had done it all himself. He started as a typist. I do not know anything about his education but he did things the practical way from his experience in the office and got qualified. At some stage, he must have been articled to a solicitor as this was a legal requirement. He agreed to take me on. No time was lost and the deed of articles of clerkship was signed on 28th July, 1948. Because of my law degree, the period was two years and forty-two days. In those times, the person being articled had to pay a premium. Mine was 100 guineas, payable in two instalments. The articled clerk was not paid anything at all. Nowadays, the clerk is called a trainee solicitor and is paid a five figure sum. My articles were a formal deed. I expect there was a standard precedent. In order to get the flavour of the legal language of the time and the rigid distinction between master and servant, I would like to set out one of the covenants that the clerk entered into:

> 4(e). That the clerk will readily and cheerfully obey and execute the lawful and reasonable commands of the Solicitor and will not depart or absent himself from the service or employ of the Solicitor during the said term without the consent of the Solicitor first obtained but will at all times during the said term conduct himself with all due diligence honesty sobriety and temperance.

Alec Jennings had another articled clerk called John Fredman, a delightful graduate from Cambridge who cultivated the impression of being idle but really absorbed quite a lot of the practice of the law. One day I had been given a drafting exercise by Alec Jennings who summoned Fredman and myself into his room while he went through it. We had both to stand facing him. I thought he deliberately knocked it about, turning clauses around with no explanation. Suddenly, he turned and said, "Fredman, why are you standing there with that smirk on your face?" To which he replied, "Sir, I am not smirking . . . just 'readily and cheerfully obeying' in accordance with my articles". Alec Jennings was not amused.

The articled clerks went around the various departments in the firm: litigation, conveyancing, probate, company and divorce work. It was very good training that we got from the managing clerks. I particularly liked litigation and going up to the High Court, often with Herbert Tann, a most experienced managing clerk who was an expert on court procedure and tactics. He used to take me to listen while he dealt with appointments in the Masters' Chambers. Sometimes, we would sit behind a barrister whom the firm had briefed.

I got used to the 9.30-5.30 routine with the walk over London Bridge where the Upper Pool was nearly always full of ships loading and unloading. Many came from Scandinavia and I used to like watching enormous planks of timber being unloaded by crane. All that trade now seems to have gone from there as many years later, I could see this stretch of the river from my room at Southwark Crown Court.

I was conscious I was not earning any money and so for a few weeks, I had an evening job at the *Daily Mirror*. I had met Duncan Campbell and his wife Audrey who lived at nearby Banstead. He was the legal adviser to the *Mirror* and was assisted by "Wat" Tyler who later went to the *Express.* They went on holiday consecutively and it was agreed that I would come in and be number two. So I used to leave Stafford Clark and Co as punctually as I could and go to Fetter Lane. There the paper would be read for any legal point, and sometimes, people would come and see us. We were not often called upon but—when something was considered a libel risk—a meeting would be called and the editor had the final say on whether the risk would be taken. I little thought that, some years later, I would be present in the court of the Lord Chief Justice when the editor (a different one!) was sent to jail!

I did not get away until 10.30 p.m. and then had to get to Sutton. I enjoyed the experience very much, especially seeing how a national newspaper was put together. I remember once after either the first or second edition, a story broke that had to have the front page lead. I was present when the paper was recast. Instant decisions had to be made on where the original lead story should go, what could be transferred to other pages, what could be edited and reduced and what had to be removed. All the transport and the presses were ready and waiting for the next edition. Any delay had to be reduced to a minimum. I was full of admiration for the skill and speed shown.

It became obvious that I could not do this for long. It was no good arriving tired at both jobs. I have still got two cartoons that were done of me, I think by 'Zak' but with respect to him I am told they are not easily recognizable!

After two years or so, I had to get down to more studying, this time for the solicitors' Finals. I knew it was a difficult exam and said to be of a higher standard than that for the Bar. After all, once admitted to the Roll, a solicitor is let loose directly on the public. I went to the crammers Gibson and Weldon and though they did their best for me, I felt it difficult. There was such a lot to memorise and learn parrot-fashion. The atmosphere was not good at home which was not helpful and I was not surprised that I failed. My grandfather was extremely understanding and he just said with characteristic simplicity that I must try again, which I did and succeeded. There was a ceremony at the Law Society on 1st October, 1951 which my mother and grandfather attended. My name was called. I shook hands with the president of the society and I was admitted as a Solicitor of the Supreme Court. Subject to getting my first job, it was the end of the road for Grandpa looking after my education. He certainly fulfilled his promise to look after me which he had done for twenty-three years.

So now, I had to look around and join a firm. My uncle Rodney had a solicitor called Eric Hanney who practised in a firm called Chapman Walker and Co. of Half Moon Street off Piccadilly. I was introduced to him and we seemed to get on well. He promised to get in touch with me but, despite several reminders, he never did. I was rather upset and not a little annoyed. Things were getting a bit desperate and there was nothing to do but to take the matter into my own hands so I went to the Law Society and searched the register to see if there was a vacancy that seemed suitable.

I saw a notice for a solicitor advocate by Amery-Parkes and Co., the solicitors to the Automobile Association (AA) for their Free Legal Defence Scheme. I wrote in and was asked to see a partner, A. C. Burrows at Fanum House, Leicester Square, which was then the Headquarters of the AA. He was a very courteous old-style English gentleman who took me to lunch at the Café Royal. He explained that the FLD (Free Legal Defence) Scheme as it was called, was for representation in the courts of AA members. It would be mainly appearing in the magistrates' courts in and around London. In those days, defendants either had to appear in person or be represented. Later, it was possible to plead guilty by letter and set out any mitigation. Normally, the scheme did not extend to trial by jury at Quarter Sessions or Assizes but, occasionally, the AA would cover the costs if there was a point involved of general interest to motorists. Again, but not often, the AA would pay for a point of law to be taken in the High Court.

I did not have much knowledge about cars and driving but I was interested in advocacy and had to make a start somewhere. I was introduced to Mr William Taylor Parkes, the nephew of the founder of the firm, John Amery Parkes who was also one of the founders of the AA. Mr Parkes was unfortunately very deaf. He had a primitive deaf aid with a box by his top pocket about the size of a modern mobile phone with a loop to his ear. His deafness resulted from the First World War when he was in the first battle at Cambrai fought with tanks. He was awarded the Military Cross. He knew a great deal about motoring law. Apparently, in the nineteen-twenties, he used to be sent by his uncle to courts around the country travelling by bike with a side car for his papers and belongings. He used to be kept on the road for several weeks as he would get messages from his uncle telling him where the next set of papers had been sent! I rather liked "Willie" who liked to put up a fight for a client when he properly could and he could be quite amusing. He had a reputation of being rather fond of and mean with money and I had an experience of this at a very early stage.

I agreed to take the job and had a service agreement with the firm for three years. The initial salary was £600 a year, the second year was £640 and the third year was £700. It was subsequently extended for a further three years with increases of £60 each year. In fact the starting amount was £50 less but I told Mr Parkes I had not been informed that I would have to work some Saturdays so he raised it.

The first case I had to do was to go to Highgate Magistrates' Court for a client who was charged with driving under the influence of drink and dangerous driving. He had elected trial at Middlesex Sessions and I was to represent him at the committal proceedings. These were very different from now when written statements are served by the prosecution, and in almost all cases, it is over formally and quite quickly. In 1951, oral depositions were taken. A witness would be asked questions. The clerk of the court would write the answers down in longhand. The defence could question witnesses but seldom did. The clerk would then read over what he had written to the witness who would then sign it. It was a laborious process. One "stipe", Geoffrey Rose, used to sit on the bench, discreetly doing his stamp collection! The prosecution did not have to call all its witnesses but sufficient to make out a prima facie case, that is, a case for the defendant to answer and the bench had to be satisfied that this had been done. The defendant could give evidence and call witnesses but very seldom did. The defence advocate would say, "The defendant pleads not guilty, reserves his defence and calls no witnesses at this stage". The prosecution did not know what the defence would be except that some indications may have been given when the defendant was arrested and/or if he made a statement to the police but, as is well known, once arrested, he would be cautioned by being told, "You are not obliged to say anything ..." etc. In recent years, the right of silence has been a matter of considerable political controversy. Over the years, the defendant's position has been weakened. The Criminal Justice Act 1967 provided for notice to be given to the prosecution when the defendant was going to put forward an alibi and the Criminal Procedure and Investigations Act 1996 provided for a scheme of more general disclosure of the defence case.

But back to Highgate Magistrates' Court and, again, in 1951 the law on driving under the influence of drink was very different. There was no breathalyser. There were no blood or urine tests from samples that had to be provided. Evidence would be given of erratic driving, the defendant would be stopped, his breath would be said to smell of drink or intoxicating liquor and he would be arrested and taken to the police station. He would then be examined by a police surgeon who would not be employed by the police but a GP on a panel who would be called out. He would carry out a number of tests e.g. walking a straight line, signing his name, subtracting seven from 100 and reading something. They varied a bit but they nearly always included a test for nystagmus which was to shine a torch in the eye and see if there was involuntary flickering—and Rhomburg's test which was standing to attention, shutting one's eyes and looking to see if there was swaying.

Once at Hendon Magistrates' Court, a rather elderly doctor was persuaded rather reluctantly to do Rhomburg's test while he was in the witness box. He started swaying and was only saved from going from the vertical to the horizontal by the quick intervention of two policemen standing nearby!

At Highgate, I thought the prosecution case was really weak, perhaps they thought they would get it through on the nod. So I boldly submitted that on the drink charge, there was not sufficient evidence to go for trial. The bench agreed and the clerk then said, "Mr Baker, have you another submission to make?" I was momentarily perplexed and thought this must relate to the dangerous driving so I said something about that and, again, the magistrates agreed. The case was not committed for trial. My client was, of course, quite delighted and gave me a big white, crisp five pound note.

When I returned to the office, I had to see "Willie" Parkes because he dealt with nearly all the Quarter Sessions cases. When I told him what had happened he was quite astonished and not one hundred per cent pleased. He asked me if the defendant had given me anything but he did not ask me to hand over the five pound note, for which I was grateful and relieved. Then it transpired that Willie had taken fifty pounds in anticipation of the case going to Quarter Sessions which he now had to return. He told me not to do this again!

I was then sent on the more usual type of work by going to magistrates' courts for the hearing of cases. The morning courts were usually in outer London where there were lay benches, places like Richmond, Kingston, Hendon, Harrow and Tottenham. I think the furthest we went was Dartford. The afternoon Courts were in Inner London where there were stipendaries, usually known as "stipes". Nearly all were barristers, with the occasional solicitor. They varied a lot. Some obviously enjoyed the job and were courteous, especially to the newcomer. Others were rather sour, perhaps regretting that they had left the Bar and taken the appointment. All had to be quick to get through the list of cases for the day. The premier court was at Bow Street where the chief magistrate sat. That court had additional jurisdiction relating to extradition cases. A new "stipe" would start there under the eye of the "chief" and then go off to his own court, generally to share it with a more senior "stipe". Sometimes, these pairings did not work out well. At Marlborough Street, "Mick" McElligott believed that foreign shoplifters, who were often quite wealthy, should be sent to prison while St. John Harmsworth thought they should be fined heavily. This meant that those jailed, would appeal and the appeal would be allowed unless it was a very bad case.

Another contrasting couple were at Clerkenwell: Tommy Davis and Frank Powell. The latter was good in every respect but the former was impatient and sarcastic, especially if a case was being contested which would lengthen his time that day on the bench. He was always hoping for a plea of guilty. One day, I was doing a dangerous driving case. I called the defendant and then a witness. There were some differences between them though not serious. If they had said exactly the same I am sure that some comment would have been made about putting heads together. When I announced that I was going to call another witness, the magistrate said, "Is he going to agree with the defendant or support the last witness or give yet another account?" I just looked at him, paused and said, "I can only invoke the well-known observation of Mr Asquith who was not only a Prime Minister but also a barrister who said, 'Wait and see!'" I have wondered if I would have done that if I had been a bit more experienced. I hope so. Tommy Davis was quite astonished. Perhaps he thought he had gone too far but at the end of the case he said he did not think it had been proved and found my client not guilty. He gave no reasons for his decision.

It was Alec Jennings, in his practical way, who stressed to me 'Know your judge". I have always followed that. I would look them up in *Who's Who* and find out something about them. Paul Bennett used to sit at Marlborough Street before the two I have mentioned. He won a Victoria Cross in the First World War and nearly always wore the Guards' tie. I once appeared before him for a man who was called Napoleon. When the case was called, in rather stentorian tones, I rose and faced the magistrate. I put my right hand across by body and under my jacket and said, "Sir, I represent Napoleon". Paul Bennett did not— often smile but he did on this occasion and asked me what course I was taking. I told him it was a plea of guilty and he said, "Ah! Fighting a rearguard action!" This put him in a good mood and he imposed a penalty about which I could not complain.

The other magistrate at Marlborough Street was Clyde Wilson, a short man with a reedy voice. It was a surprise to know that he had been a racing driver at Brooklands, the auto-racing circuit in Surrey. He was a bachelor who lived at home with his mother. One day she had to ring the court and was put through to the gaoler. The following conversation took place:

"My boy is not feeling very well this morning. He will be a bit late but he'll get in as soon as he can."

"Come along, come along, if your boy does not surrender to his bail by ten o'clock, the magistrate will have something to say. "

"My boy is the magistrate".

Clyde Wilson had one tactic which I thought was quite effective judging by the expressions on defendants' faces. He used to tell them what the maximum penalty was for the offence committed and then impose what he thought was right in the circumstances—which was usually far less—and then say, "Don't do it again". I have heard defendants say, "Thank you" with much relief.

Rowland Thomas also sat at Marlborough Street which was a very~ busy Court, then he craftily got himself transferred to Marylebone which was the nearest magistrates' court to Lords. He would want to get to the ground as soon as he could, especially on Test Match days. On one such day he saw from his list that the first dozen or so cases were prostitutes accused of soliciting in public. He said "Bring them all in". When the number was checked, he said, "You all plead guilty?" They all nodded. He continued, "I recognise you all, the penalty is forty shillings. No time to pay. You've all got that amount. Go to the office and pay it and then you can leave." They trooped out and he said to the clerk, "Call case number thirteen".

On another occasion, he was somewhat reluctantly told by a policeman that there was another case in his list.

"What is it?"

"An allegation of theft of a clock from Selfridges". A rather pathetic looking man was brought in to be greeted with, "If it's time you want, I can give you up to six months". After a plea of guilty, he was not put inside. The arresting policeman very fairly said that the clock was still going!

There are a number of other stipes I could mention, some more favourably than others but one more will have to suffice as it concerns an incident which if it appeared in a *Rumpole of the Bailey* story by John Mortimer QC would be thought quite fictional and exaggerated. The magistrate was Bertram Reece (Bertie), a large man with an imposing head and glasses and a gold fountain pen. He could never remember anybody's name. Everybody was "Yes, Mister". The exceptions were the few ladies who were in practice. He could not very well say, "Yes, Miss". He was number two at Bow Street but he often sat in the large Court One when the "chief" was not sitting. There was usually a lot of people in the court. The public stood at the back facing the magistrate. There was quite a lot of movement in the court itself as cases were dealt with quickly. One day there was more movement and buzz than usual and Bertie said with some emphasis, "I must have decorum in my court". An usher went to the door and shouted out, "Call Dick Oram!" There was no reply!

It was in that court and I think, in front of Bertie that I played a new role in court on the spur of the moment. I was waiting for my case to be called when a man was brought in accused of having paid the minimum fare on the Underground and travelled too far. The defendant was a Pole who did not understand what was happening. There was no interpreter available. I stood up and asked the clerk if I could find out if he understood German, and if so, would I be allowed to act as interpreter. The defendant did understand and the court was able to deal with the case. I did not ask for and did not get any fee to mention to Mr Parkes. If it was Bertie Reece, I am sure he would have said, "Thank you. Mister".

When I was living at home in Sutton, I decided to carve out a bit of a life of my own. I joined Cheam Hockey Club, Sutton Cricket Club, the local Liberal association (we were just in the Carshalton constituency. There were not many of us) and the Wallington Parliament. Cheam was one of the top London sides though there were no leagues. The clubs themselves decided who they would play. In addition to the weekly games around London, there were festivals at Easter at various seaside resorts. Over the years, I went to Folkestone, Worthing and Weston-super-Mare. I continued to play in goal but occasionally, I was given an outing on the left wing, but I was not fast enough. The club ran five teams. I was usually in the second team but I did play in the firsts sometimes. I was especially pleased to play against Oxford University in the Parks at Oxford. They were really a class above us and we were lucky that the score was only four-nil. I had quite a busy afternoon. I was really no good at cricket. I would like to have succeeded but I made few runs though I did take some wickets trying to bowl off-breaks. The value to me was the friendships I made. I still see people such as Tony Bennett who has been the president of the Cheam Hockey Club for some years and John Hitchin, a solicitor, who played with considerable success for both clubs. I have been regularly to the Annual Dinners of both clubs especially the cricket club which for many years has been held in the much improved club pavilion. From time to time, I have been asked to speak at them. They can be quite tough audiences especially if time is getting on and drinks are available at the bar. I got the West Indian cricketer Learie Constantine to come and he more than held his own with his stories - told with easy charm and no malice.

After the General Election disasters of 1950 and 1951, I was derided a bit for being a Liberal. The standard joke was about losing one's deposit which so many Liberal candidates did, failing to get one-eighth of the total vote; still we held the fort, fighting both local and Parliamentary elections. I had left the constituency long ago but it seemed amazing that in 1997 Tom Brake turned a conservative majority of 9,943 into a Liberal Democrat majority of 2,267. He held it in 2001 and again in 2005.

The Wallington Parliament was a debating society for political activists. A few Liberals attended regularly and made their contributions. The debates were well reported in the local press. This was done in a fair and balanced way so that the Liberals appeared rather stronger than they were locally. I just hope that in Carshalton as in Richmond, there were some stalwarts who survived to enjoy the later general election victories.

It was not long after I joined Amery-Parkes and Co. and began to earn a salary that I decided that I would leave home and go into digs. I had taken part in a number of Liberal and Young Liberal activities in Central London and I was told of a Liberal in Hampstead, Gwen Martin, who had a room she wanted to let. She and her husband were separated and she had three young children to bring up. I decided to go there. She was kind and understanding to me. We used to go to local Liberal functions and the Hampstead Parliament which was like the one I had been to in Wallington. She was a gifted pianist and taught at the Academy. The house was convenient to get to the London courts and to the office in Leicester Square.

I had a wide circle of acquaintances but no special friends. I had not been able to have much of a social life. I had, however, in 1948, met Joy Heward. I was making a speech at the Oxford Union. It must have been an important one because I went to the Liberal Party HQ in Gayfere Street, Westminster, to get some information and facts. There I met Joy who was the head of the information and research department. She was a history graduate at Newnham College, Cambridge who had been in the Women's Royal Naval Service serving on Lord Mountbatten's staff in Ceylon (as Sri Lanka was then called) and Singapore. She was most helpful and we kept in touch. We saw each other at various London Liberal functions. When I got to Hampstead, we began to see more of each other. Her brother was a solicitor with Rose, Johnson and Hicks whose offices were off the Haymarket. Joy had a flat in Buckingham Palace Road which she shared with two other girls. I had joined the National Liberal Club on 2nd October, 1946. The subscription to the end of the year was five shillings and threepence, so the annual sub, for somebody almost 21, was one guinea (one pound and one shilling). It went up by a small amount each year until the number was thirty. It was a good place to eat and see people being in Whitehall Place and the Westminster Liberals had meetings there. Joy was treasurer of the Westminster Liberal Association. One of the members was Ian Steers who was just beginning what has turned out to be a very successful career as an investment broker in the City. Like Carshalton, Westminster Liberals fought general and local elections. Once Ian and I were canvassing in the Soho ward and were surprised how few doors were being opened. We later learned that word had quickly spread around that we were from the Home Office and inquiring about immigration!

Joy knew that I was not permanently settled in Hampstead and one day she rang to tell me that there was an advert in *The Times* for a room to let in the Clergy House at All Saints, Margaret Street which is just behind Oxford Street, not far from Portland Place and the BBC I looked at it and took it. I was grateful to Gwen Martin and I am glad to say that after I left, she and her husband Jack, a piano accompanist, got together again.

Thanks to Joy, I was within easy walking distance of Leicester Square. There was a small choir school whose former pupils included Laurence Olivier. The Head was the Reverend Father Melville, who was quite interesting as he had been a cleric in Peru. The Vicar was Reverend Dr Kenneth Ross and the Curate, Tony Andrews. We breakfasted together with the school bursar. There was one lady on the premises, Miss Badderley, the matron. It was a High Church. Sometimes, there were demonstrations outside by evangelicals known as "Kensitites" who protested against "Romish practices". The clergy were very tolerant of me. For a time, I was joined by John Birch, the distinguished organist who later played at the Temple Church and at Winchester Cathedral.

It was becoming apparent that Joy and I were increasingly attracted to each other personally and that our friendship was going beyond political events though that continued. The London Liberal party was quite active socially. The President was a recent recruit from the Liberal Nationals called Sir Alfred Suenson Taylor who was associated with the London and Manchester Insurance Company. He looked far from robust and had been gassed during the First World War. He would give receptions—for which he paid the bill—at such venues as Caxton Hall. He would receive everybody, with a rather weak handshake his Scandinavian wife, who I think was formerly "Miss Suenson", standing alongside. There would be a good turn out for a "free do" and Sir Alfred would be warmly applauded and thanked. He became Lord Grantchester. This was subject to some comment and criticism as he had not done very much for the party. A Young Liberal called Dr Roy Douglas, a biologist who had stood at Bethnal Green, used to write verses and jingles about the Liberal party. To explain what follows, I should mention that the Liberal headquarters had moved from Gayfere Street to the less expensive Victoria Street. Roy wrote about Sir Alfred to the tune of, "The man who broke the Bank at Monte Carlo":

When I walked into Victoria Street with a pocketful of gold,
I had a good idea,
I could be made a peer,
So I worked liked stink,
For the Liberals pink
And I bought the party lots to drink.
I'm the man who got a peerage from the Liberals.

Joy's parents lived in Cambridge and I remember meeting them when the Liberal Summer School was held there. The Reverend and Mrs Heward were delightful people and elderly—Joy was the youngest in the family by about nine years. They were very kind to me and I shall have more to say about them later. The Methodist Church was lucky to have such a gifted and devoted couple who worked very hard and successfully.

Joy's flat was very central for London functions. We both got seats for the Coronation in 1953. I got mine through my uncle Rodney who was a Middlesex magistrate so I was in Parliament Square outside Middlesex Guildhall and opposite Westminster Abbey. In that year, I became chairman of the National League of Young Liberals. I tried to get to various parts of the country to encourage the members. We had a paid secretary, Beth Graham, and produced some quite good literature on a modest scale. I tried to see that we were represented well on all-party functions and also in the Liberal Party Organization itself. As chairman, I had a seat on the Party Executive which met monthly in London. It was not always an exhilarating experience. I got to know how small the active membership was and how difficult it was to find the money to employ the minimum number of staff to function effectively.

Joy and I shared a lot of Liberal life but our lives went beyond that. We were both fond of classical music, though she was much more knowledgeable than I was. She might have been a professional pianist if the war had not intervened in 1939. We went to concerts together, especially to the Proms at the Albert Hall in the summer. We liked to sit behind the orchestra watching the conductors' different styles and how they indicated what they wanted.

Having been brought up in Cambridge, Joy liked watching rugger and cricket, so it is not surprising that we went off to Twickenham and Lords together. We were increasingly in each other's company and so in March 1954, I proposed and was delighted when she accepted. My friends all thought I had done the right thing and in the time-honoured phrase, "They lived happily ever after". There was a bit of publicity in the press about a Liberal romance and we had some very nice letters of congratulations.

●　　●　　●

So the summer was spent making plans for the wedding. We wanted Joy's father to marry us but the Methodist Churches in Central London were very large indeed. We would have been dwarfed in the Central Hall. There was a happy solution. Joy had sat on a rather high-powered United Nations Association Committee in Westminster. One of the members was the Reverend Dr Joseph Moffatt of the Crown Court Church, Covent Garden. Mr Heward liked the Scots and their ministers. He used to go to Scotland for golf. So Dr. Moffatt was asked, a little cautiously, if he was prepared to let us have his church. I shall always remember his reply, "You can have it all day if you *want*". Nothing could have been better especially as we were able to get the nearby Waldorf Hotel in the Aldwych for the reception. So all was set for 25th September, 1954.

Ian Steers was the best man and arrived in good time at Margaret Street with a flask of brandy to keep me going! It was not wholly a Methodist occasion. We arrived at the church but Joy, coming from Buckingham Palace Road was held up in traffic — and just over ten minutes late. Just before that, Ian whispered to me, "Bang goes the timetable!" Mr Heward took the service extremely well and as it ended, there was a surprise. Dr Moffatt kindly came and was standing by my left ear and he suddenly declaimed in a very loud and resonant Scots voice, "May the blessing of God the Father Almighty etc. etc. ". When he had finished, we went to sign the register! We were able to relax at the reception at which Admiral Sir Arthur Hall proposed our health in a delightful way. We had a small page (Peter Davis) and a small bridesmaid (Sarah Dowding, now, Sarah Hill) and their photographs smelling a bouquet of flowers, appeared in a number of newspapers.

One of the members of the Westminster Liberal Association was Arthur Hostler, a splendid London cabbie who arrived at the Aldwych in a black coat and striped trousers, complete with his badge, to take Joy and myself away amidst much cheering. In fact, he took us no further than Lincoln's Inn. There, we transferred to Ian's Ford Popular car. He took us, a little jerkily, to Heathrow where we got on a plane to Palma, Majorca. Joy had on a lovely blue velvet coat and got a loud wolf whistle as we went up the gangway. We stayed at Calamayor, west of Palma and got an excellent sherry on the beach for seven old pence. From there we went across the island by local bus with fruit and poultry as well as people. When we arrived at the Miramar Hotel, Puerto de Pollenca, a receptionist produced the hotel register for me to complete. He was a typical Spaniard with olive skin, dark hair and brown eyes. I was very proud to enter Mr and Mrs Baker. I started the address 'Buckingham Palace' but there was no room for 'Road' so I just made a squiggle, something like 'Rd.' at the side of the page. He turned the book around and said in amazement, "Buckingham Palace, *importante*". We got excellent service and were well treated at that hotel which had a boat to take us to the beach at Formentor. Then we took a small plane to Barcelona. We were told it might be a bit bumpy so the passengers were given a glass of sherry before take off! In Barcelona, we stayed at an old hotel on Las Ramblas with the biggest bedroom we've ever had. The trains went on pretty late, but it is a magnificent city and benefits – as so many do – from a waterfront.

•   •   •

Then back to work for both of us in London. I moved into the flat in Buckingham Palace Road and had a small Austin Eight car which I kept in a garage in Belgravia. It had a canvas roof and perspex windows which could be pulled out! There were no security devices. It was stolen once from outside the War Office and found by the police a few days later in Willesden, quite undamaged. I paid £380 for it and drove many miles for several years without any serious mishap. She was known as 'Little Mo' after the tennis player.

In politics, Anthony Eden became Prime Minister in July 1955 and called a General Election very quickly. This was tactically correct for him because he increased the Conservative majority. Despite there being four years since the last General Election, the Liberals were only able to field 110 candidates, one more than 1951. They did very badly with 60 of the candidates losing their deposits. The six members were again returned but no gains were made. It was probably the lowest level the party had reached. Efforts were made to persuade me to become a candidate but I had not the time or the money to do it. There is no point in becoming a "paper candidate" when numbers are so small. It was clear that amongst other changes, it was time for Clement Davies to stand down, and quite soon, he did.

There was a change of work for me. I was asked by Stuart Fryer who was in charge of the office of Amery-Parkes in Arundel Street—which runs between the Law Courts and the Temple Station—to take over a scheme whereby the AA helped members who had been involved in an accident, with their claim. There was sent down from Fanum House a very large number of cases, some concerning a member and his own insurers, others concerning a claim against the insurers of the other party involved. At Fanum House, the AA had a legal department which was nothing to do with Amery-Parkes. There was no qualified solicitor but a number of clerks. They decided what cases the AA would support financially and referred them to us. Sometimes, I could see no reason for the decision. However, one had to do one's best. I had no control over the costs arrangements.

I did have discussions with Mr Fryer about what the AA were doing and he told me that I must not upset them and kill the goose that laid the golden eggs. I think the truth was that the AA was the only significant client that the firm then had. Anyway, after a time, Mr Fryer said the scheme was not working and asked me to leave the firm. I doubt whether he had any authority to do this as I was a partner—albeit a salaried and not profit sharing one. We were different personalities. He did admit he had behaved very badly and some time later, when I went to the Bar, to my surprise, he wrote a rather decent letter to me, wishing me luck and—as I shall relate—the firm sent me a good deal of work in the critical days when I wanted every brief I could get my hands on.

I could have fought the matter and called a partners' meeting but I never thought I would be staying with the firm as I felt that my professional life should not be limited to the motor car.

In a way, I was relieved to look for something else. Joy was wonderfully understanding but it was not an easy start to marriage—in effect getting the sack. However, luck was on my side and I went forward to one of the most interesting, though short, periods in my time as a solicitor.

Personally, things were going well. My parents left Sutton and went to Worthing. My mother wanted to be by the sea but when she got there, she said there were not any ships to be seen! With Joy's parents at Cambridge, we were well served for weekend visits with changes of air from central London.

CHAPTER 4

Career Changes for the Better

When I was leaving Amery-Parkes, I happened to see a barrister called Bill Glanville Brown. I saw him from time to time in the Temple and more often in the National Liberal Club. He was a big man with a hearty laugh, always ready with an anecdote though sometimes difficult to get away from. He was one of the team which included another Liberal, Sir Arthur Comyns Carr QC, who was a prosecutor at the Japanese War Crimes Trials. When they returned to the English Bar, they had to re-establish themselves and found it rather difficult as they were some years behind those who had returned from the War rather earlier. Bill though, was a good linguist and he was able to act as an interpreter. He did this to excellent effect in translating from French during a Liberal Party Conference.

Bill told me of a recently established firm of solicitors called Goodman, Derrick and Co. who had premises in the Temple both at Hare Court and in Dr Johnson's Buildings which was obviously an inconvenient arrangement. They were on the look out for another partner, so I met Mr Goodman and Mr Derrick in the restaurant in the Law Courts in the Strand for lunch. I knew Goodman by sight as he often lunched at the Law Society. His large appearance, and especially his head, was difficult to miss. It was clear that he was the dynamo with contacts especially in the literary and entertainment worlds, while Derrick was the quieter backroom man doing the traditional solicitor's work of probate and conveyancing.

I was taken on by them and would get 15 per cent of the profits. Before, I had only had a salary. One of my first tasks was to find accommodation for the whole firm though there were not very many of them: two assistant solicitors, Levene and Chody, a clerk called Hill and the cashier, Frank Usher.

Both Goodman and Derrick had excellent secretaries, Mrs Rossiter and Miss Pullen. I found accommodation in Holborn but when I reported my success it emerged that Goodman had been making his own enquiries and had got accommodation in nearby Bouverie Street at the top of the offices of the *News of the World*. He did this through Mark Chapman Walker who had gone to that newspaper from Conservative Central Office where he was in charge of press and publicity. I think they met during the war. So to Bouverie Street we moved and I remember that when I went to the premises with Goodman, Chapman Walker was there. We went to the corner room and C. W. said "Goodie, I expect this will be your room and from here you will see the Law Courts' clock. As far as I know, it is always right so it will help you to be punctual". Goodman had a reputation for being late. He had so many appointments every day as well as innumerable phone calls. It remained the same and in later life – after he had been elevated to the peerage – he was sometimes referred to as "the late Lord Goodman". I remember Sir Hugh Cubitt telling me that at the Housing Corporation there would be a phone call saying that Lord Goodman would be late and could, say, Item Seven on the agenda be deferred until he was present.

However, he was punctual once. He and I went to see a client in Tottenham who ran a furniture business. After that, I was due to go to South Western Magistrates' Court in Lavender Hill to appear, for a client in a motoring matter, the sort of case with which I was familiar. Goodman drove and I navigated. We arrived ten minutes early at ten minutes to two. With a movement of great panache, Goodman turned off the ignition, turned to me and said: "Well, Baker, if we do not make the grade as lawyers, we will make a damn good firm of taxi drivers!"

When I joined Goodman, Derrick and Co. in 1957, commercial or independent television had just begun. There had been a long, and sometimes bitter, battle to break the monopoly of the BBC. There was much resistance to the involvement of advertising with its breaking into programmes and disturbing their continuity. They have always been an irritation to me and I understand that there is now a device in the USA which will eliminate advertisements from the screen. One wonders whether it will ever be able to be marketed as there is bound to be strong opposition from the programme companies.

"A .G." as I shall call Arnold Goodman, though I first knew him as "Abe", was in his element creating syndicates that bid for a TV franchise. Like the Bar with its Circuits, the country was divided into regions and there was only one company allowed for each region. In the early days, the grant of a franchise was in the words of the Canadian, Lord Thompson, who acquired *The Times*, "a licence to print money". There was much demand for advertising space as the advantage of bringing advertising into the home both visually and orally was obvious. For a syndicate to be successful, there had to be a significant local element, supported by those with financial, entertainment and newspaper experience. "Names" were also necessary. If A. G. did not create the syndicate, he seemed to be acting for most of the others. I remember going to the offices of Associated Rediffusion in the Aldwych. I think I held one share in Southern Television to form that company but the one I was most concerned with was Television of Wales and the West (TWW). The News of the World had an interest and Mark Chapman Walker became the managing director. Jack Hylton was a director with his considerable light entertainment agency and there was also Lord Derby, Alfred Francis from the Bristol Old Vic and elsewhere, unkindly referred to by A. G. in his autobiography as a "theatrical busybody", Alec Jeans from the *Liverpool Daily Post* and Eion Meekie from the City as financial director. Among the Welsh representatives was Alderman Huw T. Edwards who seemed to know everybody in the southern part of the Principality.

Inevitably, it was a mixed bag of personalities and there was some tension between members of the board. The company had to pay its way. The larger the number of viewers, the more advertising there would be. Jack Hylton and Mark C. W. were all for popular entertainment and as Mark used to put it, "Every man likes to see a pretty girl". Jack Hylton amongst many others had Shirley Bassey on his books which was especially helpful in South Wales!

Controlling the TV companies was the Independent Broadcasting Authority (IBA) which laid down rules about balancing programme content, how much could be networked, that is, sold by one company to another and transmitted simultaneously in other regions, also the percentage of films and the amount of programmes produced locally. The companies were anxious not to fall foul of the IBA for fear of losing their franchise or not having it renewed. One sensitive point was the limitations on the amount of advertising which could only occur at "natural breaks". TWW got into some trouble over subliminal advertising.

One of my first tasks at A. G. 's request, was to go down to TWW 's offices at Cardiff and decide how the "Epilogue" was to be divided up between the various Churches in Wales. There was to be a closing ten minute programme on Sundays. I did as much research as I could into the Churches in Wales and in particular their membership. I knew something about chapels with my father-in-law being a Methodist minister, though I did not tell anybody in case they thought I was biassed!

When I entered the room for the meeting, I was not altogether surprised at the large number present, probably, about a hundred. I thought I had to give a lead so I gave the results of my research. Somebody in the audience – and I rather think it was Huw T. Edwards – asked if I was aware that, in Swansea alone, there were three branches of Methodism. I did know that the Primitive, Wesleyan and United Methodist Churches had come together in 1932 but it seemed to have passed certain parts of Wales by! The one fact on which we were all agreed was that there were fifty-two weeks in each year! I went away to allocate the various fractions of time which I did quickly as the opening day of the station was not far away and I gave my reasons. As far as I know, there was no complaint and looking back I suppose it was a good experience of appearing to act in a fair and judicial manner.

I got to know not only the directors but also, the senior staff of TWW. The secretary, called Bales, was very helpful in tipping me off about what might be coming up and when I might be asked to make a contribution to a meeting. I tried to encourage him as he was treated by Mark Chapman Walker rather like Captain Mainwaring treated Private Pike in Dads' Army though Mark never actually said "Stupid boy"! The head of programmes was a Hylton man called Bryan Michie, a big man with much good cheer and enthusiasm. He had the advantage of being a well-known voice on radio but the greater responsibility for the success of the company fell on Bob Myers who was hired from NBC in America. He had considerable experience of TV in the USA and brought much technical knowledge to making programmes economically. He was a thoughtful, kindly man whom I found easy to work with but he was a stranger to England and as far as I am aware he knew nobody, for example in the BBC, TV world. Considering his disadvantages, I thought he did a good job.

I had always been interested in TV especially as a extension of the public and political scene and I was very pleased when Bryan Michie asked if I would appear in a programme. It was called "Soapbox" and imported from Canada by Roy Ward Dickson. In each half hour programme there would be three contestants who would speak on a subject of their choice urging that something should be done, for example, that smoking should be banned from all public places. The contestant would stand as if addressing an open air meeting. There would be a studio audience gathered around and after the speech there would be questioning from a panel who challenged the ideas of the contestant. At the end of the programme, the audience would vote on which contestant had put up the best performance. I was one of the regular members of the panel, usually, three. I did twenty-six programmes; other participants were an Oxford friend of mine working in Robert Maxwell's firm, Pergamon, Sylvia Stratford Lawrence and a journalist who had been a distinguished war correspondent, a New Zealander called Wallace (Wally) Reyburn. The chairman was a barrister called Simon Kester – a forerunner of Clive Anderson. Occasionals included Katie Boyle and the author, R. F. Delderfield. I thought the format was a good one and there were certainly a lot of applications to take part and also to be "one of the crowd".

A. G. however, did not approve of my appearances. But he did nothing, contenting himself with saying that he thought we were lawyers and not entertainers. In fact, I thought I did the firm some good as there was a degree of interest in who I was. Everything was happily solved when the programme came to an end after a good run. The TV experience was to stand me in good stead later on when I became more active in the Liberal party and stood for Parliament.

TWW had a sad ending as its franchise was not renewed. This was a rare occurrence. The Director-General of ITV at the time was Lord Hill of Luton, the only man who had also held high office in the BBC. As Charles Hill he had been an MP and was well known as the Radio Doctor. He had a characteristic gurgly voice and gained a reputation for the advice that he gave people about their bowels. He had had a row with Chapman Walker, whom I know, like a number of others, held no high opinion of him. I think this happened when Mark was at Conservative Central Office and very influential. There was some score to settle and the casualty was TWW. The successful bidder was Harlech TV, presided over by Lord Harlech, a former Ambassador to the USA. The syndicate promised a number of programme improvements, especially of local content. I wrote to Mark and got back a most generous reply thanking me for all that I had done for TWW in the early days. I felt genuinely sorry for him. I once asked A. G. why Mark who was made a Commander of the Victorian Order - which is generally awarded for some service to royalty. He said it was for introducing the Queen to Prince Philip. I made no comment upon this unlikely story but thought how young all three must have been!

My television experiences whilst with Goodman, Derrick and Co. were not confined to TWW. I did some routine work for Southern TV and then one day early in 1958, A. G. asked me to go to Rochdale where there was a by-election. Granada TV held the franchise for North West England. It was effectively run by the Bernstein Brothers who A. G. knew and the firm acted for them on various matters. Granada was very concerned as this was the first by-election when TV was to play a part and there was real anxiety, shared by candidates and agents about complying with electoral law and permitted expenses. It was going into rather unchartered waters . Fortunately, there were not a lot of fringe candidates standing on one issue – or for publicity like the late Lord "Monster Raving Looney Party" Sutch. The Liberal Candidate was Ludovic Kennedy whom I knew at Oxford and within the Liberal party, so I had to be anonymous and of course, legal and impartial. Luckily, there were no hitches and quite a lot was learned for future by-elections. Afterwards, there were no complaints, so each candidate must have been satisfied especially with the two programmes when they appeared together.

The most memorable incident of this trip is when I arrived at Heathrow and was walking to the departure lounge for Manchester, when a very harassed stewardess rushed up to me and said: "Are you the gentleman for Monte Carlo?" I was so astonished that I spoke the truth. I have often wondered what would have happened if I had said, "Yes"!

Life at Goodman, Derrick and Co. was very varied and in the three years I was there it included two trips to Nigeria and one to South Africa. In 1957, Nigeria was preparing for independence following self-government. It was divided into three regions. The North is Hausa country dominated by Muslims, in the East are the Ibos good at trade and the markets dominated by women, while the Yorubas, who are mainly Christians, live in the West. It is Africa's fourth largest nation and is the most populous having 120 million people. Distances are great; from east to west is over 700 miles while north to south is 650 miles. Communication, especially by road, is not easy.

Nigeria, as events following independence in 1960 have shown, is not easy to govern. Violent coups have broken out and there have been periods of military rule which have suppressed democratic institutions. In the 1950s there were various political movements to end the three large regions and create a number of smaller states within a federal system. It was bound to be some feat to balance the power of the centre with the powers of the states as the histories of the USA, and perhaps to a lesser extent Australia, have shown.

I do not know how it came about, but Goodman, Derrick and Co., in October 1957 were retained by the Mid-West State Movement (MWSM). This was concerned with autonomy for the Benin and Delta provinces which were in the South Eastern part of the Western Region. It had a political dimension. The majority party in the region was the Action Group (I will not call it A. G. as it might be confused with Arnold Goodman!). However in the Benin and Delta Provinces, the majority party was the National Council of Nigeria and Cameroons (NCNC) who were in power in the Eastern Region. The leader of the MWSM was Dennis Osadebay — an able advocate and barrister who had an LLB degree from London University. He was a member of both the federal and Regional Parliaments but perhaps, the most powerful person was the federal Minister of Finance, Chief Festus Okotie-Eboh, an enormous man with a high pitched voice. When he came to London and met Arnold Goodman it would have been dangerous for any one else to get in a lift!

When I arrived in Lagos, I found that there had already been an article about my visit complete with photograph in the *Daily Times*. It reported that I was going "to undertake an extensive tour of Western Nigeria especially in the Mid-West area". I stayed in the large and comfortable Mainland Hotel but it was on the Western side of the Carter Bridge which was a bottleneck when it came to getting to central Lagos. Sometimes, it took half an hour to cross. Lagos teemed with people on foot, in cars, on bicycles and in buses. The buses to and from outlying towns and often going long distances, say, to Ibadan, would have slogans on the front of them often of a religious nature. One I liked as a lawyer, was: "From God's Court, there is no Appeal". I suppose this was a warning not to get in the way! The plane stopped at Rome and Kano. Aircraft ranges were short as it was before the days of the long haul jet. I arrived in Lagos in pouring rain and was greeted by a delegation of eight which included two chiefs. After checking in at the hotel, I was taken to see Chief Festus and there were two reporters and a photographer present. There was coverage on the radio and in the papers. The MWSM had some able and influential members. Festus was a member of the Itsekeri tribe and came from Warri which together with Benin and Sapele was one of the principal towns of the Mid-West. He had been a successful businessman with interests in rubber which was a valuable commodity in the Mid-West and had considerable potential. I soon got to know that in Nigeria everything has its price. "Dash" is required for almost every favour. It goes beyond the bounds of tipping. Festus was known as "Mr Ten Per Cent". How far this was justified, I do not know.

I stayed in Lagos for three days. One important matter was the choice of a member of Queen's Counsel to present the case for the MWSM to the Minorities Commission which was due to come from London towards the end of the year. An inner group had been discussing this and obviously had some knowledge of the leaders of the English Bar. Their choice was a shrewd one: George G. Baker, a Scotsman who had attained the rank of colonel in the Second World War and had contested Southall unsuccessfully for the Conservatives in 1945. I think the Nigerians wanted somebody who might have some political influence with the British Government. However, "Scottie" as he was affectionately known, never contested another seat and, as far as I know, was not active in Conservative party circles. He was a popular man, (two of his sons became judges), devoted to his family. He practised on the Oxford Circuit, became a High Court Judge and ended up as President of the Family Division. The Nigerians also wanted, quite rightly, an economist to show that a Mid-West State would be economically viable. A. G. found Professor Yamey of London University who did a lot of hard work and produced a convincing case.

I then set off for Benin which was the largest City in the Mid-West with a population of 54,000 according to the Nigerian Handbook of 1956 published by the Crown Agents in London. Benin Province had just under a million inhabitants. I flew to Benin in a small plane taking about twelve people. It flew low enough for me to get quite a good view of the country. The man in charge of the team was Chief Omo Osage who was number two to Festus in the finance ministry.

He was quite elderly, enthusiastic for the cause and had the ready laugh of many Nigerians. He was very anxious about my health and in particular, that I did not get a tummy upset by eating Nigerian food so he provided me with European food in tins.

We had a reception at Benin Airport with a crowd of about a hundred people. We then drove in a convoy of cars to the Catering Rest House. The lounge became packed as I was introduced. A number of local chiefs in robes spoke, as did Denis Osadebay whom I described in a letter to Joy as being "very intelligent". I was called upon and pledged that I would do all I could to help and there was great enthusiasm. Photographs were taken and I went to bed feeling that we had got off to a good start. I was a bit apprehensive in Benin as there was still some hostility to colonial power. It went back to 1897 when the acting consul with a party of Europeans visited the city against the wishes of the Oba (the head or chief) whose father had recently died. The convoy of visitors was attacked and most were massacred. Some months later, the British sent a punitive expedition and there were some Nigerian casualties. The Oba was deported to Calabar and his son was installed. I was reminded of this on more than one occasion and people whose families had suffered were pointed out to me. I knew something about this from my readings about Nigeria but I did not appreciate the strength of the feelings that had continued.

As the tour went on, I was extremely glad that I had been politically active in England and had done quite a lot of public speaking from Oxford Union days onward. I seemed to strike the right note of fun and humour to establish a rapport with Nigerians – who also liked a bit of old fashioned oratory.

From Benin, the touring party of five together with a journalist from the NCNC paper *The Pilot*, and the driver, drove in a jeep to the port of Sapele. Omo Osage told me that the vehicle was known as the "boneshaker". It was a pretty rough ride along a rather bad road. Sapele had a very long timber wharf and I was surprised at the size of the ships that were there as it is some fifty miles inland but I learned that the river was twenty feet deep. During the journey, there was considerable flooding and I do not think an ordinary car would have got through. We had to cross the river and then found a convoy of cars and were given another fine welcome. We were taken to a very nice modern chalet which had electric fans and good furniture. I was seated next to His Highness the Ovie of Oghara, a distinguished, wiry, thin, rather old man in a purple and gold robe. There were about sixty to seventy present including chairmen of local councils, lawyers, tradesmen and legislators. Knowing we were on the way to Warri, the local chairman of the Movement read out a prepared statement which had previously been approved. After a short shout of acclamation, he handed it to me. Then His Highness was moved to speak. He said he did not do so often but this was a great occasion. He bade me welcome and pledged his support for the Movement. A short discussion followed. Drinks were served, photographs were taken and the touring team got into the jeep with much handshaking and waving. It was explained to me that only a meeting of various leaders had been called, otherwise the whole town would have turned out. One strong feeling emerged, that administration was inefficient and that local matters had not been attended to. This was repeated elsewhere. There was considerable opposition to and frustration with the regional government at Ibadan which was 160 miles away. It may have been here that I was shown a road that had started to be built as part of an election promise but work had stopped after polling day!

We then went to the port of Warri which had a government jetty with a draught of seventeen feet. When I returned to England, I was told that there had been a dispute at the dock about goods that belonged to Chief Festus getting loading priority! Warri was the headquarters of the Delta Province which had some 580,000 inhabitants which was about two thirds of Benin Province so I had a potential of one-and-a-half million clients and most seemed to support the

MWSM, at least where I was taken! The road to Warri was again rather bumpy. We passed masses of rubber trees and some palms. I was glad that there was some other traffic in case anything happened to the jeep.

My chalet at the Catering Rest House with two rooms and a bathroom was very comfortable, a good creation from colonial days. After dinner, the team went to a well-appointed house where there were about twenty people. There was no oratory but a lot of hard thinking and questions. I found this a considerable ordeal but the other members of the team were first-class and we really became a Brains Trust. I certainly learned a lot which was to be a great help when I prepared the brief for G. G. Baker. At breakfast the next day, by chance I heard the eight o'clock news and there was an accurate account of what I had been doing the previous day. The PR of the MWSM continued to be excellent. I never knew how it was arranged and how far it was done centrally or locally or both.

We then returned to Benin City and on the way, stopped at a Shell prospecting station. I had a chat with the Dutch local manager who seemed quite optimistic about Nigerian oil potential. The previous December, Esso had opened a terminal at Apapa near Lagos whose tanks were capable of holding four million gallons of oil. At first, this was going to come mainly from the West Indies. The Mobil Company was also active. They were in the Northern Region based at Sokoto whose Chief, the Sardauna, was the Premier of the Northern Region. One evening at a Catering Rest House when I was on my own, it was probably in Benin City where I stayed longest, I spoke to a representative of the French oil company, Total. He was not only concerned with Nigeria but the Southern Sahara as a whole. He believed that there were great opportunities for successful exploration.

In the latter part of 1957, the prospects for Nigeria were good. In a survey published in December by the UK Trade Commissioners in Lagos and published by the Board of Trade in London, it was observed that, "In a little over a decade, the volume of Nigeria's export trade has increased more than sixfold". Britain was Nigeria's best customer and principal supplier. A warning was given not to be reluctant or tardy otherwise foreign firms and technicians would move in. I had some experience of this when an important crossroads was pointed out to me and the German Volkswagen Company had acquired the adjoining land which would be a convenient place for their vehicles to be brought for servicing.

After lunch in the Catering Rest House — which was a rather disappointing stew — the team set off for Auchi to the North East. At 3.0 p.m., there was a meeting of about fifty people, some of whom had been there since 9.0 a.m. and some had come from fifteen miles away. We were received by the ruler, the Oturo, sitting on a throne in a small dark room. He heard what we had to say and then said virtually nothing. He was, I think, our one complete failure because when the commission was taking evidence, and I will be dealing with this later, this Chief spoke against the MWSM. Perhaps wisely, he gave no hint of this to us, or perhaps his decision was made later!

After Auchi, we went to Asaba and had what turned out to be the best meeting of the tour. The town is on the River Niger which formed the boundary between the Western and Eastern Regions. It is on a hill and has a Catering Rest

House which was the creation of one of the founders of Nigeria, Lord Lugard. The team entered the Town Hall at 5. 30 p.m. which was full with about 150 people. In the front row were six chiefs in white wearing with headdresses of a red fez type with a circle of white feathers. As the team came in, everybody stood up as one man with military precision. We mounted the platform and I was taken to the central chair. I bowed to the chiefs and to the meeting. Everybody sat down, making noises which I was told, signified their pleasure. This was the home of the leader of the MWSM, Denis Osadebay, who represented it both at federal and regional level. He made a great oration in English which was duly interpreted. I was asked to speak next. This was not easy as I could not identify myself as one of the Movement but I could and did say that I had come to help present their case to the commission. I knew how deeply they felt and how they wished to maintain their traditions as they moved forward to independence.

I think it was at this meeting—but it may have been in Benin—that Chief Omo Osage made a wonderful remark in his speech which I have often quoted though with care and discretion. However, I think it is worth repeating here. The reader has to imagine an extremely charged meeting in Nigeria and the speaker working himself up in faultless English and theatrical delivery; the robed Chief declared: "I have been in public life since 1929 and, by now, I am almost—I repeat —almost incorruptible". Just a reminder that he was number two at the Ministry of Finance!

After the meeting, the team and some others went to the Rest House for Dinner. We then returned to Benin. I was told it was eighty-eight miles and we arrived about 10. 30 p.m. I was also told that at Asaba I had been made an honorary chief but I never heard further about it so I do not know anything about the initiation ceremony! I had to look a bit sharp in the morning and get packed up before giving an interview after breakfast to the Nigerian Broadcasting Company.

I was taken back to Lagos to report to Chief Festus on my tour. He seemed to know all about it anyway! The meeting was very useful because there and then he went through my expenses—which I explained to his satisfaction. He paid them together with the fees of Goodman, Derrick and Co. but I did not give him any reward for prompt payment!

Having said my farewells and said that the MWSM were very kind and appreciative, I then flew to Kano to catch a plane to Johannesburg.

I travelled to Kano with the left wing Labour MP for Reading, Ian Mikado, who had been to Ghana and then to Lagos on business. He made a good companion and had sent a libel case to A. G. so that was a good point of contact. Our paths were again to cross unexpectedly during the General Election of 1959 when we represented our respective parties in a BBC broadcast with Harold Watkinson, Minister of Defence, for the Conservatives. I remember the other two getting rather cross with each other but I got the last word with just enough time to make references to Tweedle Dum and Tweedle Dee and my supporters ended the programme with a great cheer which I hope was helpful to the Liberal cause.

There was a delay of some hours at Kano which worked to my advantage I hired a taxi from the Airport Hotel and went around the old city. It got dark very quickly but the car headlights made the buildings look quite remarkable. The atmosphere was notably Arabic and Muslim. The Mosque was the dominant feature. According to the census figures of 1952-3, which were the latest available and like all such figures, may not be completely accurate — the population of the Northern Region was just under 17 million, more than the combined figure for the other two regions which was 14.36 million.

I now appreciated even more what an artificial creation the country of Nigeria was. I hope it is not too simplistic to suggest that its boundaries were determined by the places that British explorers reached. The colonial power was able to hold it together but it was another story after independence came in 1960. In any democratic constitution based on "One man, one vote", for a northern dominated Parliament to rule Nigeria from Lagos was fraught with difficulties and I realised how important devolution was in a federal state.

I left Kano some hours late but before I left Lagos I had a cable about the arrangements to meet me in Johannesburg. The KLM flight there was uneventful except that there was a little ceremony for the passengers, which included me, who had never before crossed the Equator. I still have the rather flowery certificate and, by and large, I think that the gods have since been on my side! When I arrived, I had an unfortunate experience with the official at the immigration desk. I produced my passport and he said: "What are you"? I replied, "British subject by birth". He continued, "It says you were born in Calcutta". I then made the mistake of thinking that the official, obviously a Boer by his accent, might have had a sense of humour and said, "Yes, my mother happened to be there at the time". He then pointed out that I had come from Kano and asked what I had been doing there. I then said that, as a solicitor, I was on legal business. He stamped my passport and threw it at me. This was my introduction to the workings of apartheid. I was rather shaken and wondered what to do. This incident had taken up some time and Mr and Mrs Marks, who I did not know until then, were waiting for me. I decided not to mention anything about it. Perhaps, it was the easy way out but it would have been word against word as nobody else was present and, had there been an investigation, I am sure it would not have helped if it came out that I was active in the Liberal party in England and a member of the Party Council.

This is not the only time, though it was the most dramatic, that I have been grateful to my mother for appreciating the consequences to me of the British Nationality Act 1948. India had obtained Independence in 1947 and not only myself but my father and his father were born there. After I was engaged to Joy in 1954, I applied to be registered as a citizen of the United Kingdom and Colonies.

I was successful in this as I was ordinarily resident in the UK and indeed, had been since I came here in 1926 as I described in *Chapter One*. Needless to say, I value that document and it has had to be produced occasionally for passport and visa purposes.

Mr and Mrs Marks took me to my hotel and looked after me very well during my visit of three to four days. The purpose of it was rather obscure. A. G. had asked me to see some businessmen to find out about certain companies and their links with London. This I did and when I returned I was astonished to be visited by the head of the fraud squad of the City of London Police who was called Lea, a distinguished looking man and the only policeman I have ever seen carrying a black rolled-up umbrella while on official duties! He knew about my visit to Johannesburg and asked me about two of the men I had seen. However, I knew very little about them. When I told A. G., he seemed rather unconcerned. His mind was on other things, probably, several at once.

The second part of my visit to South Africa took me to Cape Town where I was to visit A. G's Uncle, Morris Mauerberger. According to A. G's biographer, Dr Brian Bnivati, the two men did not get on at all well but A. G. gave me no indication of this, though the two men were very different. M. M. was a successful businessman concerned with fruit canning amongst other things. He was determined to be a success and as far as I could tell had no interests outside his work and family. He certainly did not have A. G.'s concern for the arts and good living with congenial friends. M. M. clearly controlled his businesses himself and quarrelled with his family especially his son Joseph, known as Joey, who had divorced his wife and married Marcia, who was not Jewish. He dismissed Joey and there was a dispute about the shares that he held which M. M. wanted returned. With some reluctance, A. G. responded to M. M's request to come out to South Africa to try and settle the matter which he did. This was some two years before my visit and, by the time I arrived, there had been a reconciliation with all the family so that there was, so to speak, a "full house" for the traditional gathering on Friday evenings to which I was kindly invited. With great pride—and he was proud of all he did—M. M. showed me grapefruit growing in his garden. He spoke English with a thick accent which was not always easy to understand especially when he got excited. The Mauerbergers came from Lithuania. I stayed with Joey and Marcia in a lovely Dutch-style house to the west of Cape Town. They were very kind and hospitable.

One day, M. M. drove me there and when two ostriches slowly crossed the road in front of us, he said: "My boy, look vot a vonderful show I put on vor you"! He kept saying that he had bought a "drimaus" for all his children. I could not understand this and I quietly confided in Marcia who said it was "dream house".

I was pleased to see one of N. M.'s managers called Coates as we had met in London. In Cape Town we were watching some black Africans digging a trench in a road and he surprised me by saying, "One day the white people will be digging the trench and some black people will be watching". This was the only reference to apartheid that I heard during my visit. After a few days, I mentioned something to Joey in an unprovocative way and again I was surprised when he said that separate development had a lot of support. I thought it better not to take the matter further. The Mauerberger family like many Jews, had clearly been generous in their support of Israel and people they knew who had settled there. What puzzled me was that while they appreciated the evils of persecution and oppression of Jews in Europe, they did not seem to be aware of the increasingly urgent situation in South Africa.

Support for the Liberal party in South Africa was extremely small and those who advocated any form of racial tolerance in public were heroes. They were generally dubbed "communists". A number like Peter Hain (formerly leader of the House of Commons and currently Minister for Northern Ireland) and his family left the country. Others, like Randolph Vigne, whom I knew at Wadham, were under house arrest.

M. M. knew of the growing success of Goodman, Derrick and Co. "I hear you have got all de good business in London" was how he exaggerated it. He had nothing for me to pass on to A. G. who did not send any message to him. So it was a pleasant interlude for me and I learnt a lot by listening and also enjoying the wonderful scenery of the Cape. Joey and Marcia came to London about two years later and Joy and I were pleased to ask them to our house in Richmond. I have not seen any of the Mauerberger family since and, as far as I know, none came to A. G's memorial service.

I returned home to a much colder England and I was pleased to find out how well Joy had been keeping. She was expecting our first child in March. She had spent some time with her parents in Cambridge and they had visited her.

Apart from my African travels, 1957 was an eventful year for Joy and me. The flat at Buckingham Palace Road was not suitable for a family, being on the second floor above a restaurant and having no garden. In any event, the lease was coming to an end. So we started to look elsewhere. For some reason, we thought we would like to live in Kent but we had no luck. Then one day in February we were going to a rugger international at Twickenham. As I have already mentioned, Joy, having been brought up in Cambridge, knew a lot about both rugger and cricket. I have always been delighted that her interest has continued and we have been to many matches together over the years. She was especially pleased in January 2002 to go to the Long Room at Lords for the first time. "The Holy of Holies" as she kept calling it. The occasion was a supper and a showing of films of Wally Hammond and Denis Compton to which members could bring guests including ladies. It was a great success,

On our way to Twickenham, we got out of the train at Richmond. I went into an estate agent's opposite the station called Pennington's and asked if there were any houses for sale in Richmond. I was told that there were not. I pointed out that it said outside that the firm was established in 1868. "Surely", I said, "with all your experience, you must have one house for sale in Richmond." The man asked if I was in a hurry. I said it was not an urgent matter and he revealed that he had a friend, an architect, who lived off Richmond Hill and wanted to move next May. I said that was all right for us. I got the address and Joy and I saw where it was on the next day. The day after that we visited it with her father and we bought it for less than £5,000. The price today, judging by neighbouring properties that have recently changed hands, would be well in excess of one million pounds!

We moved there in May, 1957 and have remained there ever since so that is the only home our two children have ever had until they were grown up and left to live their independent lives. For the Heward family, to return to Richmond was to go full circle because Richmond was the first Church (Primitive Methodist) that Mr Heward, my father-in-law, had after he was ordained at Bridlington in 1907. I know this from the inscription in the Bible which was presented to him, our house was near the Methodist Training College and 'Pop', as we called him within the family, found a member of his congregation living in our road! Their church, or rather chapel, later became a synogogue. It is not for me to draw any theological deductions from that! My brother-in-law, Edmund Heward, was born in Richmond in Selwyn Avenue.

We soon settled in Richmond, joining the local Liberal Association, the Richmond Society and the Friends of Richmond Park. Although I was brought up an Anglican, I went with Joy and later the children and 'Pop', who came to live with us after he was widowed in 1961, to the Methodist Church in Kew Road which had a very likeable and able minister in Wallace White. I have always liked a stimulating sermon especially one that is not obviously read and flat in delivery which, I am sorry to say, so many Anglican sermons are. Kew Road was lucky in that it could and did call on four teachers at the Methodist Training College to preach. They were gifted men. The principal was Dr Harold Roberts who had all the eloquent passion of a Welsh orator. He would go into the pulpit, open the Bible, read out a verse for his text, shut the Bible and preach for half an hour without a note. Like another gifted preacher, Canon John Oates, who was vicar of Richmond and then rector of St. Bride's Fleet Street, I never knew how much was *ex tempore* or whether any part was learned by heart or whether they just kept headings in their minds. Other preachers at Kew Road were Marcus Ward who had been in South India, Clive Thexton and Norman Goldhawk. I learned a lot from them. They became personal friends and all were very kind to 'Pop' and invited him to various functions at the College which he enjoyed. Of course, he was familiar with students, not least Methodist ones from his time at Cambridge. Indeed he had been a Governor of Wesley House where Marcus Ward, a great authority on St. John's Gospel, was unlucky not to have been the principal. Once he was too young and the next time, too old. Life can be like that.

Having begun to settle in Richmond, Joy and I took a holiday in Villefrance-Sur-Mer. We went to Nice by train having a couchette for the overnight journey. The holiday was a success. We used to go by bus along the coast to the fashionable resorts of Cannes, Monte Carlo and St. Tropez and this intensified my love of France which has continued ever since. I sometimes wonder whether this might be influenced by the fact that I have a Huguenot ancestry.

Nineteen-fifty-seven brought a number of memorable experiences in the legal world. In February, I was in A. G's room at Bouverie Street when he told me that Aneurin (Nye) Bevan had asked him to act in a libel action. It was not long before I was to learn rather more. Bevan, together with Richard Crossman, another leading Labour MP, and the secretary-general of the Party, Morgan Phillips had attended the Annual Congress of the Italian Socialist Party and their behaviour was the subject of a report in the *Spectator* which referred to their occasional appearance and "capacity to fill themselves like tanks with whisky and coffee". Bevan was furious at such an attack and wanted a complete withdrawal and apology. He was not concerned with damages. Crossman was a very clever and mercurial man, capable of changing his mind with some frequency. After he had once spoken in the House of Commons in a contrary sense from one of his recent speeches, Winston Churchill effectively said, "I follow the Honourable Member with all the mental agility that my mind can muster". He was also one of those MPs who write regularly for newspapers and are not always popular with full-time journalists. He has been referred to as: "Slick Dick of the Sunday Pic." He was reluctant to get involved in litigation with a newspaper or journal. This was to have repercussions later, but he really had no alternative than to support his senior parliamentary colleague and demand an apology.

Morgan Phillips had to do the same but as I already knew and it was known generally in political circles, he had a reputation for being a heavy drinker and this, too, had repercussions as the case proceeded.

What happened is well set out, if I may say so, in the biography of A. G. by Brian Brivati and I am grateful to him for his acknowledgement to me of my contribution to his account. However, I feel I must repeat some of the salient features in order to put some comments I would like to make, in the context of the events.

I played no part in the to-ing and fro-ing of draft apologies but A. G. did say to me in some anger that Crossman had been going around Fleet Street behind his back and trying to get an apology himself. This put A. G. in a most awkward position. He was exchanging drafts with Peter Carter Ruck of Oswald Hickson and Co. who were acting for the *Spectator*. Also, and as important, A. G. had to consider the interests of his other two clients. The situation became rather tangled. Crossman met Ian Gilmour, the proprietor of the *Spectator*, at a lunch hosted by Roy Jenkins, the future Chancellor of the Exchequer and Home Secretary. Crossman drafted his own apology and let Gilmour take it away for consideration. He made some significant alterations and then sent it to A. G. who rejected it.

The *Spectator* paid some money into Court and published an apology which they knew was unsatisfactory to the plaintiffs. So the matter came to trial with a jury. Very unusually, the Lord Chief Justice, Lord Goddard, decided to take the case himself. He was not a libel specialist and was known for his right wing views on capital and corporal punishment, publicly expressed from time to time in the House of Lords. He had stood for Parliament as an Independent Conservative objecting to the reform of the divorce laws. He was at the opposite end of the political spectrum to Nye Bevan who had once said that those who voted Conservative were 'lower than vermin'. The Plaintiffs could be forgiven for being downhearted. They need not have worried because it became clear at the first day of the trial that there was one suggestion that Lord Goddard, who was very fond of port, abhorred and that was to accuse a man, wrongly, of not being able to hold his drink. Bevan and Crossman gave evidence and I thought they were clear in their denials of being drunk and stood up well in cross-examination. After all, they had been used in their long political lives to answering awkward questions. I took the three clients to lunch at a restaurant in the Aldwych pursued by the press to whom we said nothing. At lunch, Nye Bevan who ate fish and chips—as he put it—with some gusto, was anxious to know from me how I thought things were going. I was quite upbeat. For some reason that I do not remember, I did not attend the trial in the afternoon but A. G. did.

What I do remember is that when I saw A. G. after court, he was very downcast and told me that Morgan Phillips had been terrible in the witness box. He did not elaborate or suggest any change of tactics. In any event, it would have been a disaster for the reputation of the plaintiffs if, at that stage, they had accepted the money in court which was £500 each and the apology. For one thing, unless something else was agreed, they would have been liable for costs up to the moment the money was accepted which would have included the first day of the trial. Whatever may have been in A. G.'s mind, again, he need not have worried because when the turn of the defence came, Lord Goddard went for Ian Gilmour with great verbal ferocity but before that, A. G. himself gave evidence.

In view of what happened after the case was over, I regard this as being of some importance. He was called to deal with the apologies that had been offered and why they had been rejected. I was there for this. There was one amusing moment when he was asked by Fearnley-Whittingstall, QC for the *Spectator*, how a conversation with Peter Carter Ruck had ended: "I have no specific recollection but I trust with my usual courtesy". "No, Mr Goodman, I put it to you that you said: 'Mr Carter Ruck, you must grovel further". "Oh, no, no, no", (said with much derision and disbelief) and continued until drowned by laughter.

What annoyed Lord Goddard was that the defendants made no attempt in court to justify what they had written by calling witnesses. Their only witness was Ian Gilmour who contended that the article was not defamatory. As the Lord Chief Justice and Gilbert Beyfus, QC for the plaintiffs, tore into him, extracting particulars of his education at Eton and Balliol and asking him what he thought the words meant, I felt a bit sorry for him. The witness box is a lonely place and Gilmour was in a hopeless position which got worse because Lord Goddard then weighed in about the apology:

L. C. J. : "What was wrong with Mr Crossman's draft?"
Gilmour: "Nothing, my Lord".

This was a very strange answer, because as I have already pointed out, Gilmour amended it in a number of respects. The questioning continued:

L. C. J.: "Then why not publish it? You were saying all along you wanted to apologise. Why didn't you? "

I have read and re-read the answer to this and quite frankly, I cannot understand it.

Gilmour: "We took it for granted that an apology acceptable to the other side would be better than one they did not approve. I was under the impression it was universal practice to agree an apology."

If Crossman's draft had been approved by Gilmour, there would have been an agreement. A. G. could not veto it but the other two plaintiffs would have to agree before the case could be settled. I very much doubt if A. G. would have advised them to reject the Crossman draft, however irritated he was at how it came about. Lord Goddard summed up to the jury and there was no doubt where his sympathies lay, but if a judge goes too far in one direction there is a danger that a jury will rebel and show their independence. This jury did not and found for the Plaintiffs, awarding them each damages of £2,500. In fairness to

Lord Goddard, he did tell them that if they found for the plaintiffs, the damages should not be excessive.

One nice spin off was that Morgan Phillips, with his money, paid off the mortgage on his house which brought a little work for "Mac" Derrick to do, so all three partners of Goodman, Derrick and Co. were involved in the case!

Shortly after the verdict, I met Crossman by chance in the House of Commons. In fact, in a friendly way, he approached me and was in an elated mood. He showed no misgivings and made no criticisms of A. G. He gave every indication of being a satisfied client. This is important in view of his subsequent activities. Never able to hold his tongue and always wanting to be congenial, he began to talk to all sorts of journalists and writers indicating that, in fact, they *were* drunk in Venice. Assertions began that perjury had been committed and that A. G. was a party to it. This continued and in February 2002 a piece in the *Observer* by Richard Ingrams referred to A. G. acting for three perjurors. I have written to several papers in defence of A. G. whilst Michael Foot took up the cudgels for Nye Bevan whom he knew very well and whose biography he wrote. I have no doubt that right wing circles wanted to get at Bevan whenever there was an opportunity and Crossman really should have appreciated this. Various stories went the rounds including that the *Spectator* tried to get some Italian waiters to attend court but they would not come unless they were found jobs in England. As Brian Brivati tellingly points out, there was never any suggestion that anybody attending the conference was prepared to come forward and testify to the behaviour of the plaintiffs during its sessions.

My feeling throughout was that a solicitor has to accept what his client says to him. Of course, he can probe and test it and say that it is unlikely to be accepted by a jury. Again, he must not present a case to a court that he knows to be false because he would be party to the perjury. A. G. always maintained that each of his three clients told him that he was not effected by drink and did not behave in the way alleged in the article. In these circumstances, I consider that A. G. behaved quite properly in acting on behalf of his three clients. My belief is underscored by the fact that he was prepared to go into the witness box himself. I do not believe he would have done that if he knew, or even suspected, that his clients had just committed serious perjury to save their reputations. The article in the *Spectator* would have gained very little publicity if it had not been for the libel action. It is true that A. G. was called to speak about the apologies but cross-examination is at large and he could have been questioned about anything that was relevant to the case. If some attack on his integrity succeeded, even to the extent of causing suspicion of his conduct, he would have left the court a ruined man.

I also do not believe—as has been suggested by Crossman and others—that he was determined to win this case for the publicity and his own reputation. While he was no doubt pleased that the still new firm, largely created by him, had been involved in such a case, I do not think that his mind worked in that way. He took, with gratitude and enthusiasm, every case that came along and did it to the best of his considerable ability. It may seem strange, but I do not think he was a political animal who revelled in the cut and thrust of debate and the excitement of winning elections and getting office. He was approached to be the Labour candidate for Hampstead and declined. When he became a peer, he sat on the cross-benches.

Over the years, we kept in touch about various press comments concerning the case. Quite early one day, he rang and asked me to read out a rather full letter I had written to the *New Law Journal*. When I had finished, he just said, "Sir, I shall now go and enjoy my breakfast". I have always regretted that so many people have accepted the post-trial Crossman version of events. A. G. did not deserve the criticisms and censure that have been heaped upon him but it certainly brought him into the limelight and it was not very long before he was being consulted by Harold Wilson.

CHAPTER 5

Hopes, Disappointments and Nigeria Once Again

In September 1956, the Liberal Party Conference (then called the "Assembly"), met at Folkestone and the leader of the party since 1945, Clement Davies, stepped down. It was a sad moment for those Liberals who had been active in the party during his years, but he was over 70 and although his powers of emotional Welsh oratory were undiminished, there was a growing feeling that the time had come for a younger and, hopefully, more charismatic figure to take over. Clement Davies had been the MP for Montgomery since 1935. His style and political presentation were not suited to the age in which television was to become the prime medium of communication. There were only six Liberal Members of Parliament, less than one per cent of the total. The joke was that they could all get into one London taxi! In 2005 the 62 Liberal Democrat MPs would fill a London bus.

There was no dispute across the whole range of political activists and commentators that the best person to succeed Clement Davies was Jo Grimond who had been in the House since 1950 and had always defeated both Labour and Conservative opponents.

He looked like a leader. He was tall with a characteristic forelock and impish sense of humour, he also had a compelling, resonant voice. He could not only be an old style orator captivating a big meeting but he was a highly successful performer on TV where he could do the straight talk and more than hold his own in interviews and discussion programmes.

One man though, however gifted, cannot make a national political party and Jo Grimond was fortunate in that, when he became Leader, the Liberal party was doing quite well in by-elections but not well enough to win a seat. There were some creditable near misses and the general feeling was that the party was on the "up". Another factor was the general political situation. The Suez crisis had resulted in the resignation of the Prime Minister, Anthony Eden, who was succeeded by an older man, Harold McMillan. The comparative youthfulness of Jo Grimond was an asset. He showed considerable skill in keeping the Liberal party together after the embarrassment of seeing a pro-Suez Liberal candidate at a by-election in Carmarthen! The situation was aggravated by the fact that it was caused by the death of a Liberal MP, Sir Rhys Hopkin Morris, and that the successful Labour candidate was Lady Megan Lloyd George who had been a Liberal MP, indeed deputy leader, until her defeat in Anglesey in 1951. One amusing story about her was that, at her first meeting, she started to speak in Welsh but, coming from North Wales, she was not understood in Carmarthen!

Once the by-election was over, Jo Grimond was able to concentrate on the big issues of the day and he was fortified by another by-election near miss in Rochdale. He became much loved by the media not only for his intellectual ability and clarity but his shafts of wit which were often good for a headline. By-elections are often a matter of chance. Only seldom does an MP resign and deliberately create one, most often an MP dies or is seriously ill or, in the days of hereditary peerages, the father of an MP died, sometimes inconveniently, and the MP, if the eldest son or nearest male relative, succeeded to the peerage. An unplanned by-election took place in the Torrington, Devon constituency in March 1958 where there was a Conservative majority of 9,000. Actually, the member had stood as a National Liberal and Conservative. This stems from the split in the Liberal party in 1932 when some Liberals under John Simon decided to continue to support the so-called National Government which had been formed after the General Election of 1931. They were called National Liberals while other Liberals under Herbert Samuel broke away and became an independent party and were called Liberals.

They used to sit at different ends of the large smoking room in the National Liberal Club. This schism persisted until the nineteen fifties. In fact, though there was a joint Whip, the National Liberals became indistinguishable from Conservatives and, as in Torrington, one candidate stood under both labels.

A local prospective Liberal candidate, Ambrose Fulford, gallantly stood down to make way for Mark Bonham Carter who had fought the adjoining constituency of Barnstable in 1945. He was the son of Lady Violet Bonham Carter who was the daughter of the Liberal Prime Minister, Herbert Asquith. In addition, his sister, Laura, had married Jo Grimond. His pedigreee was therefore, impeccable but he was an able man in his own right. He had a good mind. Personally, he could be somewhat austere and aloof. However when he took to you, he was a very good companion. He liked the social life and was one of Princess Margaret's "set" - and remained a life-long friend of hers in all her later ups and downs.

The National Liberal and Conservative candidate was Anthony Royle who had been nursing the constituency for some two years. He had served in the Life Guards and the SAS and was a polio victim, which caused him difficulty in walking. He was married to a well-known fashion model, Shirley Worthington.

The Labour candidate was Leonard Lamb. He was really not in the race but his name caused an amusing incident for which I am grateful to the Liberal agent, Edward Wheeler. Anthony Royle's election address included a picture of his most attractive wife cuddling a small lamb. A real Devonshire character went up to Royle and said: "I see your wife is having an affair with the Labour candidate!" Royle was totally non-plussed as he had either forgotten or did not understand the significance of the remark!

Mark Bonham Carter was anxious to make his own impression and asked his mother not to come during the first week of the campaign. It was the right decision, but Lady Violet was rather upset. She relished political campaigning and the excitement of the hustings. She took great trouble, like Winston Churchill did, in preparing her platform speeches. She would rehearse them and they were like stage performances with every word and pause carefully put in place. She could be quite withering. She once said of the Labour Chancellor, Sir Stafford Cripps: "He has a brilliant mind ... until he makes it up!" Once she did enter the campaign, I know from friends in the constituency that her enthusiasm was unbounded. She described the recount as: "I don't think I have been through a greater agony", and these words were clearly not rehearsed but came straight from the heart. As is customary, polling day was on a Thursday but owing to the considerable geographical extent of the constituency, counting did not take place until the next day. After the recount, Mark Bonham Carter was declared the winner by 219 votes.

I have kept copies of that Saturday's *News Chronicle, Daily Express* and *Daily Mail*. The coverage on the front pages was very extensive, far greater than the references to the sadness of Princess Margaret when visiting Germany and speculation that her relationship with Group Captain Peter Townsend was ending. That would not be the position today.

Following the result, the scenes were remarkable. The headline in the *Daily Mail* was "Triumph by Torchlight" and above that, "Cock-a-hoop Liberals stage march of 1,000 flares". The crowd was put at 3,000. The *News Chronicle*, basically sympathetic to the Liberal cause had: "On to More Victories" followed by, "Torrington carries the torch". That Saturday was Grand National day and the coverage of the *Daily Express* was in racing terms. It began: " Mark Bonham Carter on his famous dark horse. The Liberal raced home by a whisker yesterday to win the Torrington Grand National by-election. It was a sensational race, complete with an innocent bit of nobbling, a photo finish and an objection to the winner. The result went into the frame at 2. 53 p.m. yesterday."

Mark Bonham Carter (L)	13, 408
Anthony Royle (Nat Lib and C)	13, 189
Leonard Lamb (Soc)	8, 697
Majority	**219**

It continued in similar vein and then went into straight reporting. It covered about half the front page and a column in the second page with only a small photograph by present standards, but it showed Mark Bonham Carter gloriously triumphant. When one considers the reducing figures of people voting since 1958, it is interesting to note that 79.98 per cent voted in this by-election while at the previous General Election in 1955, the figure was 69. 19 per cent.

Knowing that I was likely to be a candidate at the next General Election, I kept and have still got a copy of Mark Bonham Carter's election address which I think is a model of its kind. The front is a good photograph topped by "Vote Bonham Carter' black on yellow and a similar strip below, "For Torrington". The back page asks that this should be displayed in the window and a very effective poster it made. On the inside, is a letter with a facsimile but clear signature which really does pack a punch in setting out the reasons in straightforward language for voting Liberal. The inside right hand page has two features. The top half is a brief CV and a delightful photograph of his wife, Lesley, and two daughters. The lower half is entitled "What the Tories and Socialists have done to your pound". It is a graph starting in 1945 with the pound at twenty shillings (pre-decimalisation). By 1951 under Labour Governments, it had fallen to fourteen shillings and threepence (around 70p today). Under the succeeding Tory Governments by 1958, it had fallen to eleven shillings (55 pence today). This is in black and white and gives a clear message in another form.

The back page in straightforward black and white print is headed "Brief

Points of Policy". It is positive and pithy and covers much ground. Foreign Policy and Defence, H-Bomb, Cost of Living, Agriculture, Rent Act and Old Age Pensions. It was the complete answer to the gibe quite often made in Conservative circles that the Liberals had no policy. Whatever trouble was taken in preparing this document, it must have paid off and, in those days, more people used to read such items than they seem to do today.

Mark Bonham Carter added greatly to the quality of the still small Liberal Parliamentary Party and became spokesman for Foreign Affairs. He was to have considerable clashes with the so-called Young Liberal "Red Guards" in which Peter Hain was prominent. He used to win the decisive arguments and kept the party away from the Campaign for Nuclear Disarmament (CND) and unilateralism as well as being pro-Europe. He was a great asset to his brother-in-law, Jo Grimond, who had shouldered so much responsibility not least because he was forever in demand by the press and television and he did not want to disappoint them.

The sad thing was that after so much excitement and euphoria, Mark Bonham Carter was to lose his seat in the General Election of 1959. This was a great disappointment to many people but especially to Jo Grimond. Mark, however, remained supportive and loyal. He had been in Collins the publishers but he left after some of the directors indicated that they did not think his political activities were helpful to the firm. He then became chair of the Race Relations Board. Another member was Sir Learie Constantine, of whom more later. The two no doubt shared their mutual enthusiasm for cricket. Mark fought Torrington again in 1964 but lost for the second time. He did not contest any other seat but his Parliamentary qualities were able to be used again when he was made a life peer in 1986. He remained a central figure in the party and spent some time trying to improve its organization to try and make it more effective and efficient and achieve the breakthrough that had been so elusive. The last letter I had from him was in 1994 after the death of his sister Laura Grimond. He himself, died six months later. Jo Grimond died in October, 1993 so—within less than a year—the cause of liberalism in the broadest sense and the Liberal Democrat party in particular, had lost three of its most gifted and tireless members.

• • •

I am going to leave the disastrous Assembly of 1958 until later because I want to say something more about what happened when I returned to Nigeria in December, 1957. The Minorities Commission arrived in Nigeria on 23rd November, 1957. It left on 12th April, 1958. The relevant term of reference was: "If, but only if no other solution seems to the commission to meet the case, then as a last resort, to make detailed recommendations for the creation of one or more new States". From this, it is clear that any separatist movement had an uphill task. One wonders if those in London who, presumably, finalised the terms of reference, really appreciated the strength of feeling that there was in Nigeria and the dissatisfaction with the three large and unbalanced existing Regions. I certainly feel that a more level playing field would have been appropriate and that the subsequent violent history of Nigeria bears me out.

The chair of the commission was Sir Henry Willink who was Master of Magdalene College, Cambridge from 1948 to 1966. He was MP for Croydon, North from 1940 to 1948 and Minister of Health from 1943 to 1945. He was an authority on ecclesiastical law and Dean of the Arches from 1953 to 1955. As far as I know, he had no experience in Africa but that did not stop him from becoming a firm, perhaps a little forbidding, chair. For African knowledge and custom he probably relied on his three colleagues. Gordon Hadow had been in neighbouring Gold Coast, now Ghana. John B. Shearer was a career diplomat in India and Pakistan while Philip Mason was the Director of the Institute of Race Relations.

"Scottie" Baker and I set out from Lagos with a few supporters to go to Benin. On the way, at Owo, by complete chance, we met the commission and their staff. It was a somewhat embarrassing occasion and all one can do on such occasions is to laugh it off and make it brief, as otherwise, rumours would begin to spread — and this could happen easily in Nigeria. However, the meeting was useful in a practical way because we were introduced to the small secretariat and two typists, especially Irene Munn, were unofficially very helpful as we had no secretarial facilities ourselves.

When we arrived in Benin, it became clear that more basic preparation was needed in deciding what witnesses were going to be called and in what order and, of course, what they were going to say. Fortunately, we did have a little time for this. Normally, it is solicitor's work to prepare a case including taking witness statements but Scottie was really helpful to me. This was not a Court case but an inquiry, so Scottie who had no "side" to him went along with me to get the best witnesses we could and "hard" evidence of discrimination and inefficiency with specific acts and omissions set out. The other thing was to inculcate some sense of time. On the whole, we did quite well but there were hiccups including at the beginning when the commission started sitting at Benin. Our first witness was going to be the Olu of Warri but he sent an apology and did not turn up. Scottie was very philosophical and phlegmatic about it. I expect I showed more tension and anxiety. He passed me a note:

The Olu of Warri
Said, 'Sorry'.
So we had to begin
With the Oba of Benin .

I thought that our witnesses did well and made a persuasive case. It was at the lunch adjournment that an amusing and interesting incident occurred. During the morning, there had been a reference to a resolution of the Benin Council. There was some dispute about it so I said to our supporters who had gathered around me that this matter could be resolved if the council minute book was produced and it would be most helpful if that could be done by two o'clock while the matter was fresh in everybody's mind.

A man I did not know stepped forward and said he could do that but I must pay him half a crown. I demurred at that and another man stepped forward looking like the perfectly dressed barrister of those days: white shirt, striped trousers, black coat and waistcoat. He told me that if we were in London and someone offered to produce an important document, I would take him to lunch at the Savoy and that would cost me more than half a crown! I did not pay myself but someone must have done as the minute book was produced and was quite helpful.

At Benin, the hall had a gallery and, after some days, I told Chief Omo Osage that I had noticed it was nearly always occupied by our supporters — and I asked whether they had been told to arrive early each day. He explained that there were admission cards for the first day which he had looked at. He urged our supporters to get them and hand them to him at the end of the day. He then had them overprinted for all the days on which the commission sat!

I think it was at Benin and not Warri that Chief Festus Okotie-Eboh gave evidence. I have already referred to his great size but this was matched by the Attorney-General for Western Nigeria, Chief Rotimi Williams who cross-examined him. There were allegations and denials which became increasingly heated. A man stood on a chair in the front row of the gallery and started making noises either of approval or dissent. This caught the attention of Sir Henry Willink who asked him what he was doing. The reply came down: "I am enjoying the battle of the elephants!" There was much laughter. I do not think he was removed but he had to sit down.

When the commission left Benin for Warri, I went ahead of Scottie to see how things were going. Scottie followed in the Mercedes of Chief Festus, probably one of the best cars in Nigeria. It was driven by a man called Goodwill. When he arrived, he looked very sad and forlorn. I enquired why and he explained that the "Master" wanted to do some work and asked him to drive more slowly. As a result of this request, he was overtaken by another car for the first time in three years!

After we had called our last witness, Scottie made a powerful and closely argued final speech reviewing the evidence and pulling all the arguments together. He spoke with some emotion but it was carefully controlled. He had clearly taken a good deal of trouble over it. Quite properly, our supporters were well pleased. The atmosphere was very happy as the two of us left for Lagos, again driven by Goodwill.

On the way, we stopped outside a house for no apparent reason. Goodwill jumped out and came back with bunches of plantains (rather like large bananas) which filled the boot of the car. He explained that he had to take them to market. Scottie and I did not ask any questions!

When we arrived at Lagos, we went to see Festus and as we entered his room, he said to Scottie, "I hear you made a good speech". He had been correctly and speedily informed.

So we left Nigeria in a *Britannia* which had two decks but there was no class distinction and everybody moved about in what became a good party atmosphere for Christmas. I have not been back to Nigeria since but I did keep in touch with events. The Commission Report was presented to Parliament in July

1958[1] but before I say something about it, I want to refer to an astute move made by the Government of the Western Region shortly before the commission arrived in Nigeria. On 20th October, 1957, a Ministry of Mid-West Affairs was appointed with a Mid-West Council with advisory powers. The minister appointed was a very able man, Chief Anthony Enahoro who was also the Minister for Home Affairs. He came to prominence in the UK in 1962.

The previous September, a quantity of arms was discovered by the police in Lagos and some thirty prominent politicians were arrested and charged with treason. They included Enahoro who escaped to the UK. His children were here and he obtained assurances that it was safe for him to come. However, once he was here, the Nigerian Government applied for his return. Being a commonwealth country, this was done under the Fugitive Offenders Act 1881 under which political considerations were relevant. If he had been a "foreigner", it would have been easier for him.

There was much feeling in Parliament after the Home Secretary, Henry Brooke, made the order of deportation. Dingle Foot MP was prominent in the House of Commons and there were a number of applications to the courts especially for *habeas corpus* as Enahoro was detained in custody. There was also an unprecedented complaint to the benchers of Lincoln's Inn against the conduct of the Attorney-General, Sir John Hobson. All matters failed and Enahoro was deported to Nigeria. He was tried by the High Court at Lagos and convicted. He appealed and that was dismissed. His solicitors in England and especially Noel Sleigh who bore the brunt of the considerable work in this case helped Enahoro's children who remained in England. Lawyers are often regarded with suspicion and, indeed, derision being considered as making a lot of money out of other people's misfortunes. It is a pity that their acts of kindness and humanity are not better known — but those who do them are not out for publicity.

Thanks to the help and courtesy of the staff at the Foreign and Commonwealth Office, Whitehall, I have re-read the Report of the Commission which, on the whole, I still find disappointing because, somehow, it does not capture the feelings and aspirations of politically active Nigerians at the time. It is an arid document. However, it was right when it observed that the Mid-West State was supported by the Government of the Western Region, the Action Group and the Mid-West State Movement with different degrees of warmth. The Action Group wished to bring together all the Edo speaking peoples which meant crossing regional boundaries. The commission expressed "some doubt" as to the sincerity of the Western Region Government's recommendations. Of the Mid-West State Movement, it said that a new State would have been received with delight in the Benin Division but elsewhere, the reception would have been lukewarm and some minorities were hostile and feared further fragmentation. I am bound to say I did not myself detect such differences between the hearings at Benin and at Warri. The commission pointed out that there were very few Yorubas in the Benin and Delta Provinces. They said they had made a detailed examination of fears of Yoruba domination in appointments including economic discrimination especially of rubber and cocoa and also discrimination in public

---

[1] Command Paper 505: price 9 shillings and sixpence: less than 50p today!

services and Parliamentary seats. There were 4,302,000 Yorubas out of a population of 6,085,000 in the Western Region.

The conclusion of the report was that there was "no evidence of vindictive and deliberate discrimination or even culpable neglect". I would have thought it would have been helpful though, no doubt, time consuming, to give some basis for arriving at this conclusion – but perhaps, it was felt more diplomatic in view of forthcoming independence, not to set out the commission's view of the evidence that had been given. Perhaps it may be too harsh to say that the commission had a plausible get out with the recent creation of the council for the Mid-West. It thought it should be allowed to develop. In fact, it had not yet met! The commission thought that the members should not be nominated by the Western Region Government but be widely drawn. One comfort for the Mid-West State Movement was that, with some adjustments (unspecified), the Benin area should be designated a minority area.

The report was debated at the resumed Nigeria Constitutional Conference held in London during September and October 1958 under the chairship of the Secretary of State for the Colonies, Right Honourable Alan Lennox-Boyd MP. The report had stated that the case for new States had not been made out and so the issue was discussed again. There were a large number of Nigerian delegates including Chief Festus Okotie-Eboh whom I introduced to Arnold Goodman who gave a party in his flat in Ashley Gardens for him and a number of other Nigerians. It was a cheerful occasion and Joy and I left late, though before the end! Nigerians have a great gift of happiness even in unfortunate circumstances. However, all was not lost in London as there was a recommendation that there should be a Mid-West Advisory Council and a minority area of the whole of the Benin and Delta provinces with some exclusions including Warri. A recommendation for a Niger Delta Development Board was approved.

One of the Action Group delegates was Ayo Rosiji. I did not know him then but in 1966 after various troubles in Nigeria he came to England and joined my chambers in the Temple. This was made possible by Dingle Foot whom he had met in Nigeria. We remained good friends until he died in 2000.

This is not the book to relate the turbulent years in Nigeria as I was not involved in them. There were a number of constitutional changes. My only contacts were a pleasant exchange of letters in January 1960 when Chief Festus was re-appointed Minister of Finance and another letter from him in July 1963. There was also one from Denis Osadbay the following month. They referred to a successful referendum on the Mid-West State and they were looking forward to help build a new region. They both thanked me very warmly for what I had done in 1957 which I much appreciated.

For my last contact with Nigeria itself – personal friendships apart – I must jump ahead. When I was in Sir Dingle Foot's chambers, we were joined by the great West Indian cricketer and former High Commissioner for Trinidad and Tobago, Sir Learie Constantine who received a life peerage shortly before he died in 1971. At the beginning of 1966 there was a military coup and a number of political leaders were arrested. The federal Prime Minister, Sir Abubakar Tafawa Balewa, a Hausa from the North, was kidnapped. Civil war broke out and Sir Learie was asked by Amnesty International to go out and do what he could to preserve life. It was an impossible task but he saw important people and did what he could to examine personal cases. One mystery was what had happened to Chief Festus. It seems that he was taken up in an aeroplane and asked for the numbers of his Swiss bank accounts.

He refused to give them and was pushed out of the plane to meet a terrible death. It is an appalling commentary on what happened in Nigeria. One can only hope that after these horrific and damaging experiences, democracy can again establish itself and the country begin to realize some of its considerable potential. My overall impression is that at the time of Independence in 1961, while there were a number of able people in Government and in other public services, they were not sufficient in number to run the country at local level. This led to inefficiency and corruption.

My final dealing with Chief Festus was some month's after Learie's return when I was asked to see John Mortimer QC - of *Rumpole of The Bailey* fame - in his chambers. He specialised in wills and probate and the matter of Festus' estate had been referred to him. I gave what help I could and heard no more.

•　　•　　•

When I returned to England, I again found Joy very well though of course, getting bigger as our first child was expected in March. She duly arrived on the 17th of March safely in Queen Charlotte's Hospital where, as was then customary, Joy spent ten days. Nowadays, mothers seem to be in and out in a day or two. We called the baby Sarah Caroline for the very good reason that we liked the names! She has always been known as Caroline— though being known by one's second name does cause problems with letters and other communications. Joy knew about this as Joy is her third name. She dislikes the other two very much so I will not refer to them.

At an early age, about four, it was clear that Caroline was going to be musical. She had a good ear and perfect pitch. She seemed to go to the piano naturally. Later, she took up the oboe and her talents were fully exploited at St. Paul's Girls' School which had a thriving music department. She had three wonderfully happy years at Cambridge where she read music. She was at Newnham College, as were Joy, her Aunt Con Heward and her sister Jenny. As an Oxford man, I was the odd one out! Caroline, however, had other interests than music and took to politics becoming chair of the Liberal Club and successfully moving a motion at the Cambridge Union in favour of the ordination of women. She was also chair of the University Methodist Society. She had piano lessons from Hilda Bor amongst whose former pupils had been Princess Margaret. Miss Bor wanted Caroline to continue her studies in Paris but Caroline felt that the life of a professional musician was not for her. She did not have the necessary single-minded and total dedication and commitment. Her horizons were also broader. She has not played the oboe for some years but has always kept up her piano playing and plays locally from time to time.

It seems a long way from music, but Caroline has pursued a successful career in the world of housing. She trained with the Hyde and South Bank Housing Association with which her uncle, Edmund Heward, had been involved. She started up an advisory agency called Dome which was more successful than the more notorious millenium venture! She went back to Hyde as deputy director. It is based in Lewisham and has expanded so that it is now responsible for more than 25,000 properties. The squeeze on the finances of local authorities has meant that their involvement in housing has greatly declined and, also, during the Thatcher period, many council houses were sold. This has brought increasing regulation of housing associations and there have been direct transfers to them from councils. The Hyde Association took over 5,000 properties from Lambeth and a similar number from Dartford.

Caroline met Robert Titley at Cambridge. They were both Methodists. He was a classisist at Christ's College and just missed a first class degree. He became a trainee manager in the Coal Board and then felt the call to the ministry. He became an Anglican and returned to Cambridge, resuming his studies at Westcott House. They were married in Cambridge on 19th December 1981 in icy weather. Robert was ordained in Southwark Cathedral. I was struck by the fact that so many of the candidates were mature men, many older than Robert, who had come from a number of walks of life such as doctors and from the City of London. I felt that this variety was good for the church. There were very few 'curates pale' straight from the shelter of a theological college.

Caroline has always been committed to doing a number of things simultaneously and successfully—and although she was busy, apart from her job, helping Robert in his first parish in Sydenham, it was no surprise that she became the Alliance candidate for Lewisham West in the General Election of 1987. Great things were expected of the Liberal/Social Democrat Party (SDP) Alliance but although the total vote was large, the number of seats gained was small. On the back of Caroline's election address was a nice picture of herself between David Owen and David Steel. An abrasive political pundit could suggest that it would have been good if she had banged their heads together, metaphorically, of course! Caroline got 7,247 votes which was 15. 9 per cent—not at all a bad performance especially considering that the squeeze was on. That time John Maples won by 3,772, but his Labour opponent, Jim Dowd, fought again in 1992 and won the seat by 1,809 votes.

Caroline did not fight again and has not done so since. Even she found it more than she could manage but she has sat on the Housing Panel of the Liberal party. Laura Grimond wanted her to become the chair but it meant rather frequent visits to the House of Commons. She has, however, been able to help Simon Hughes the MP for nearby Bermondsey. Her first child, James, was born in 1990. By this time, Robert had moved to Whitelands College, Putney and became the chaplain there. He enjoyed working with the students but after a time, he wanted to be with a broader section of the population. All Saints' Church, Rosendale Road, Dulwich had been looking for a vicar for about a year and had turned down a number of candidates. The Bishop of Southwark asked Robert and Caroline to consider it and they agreed to be interviewed. The previous incumbent was a bachelor and the parish was looking for a married couple. The Titleys were successful and moved into the vicarage next to the church but only after Caroline, with her experience in housing, had succeeded in having certain things done to it. The move took place in 1993. All went well at first. The church was a huge Victorian red brick building in the style of Lincoln's Inn and Keble College, Oxford. It was known as "the Cathedral of the South East" and had never been fully completed. More important, it had a lively and dedicated congregation with an excellent choir and music under the direction of Tim Penrose. The main Sunday morning service would attract between 150-200 people. It was a High Church and Robert adapted easily to the rituals. At his installation as vicar in 1994, Joy and I were near the front and a priest kept on swinging incense very close to me which made me sneeze. I did my best to suppress the sneezes but, sometimes, they came at rather solemn moments which was an embarrassment. I have never been a High Churchman and this experience was a deterrent! Julia arrived in August 1994 and the Titley family were well-regarded and popular. Robert was able to resume his theological studies and obtained a doctorate from London University.

Then in June 2000 disaster struck. On June 9th about 5.0 a.m., there was a ring at the vicarage door. Sometimes this happens as tramps and others call to ask for help — but this time, the caller told Robert that the church was on fire. Many fire engines came quickly but access was difficult and it turned into a major blaze. The vicarage had to be evacuated and Caroline thoughtfully rang us so that we would not hear it on the news for the first time. There was a lot of publicity, especially about Robert preparing a sermon for Pentecost with its references to the fire of the Holy Spirit descending on the disciples! Robert's reaction was very dignified and hopeful that something good would come out of the disaster. The Sunday morning service was held in the vicarage garden which was crowded with worshippers — and was featured on television.

The cause of the fire was an electrical fault in the vestry. Joy and I did what we could to help but, fortunately, after a few days, the building was declared safe and the family was able to return to it. What surprised me was the great delay there has been in getting any repair work done to the church itself. I have not been involved in this, but I do know that insurance companies and assessors have not been able to agree about the claim and the restoration work to be done. It is a Grade 1 listed building. I appreciate the care that must take place for the approval of plans and a lot of interested parties are concerned but it did sadden me on my visits, to see the roof completely uncovered and there was much rain in the winter of 2000. However, much has been done to dry out part of the building which has a very large crypt where many and varied community activities used to take place.

At Easter 2001, this had been cleared and dried sufficiently for services to restart. The congregation has remained intact so that at the Easter morning service, there was a congregation of some 250. In its report of 10th June 2000, *The Times* put the estimated cost of repair at six million pounds and I understand that this is pretty accurate. There will be a shortage of about one million pounds between what the parish would like to see and the figure that the insurers will pay. There have been a number of fund raising activities and Joy and I have been to prestigious concerts at Dulwich College where James Titley started in September, 2002. The college and the artists have been very generous in their support. The soprano, Ruth Holton, is a member of the congregation and the counter-tenor, James Bowman a friend of Tim Penrose. Robert is at the centre of this and has borne up very well. Fortunately, a number of volunteers have come forward to help him. I hope Joy and I will be able to be present when the church is officially re-opened. Robert is scheduled to leave in 2006 having been appointed a canon of Southwark Catherdral.

●   ●   ●

To return to 1958, after the arrival of Caroline, Joy's mother Mrs Heward, always known as Mears, came and stayed with us for a month. She was a great help and Caroline developed healthily. She was sometimes taken out in a carry cot. In later life, she could boast that she had slept on Lord Goodman's bed! The family went off to Torquay for the Liberal Assembly. We stayed at the Queen's Hotel. I did not mention that my Uncle Kenneth Swiss, had commandeered it during the war for use by the RAF!

After the success of the Torrington by-election and the leadership of Jo Grimond, Liberals arrived in buoyant mood but that particular assembly became notorious in party history as a disaster. Commentators like Anthony Howard and the late Bernard Levin have continued to refer to it over the years. The root problem lay in long and complicated resolutions which delegates could amend having given prior notice. The Agenda Committee was empowered to select amendments and there was sometimes controversy over this. The agenda would be full of lengthy resolutions and amendments. There would be further trouble if some delegates were in favour of part of a proposed substitution and against the rest. Separate votes would be asked for. The history of this type of agenda went back to the times when the Liberal party was in Government and the resolutions were like draft Bills which the assembly would like the Government to enact.

This procedure exasperated the journalists who were trying to cover the event and get worthwhile stories. There were no sessional chairs and the president presided throughout. He was Sir Arthur Comyns Carr, QC, a resplendent figure in a wing collar. The trouble was that he kept getting his papers — and they were quite large — between himself and the microphone. When he was asked to speak up and use the microphone, he replied in a phrase that Bernard Levin used on a number of occasions: 'The trouble is that I am a foot too tall for the thing'. The abyss was reached when, before the assembly was due to start, on either the second or third day, Miss Frances Pugh a veteran Devon Liberal who looked like the headmistress that she was, pointed out that in the debate on education the previous day, by passing an amendment to the resolution, certain words had been deleted which could not have been meant to be done. Nobody had any notice of this, so some delegates who were interested in the subjects may not have been present. However, Miss Pugh succeeded — and the assembly reversed the decision of the previous day. Jo Grimond must have been exasperated by all this, but he cheerfully overcame it as he was to do various problems throughout his leadership. At least Liberals were doing their business in the open and not behind closed doors, he said, putting on a brave face. The result was that a committee was set up to reform the proceedings and procedure of the assembly in which I played some part.

Outside the assembly sessions themselves, there were some good events. I remember Ludovic Kennedy, fresh from Rochdale, giving a thoughtful and compelling speech called 'The Mood of Liberalism' while Tom Kellock who was to be the candidate for Torquay in 1959, began to make an impact. He was especially knowledgeable on Commonwealth matters and later was a colleague of mine in chambers. He became the first legal director of the Commonwealth Secretariat then returned to the Bar, took silk and after that, became a Circuit Judge in Nottingham.

Shortly after he retired, he died suddenly after a heart attack in the Temple , where he lived with his wife, Jane. He was a bencher of the Inner Temple and his funeral and memorial service were attended not only by members of the legal profession but also by many representatives from Commonwealth countries. He married Jane in 1967. She was the secretary of the Africa Bureau and editor of the *Africa Digest*. She was to become a magistrate in both London and Nottingham as well as being on what is now the Independent Police Complaints Commission and former Race Relations Board. Busy lives though they both led, they were most hospitable giving parties for people from many countries. Tom had a string of overseas pupils and kept in touch with many of them. He used to say that, in later life, they were either in power or in gaol! I was glad to pay a tribute to him when I wrote his obituary for *The Times*. A warm and kind personality, he really was one of those people who was much missed by a wide circle of friends and colleagues. The sad thing was that his efforts to enter the House of Commons had been unsuccessful but he remained faithful to his Liberal principles and to the Liberal party.

The year 1959 was to turn out to be one of the most important years of my life but it began on a rather sad note. On 31st January, at the early age of 52, Philip Fothergill died. He was one of the most prominent Liberals to emerge since 1945. A short man with a trimmed military moustache, he was a non-conformist teetotal Yorkshireman. He overcame ill-health with considerable courage. He once told me that he put his gout down to the sins of his ancestors. He never married and was unfailingly courteous and optimistic so that you always felt better for talking to him. He was in the textile industry and was fortunate in being able to arrange his business interests so that he could devote a great deal of his time to the Liberal party. His business life seemed to revolve around the wool trade. From 1946, he held high office combining chair of the Executive Committee and president as well as joint treasurer.

I was especially pleased that after I was chairman in 1953, Philip became president of the National League of Young Liberals in the following year. His three attempts to enter Parliament failed but he was never dispirited. There were very few successful Liberal candidates in the nineteen-fifties. He had a great gift for the quote and used to make statements, calling a few people together in either party Headquarters or the National Liberal Club, and would give an instant reaction to a topical piece of news which would often start: "Mr Philip Fothergill, speaking in London yesterday, said : 'His other gift was to try by his cheerfulness to keep the party together. He used to get quite upset by disagreements. He once said to me when Lady Violet Bonham Carter and Lady Megan Lloyd George were having some waspish spat, 'We cannot afford a dynastic feud'. Francis Boyd, the much respected political correspondent of *The Guardian* used to say that Philip Fothergill was the nearest the Liberal party ever had to a Herbert Morrison; in other words, someone with an acute political brain who knew the importance of organization. His thanksgiving service was held in the City Temple and, after it, Jeremy Thorpe asked me if I agreed with the remark in the address that Philip Fothergill was the outstanding Liberal since the end of the war. I do not think I felt able to comment. Anyway, Jeremy Thorpe's time was to begin in 1959 as I shall relate.

Before that, in March I had a call from Laura Grimond now living at nearby Kew which was part of the constituency called Richmond and Barnes. She would not say what it was about but wanted to come and see me. So she came and told Joy and myself that the local Liberal Association was not satisfied with the candidate who had fought in 1955, Eva Haynes, who got 5,266 votes out of a total of 47,567. The Conservative majority was 12,955 but Richmond was thought to be a seat of some potential for the Liberals who were doing much better in local elections. The purpose of the visit was to know if I would be the prospective candidate. I was a bit chary about this as, although there had been no meeting, Miss Haynes wanted to carry on and must have had some supporters. Like Philip Fothergill, I did not want any disagreement to arise. Laura was reassuring and did not think there would be any dispute about my candidature. I said I would think it over. Joy and I agreed in principle. She was such an asset, not only having been in the Information and Research Department of the party, but also she had worked hard in the Westminster Liberal Association. It did not have many members but they always put up a Parliamentary candidate and fought a number of local elections.

I saw A. G. and he said he had no objection provided that I did not get in! This was a characteristic sally and before the momentous by-election at Orpington which, on the face of it, was as difficult a seat for the Liberals to win as Richmond.

So I told Laura that I would let my name be considered. I knew a number of the officers and members but by no means all as the constituency stretched from Hammersmith to Kingston. The electorate was about 60,000 and it was divided into a number of different places: Barnes, Kew, Mortlake, Sheen, Richmond Town, Richmond Hill, Petersham and Ham. The annual general meeting of the Richmond and Barnes Liberal Association was held on 25th March and according to the *Thames Valley Times*, about a hundred people were present including Eva Haynes. However, she remained silent and nobody else spoke about her possible candidature, so I was adopted without dissent. I made an upbeat speech about the improvement of the organization of the party at all levels and said that it would not be fighting the forthcoming General Election in a negative way but would present a positive alternative Liberal policy. Unfortunately, Laura Grimond resigned as president as she was expecting a baby in May, but she was elected a vice-president and never lost touch with what was going on. Indeed, in July there was a fete in the Grimonds' garden in Kew and I have a picture of Joy, Ludovic and Moira Kennedy and Laura Grimond each with offspring on their laps. I am standing incongruously behind the mothers. Jo Grimond was doing something else!

In June, I was one of eight members elected by the Party Council to the

Executive which met monthly and was responsible for the day -to-day running of the party organization. I had been on it before *ex officio* when I was chair of the National League of Young Liberals. I was going to be kept busy as I was appointed chair of the party's Assembly Agenda Committee. This was quite a responsibility after the poor performance of the previous year.

I was determined that there should be a number of changes to try and make the proceedings more understandable and relevant to the issues of the day as well as recognising the importance of TV coverage, A lot of hard work was done but, in the end, the assembly at Scarborough in September did not take place — as the polling day for the General Election was going to be on 8th October. But the work was not wasted as the assembly took place as usual in the following year at Eastbourne.

So I began to get known in the constituency. This was not difficult as I lived there. It was good to get out and about, to be there and to talk. There was much goodwill but there was a barrier that was very difficult to cross. In a seat with a large Conservative majority, if I was to make any impact at all, I had to get Conservative voters to change to me. Many were sympathetic. The Conservative party, which had been in power since 1951, had not done well either at home or in international matters. The Suez escapade in 1956/7 had been a disaster and Britain's esteem had been lowered in many quarters especially in the Middle East. This was to have consequences for many years to come and still does.

Conservative voters, however, were very fearful of the return of a Labour Government. They feared more nationalisation and higher taxes; a threat to their pockets and standards of living is a very powerful feeling. This gave rise to the 'split vote' argument. Time and time again, I was told that the Liberals would let Labour in and that the anti-Labour vote must not be split. It was not a high-minded view of politics but it was a powerful factor in preventing a Liberal recovery. I did my best to get people to vote positively for what they believed. If they would like to see a stronger Liberal party, the only way to achieve that was to vote for it. I also tried to put across the view that there was no such thing as a 'wasted vote'. Some people were very despondent and took the view that if you were not likely to win you were not worth voting for. It was rather like the approach to a horse race, you want to back the winner. I used to say that every Liberal vote increased the authority with which Liberals spoke in Parliament and the influence that the party had in the country. I think I had more success with this when trying to counter the 'split vote' argument.

The election was announced in September and I had a very good and enthusiastic adoption meeting. It was an Asquithian occasion. The Grimonds gave supper for Joy and myself. Unfortunately, I was late arriving as I was held up at Goodman, Derrick and Co., something that was not unknown — but everybody was very understanding about it. Both Lady Violet and Mark Bonham Carter were there and both spoke. Both speeches were really of a very high standard and all Liberals enjoyed hearing from a recent election winner in Mark.

The poignant factor was that my Conservative opponent was to be Anthony Royle, the loser at Torrington. Everyone thought that, as the contest was so close, the two would be fighting it out again but, after his defeat — and it was said somewhat furtively — Royle began to look elsewhere. While he was trying for

Folkestone with Alan Clark, he was also considering Richmond which he got. He died in 2001 and in his obituary in *The Guardian*, Andrew Roth recalled that he was known as 'Runaway Royle'. This may well have been so in Devon but I am bound to say I never heard anything of it in Richmond and never referred to it myself. At first, he was rather abrasive towards me, no doubt having been stung by being defeated by a Liberal, but later on he mellowed. We saw each other from time-to-time and he wrote me a very decent letter after the 1964 election and also when I became a judge in 1973. He became Lord Fanshawe of Richmond in 1983. For reasons I do not know, and I find it rather surprising as he had a yen and keenness for politics, as far as I know, he never spoke in the House of Lords. In one way this was a pity as he was staunchly pro-European and it would have been good to have the positive case put more frequently when there was so much anti-Europeanism and scepticism during the Thatcher years.

Polling day was October 8th. My agent was Madeleine Huxstep who was very good. She had been at Oxford just before me and was active in the Liberal Club. She helped Basil Wigoder at Bournemouth in 1945 and in the subsequent by-election. She had bad luck in local elections standing for Barnes several times and once losing by two votes after several recounts. She led on the first count.

The Central Committee Room was on Richmond Hill and we were able to have a banner across the road. We had other Committee Rooms in Barnes, Kew, Sheen and Ham We seemed to have an adequate number of helpers for the basic work, though at times we could have done with more canvassers. In those days, the candidates held more public meetings than they do nowadays, ending with a traditional eve of poll meeting. Mine was surprisingly successful as there were about eight hundred people present but I know that the other candidates had good meetings as well. There was an interest in politics in Richmond and people made an effort to get informed. The colours of the posters were not standardised as they are today and, in Richmond, the Liberal colour was green. I personally liked that as it was the colour of the football team that I had always followed, Plymouth Argyle. I also knew that it was said to be unlucky, especially by sailors.

Money for the campaign was short and my election address was limited to black and white printing. I did, however, have a green and white visiting card which was well designed. My election address followed the pattern of that of Mark Bonham Carter in Torrington that I described earlier. A photograph and slogans were on the front so that it could be used as a window poster. Inside, I was able to write a message from my home address. There were eight brief points of policy. The one on the H-Bomb seems the most dated while others, such as a call for wider home ownership and also of shares remain topical. There was also a mini CV and a very nice picture of Joy and Caroline.

Not only Joy but also Caroline was an electoral asset. Caroline's pram was decorated with posters and she was wheeled along the terrace by her grand-father. The four of us featured in a perceptive article by John Rosselli entitled 'Politics on the Doorstep: A Day with the Candidate' published in *The Guardian*. I am sure it was helpful. It was reproduced in the *Bedside Guardian*. It came to a pretty accurate conclusion, namely that I ought to do better than my predecessor but that there might yet be many days of work ahead for me and Caroline. She was also named as the youngest election worker in a short piece in the *Evening News*. On polling day, A. G. lent me his car and his chauffeur so that I was able to go around the constituency in some style. The result was quite good. My main workers seemed pleased. I think I was a bit disappointed that I had not reduced the Conservative majority which went up. The figures with those of 1955 alongside them, were:

	1959	1955
A. Royle (Con)	27,161	27,628
C. H. Archibald (Lab)	12,975	14,673
J. A. Baker (Lib)	7,359	5,266
Con majority	14,186	12,953

At least, I was well above deposit level which was then one eighth of the total votes cast and the Liberal vote had gone up by over two thousand while that of the other candidates had gone down. Everybody was very generous to me and thought that the Liberals had put up a good fight. The only sour note was struck by Eva Haynes who, having helpfully done nothing during the campaign, wrote a letter to the local press saying that I had not done well and that my agent had told her before I appeared on the scene that the Liberals should poll 10,000. I do not think anyone replied to it.

Nationally, the result was a disappointment to the Liberal party because they still only had six seats and the Conservatives were returned with an increased majority despite being in power since 1951 and the many criticisms that could cogently be made of their performance in Government. If disappointing for the Liberals who had high hopes of getting some extra seats, the result was a grave indictment of Labour and the clear refusal of the electorate to trust it with the responsibility of Government.

The loss of Mark Bonham Carter in Torrington was compensated by the gain in neighbouring North Devon by 362 votes by Jeremy Thorpe, aged thirty. He had come second in 1955. Ominously, as it turned out, across the River Tamar in the Bodmin division of Cornwall, Peter Bessell came within 2,801 votes of winning—but he did succeed in 1964 by 3,136 votes. In 1979, the two men were to face each other in number one court at The Old Bailey.

Peter Bessell was a witness for the prosecution and Jeremy Thorpe was in the dock charged with conspiracy to murder. Bessell was discredited and Thorpe and the others were acquitted. It says much for the underlying strength of the Liberal cause in Britain that the party and its successor, the Liberal Democrats, have survived so well from such events, to which I shall return later.

However, the 1959 result was not all gloom because the Liberals more than doubled their 1955 vote and got 1,641,000 but it was under six per cent. The task was to remain optimistic. There were a number of near misses and the general political position was favourable, especially if Labour continued to do badly in by-elections during the new Parliament and in local elections.

So it was back to Goodman, Derrick and Co. ready to pick up where I had left off. But the fascination of the firm was that there were always different and interesting people appearing on the scene. One was Spike Milligan and I was asked to act for him as he had separated from his wife. His life story, which sadly due to his death at the age of 81, saw the last of the Goons, is well-known but I suppose that everybody who had anything to do with him has some experience or story to tell and I am no exception. One day, he was late for an appointment and he explained that, on his way, he was passing the Israeli Embassy and heard the phone ringing. He stopped and went in and told them. He added that he was staying there until it was answered as for all they knew the Third World War may have broken out! It was such an original explanation for lateness that I had not the heart to query its truth!

One thing he did tell me about his life with the Goons was repeated on TV by Eric Sykes in his tribute to Spike so this time, I had some corroboration. The Goons were rehearsing at Lime Grove Studios, Shepherd's Bush. All went well and they were released for a time so they walked around and came to a funeral director's shop. Nobody was inside so they went in: Spike, Harry Secombe, Peter Sellers and Michael Bentine. There was a counter with a green baize top and a bell on it. Harry Secombe lay on the floor on his back with his hands across him, in front of the counter. The others stood alongside him. The bell was rung. A man appeared and those who were visible pointed in unison with heads bowed down to the floor. The man looked over the counter and saw the motionless Harry. The others ran out of the shop so Spike said he was unable to tell me what happened! He told me that he was rather upset that I could not continue to act for him as I left Goodman, Derrick and Co. in very unusual circumstances.

I was having a conference with Dingle Foot and as we finished and he was tying the pink tape around his papers, he said to me, "Have you ever thought of going to the Bar?" I explained that it had always been my ambition but I had no resources or links with the Bar to enable me to start, especially after the war when it was very overcrowded. I think he knew that I always liked advocacy. He said he had not taken anybody into his chambers for some five years and they were turning work away. He asked me to think it over for a week and then let him have my decision. If I agreed, he would propose me for Gray's Inn, where he was a bencher.

This was a total bombshell. I was married with a young child of some 21 months and aged 34. I went home to Joy and she was incredibly supportive. She knew the extent of the challenge as she knew about the Bar and the hazards of self-employment. There were and had been a number of solicitors in her family. She thought I could not get a better way to start at the Bar and had confidence that work would come my way from my experience as a solicitor. I am glad to say that she proved to be correct. She had done some political work for Dingle Foot in his Liberal days.

I then had to tell A. G. He was quite first class. He could have been rather angry, having given me a great chance to succeed as a solicitor—but he said I must do as I wanted. I think he probably thought I had gone mad but we parted on very amicable terms and his character and kindness are shown by the fact that he sent me one of my first briefs. He was rather amused because he replaced me with a barrister, John Montgomerie, who in the 1959 General Election was the Liberal candidate for Sutton and Cheam. He did very slightly better than I did polling 7,600 votes. Another strange thing is that in due course both Richmond and Sutton were to become Liberal Democrat seats though I have to concede first success to Sutton for it became a Liberal seat in a famous by-election in December, 1972 which produced one of the largest turn over of votes ever known.

Having made my decision, I told Dingle Foot who quickly made me a member of Gray's Inn as he had promised. I then had to find out what was required before I could be called to the Bar. I knew I had to lie fallow for six months. This could have been a financial hardship but, fortunately, I had not drawn all my earnings during the time I was at Goodman, Derrick and Co. What I had to do took an irritatingly long time, though the under-treasurer at Gray's Inn, Os Terry, was most helpful and did what he could. Eventually, it was decided that as I did not get a good law degree at Oxford I had to take the Bar Final Examination and some of the papers in Part I. It was imperative to do this as quickly as possible and to get through successfully in each paper. Knowing my poor record as an examination candidate, this was a worry. So I enrolled at the crammers Gibson and Weldon in Chancery Lane and I knew that they would do their best for me to succeed.

I used to meet Jo Grimond from time-to-time and when I told him what I was doing, he offered to let me have his wig. He told me he had practised a little in East Anglia but that was many years ago. I was very grateful. Some weeks later after I had heard nothing and reminded him as it was approaching Call Night – the formal occasion when newly qualified barristers are called to the Bar – at Gray's Inn he confessed he could not find the wig! I had to act rather quickly to get another one.

The class I joined at Gibson's had some mature students apart from myself. I recall Hugh Mainprice who had been in Kenya and was a tax inspector, Hunt who had been in the Colonial Service in Nigeria so we had a number of mutual acquaintances and Brown who was a company secretary in the City. Of those who were just about to begin their careers, there was Sally Ehlers who years later emerged in Richmond as Lady Weston, the wife of Sir John Weston since retired as our permanent representative at the United Nations. Then there was John Bull, now the longest serving judge at the Guildford Crown Court. With a name like that he was the butt of one of the lecturers called Padley who taught us divorce law with a booming voice and making personal and sometimes, insulting illustrations. He used to link John Bull ("the spirit of Olde England") with a striking girl called Christine Gorna who later practised on the Western Circuit with chambers in Exeter. Padley's gift was to make his pupils remember some of the outrageous things he said. He was reputed to be at his best after lunch.

I shall always remember him striding in one afternoon and exclaiming: "Well now, Bull, to-day we come to a subject near to your heart and no doubt other parts of your body, adultery. Now, Bull, suppose you've been romping in the hay with Miss Gorna and you are so indiscreet and careless that Mrs Bull finds out and petitions for divorce—remember, Bull, you are a C3 man, because in Answer to the Petition, you can plead; Connivance, Collusion and Condonation". I am sure all the class remembered this.

But the verbal joustings were not all one way although I do not think Padley was used to being answered back. One morning, however, he did get his comeuppance from John Bull and I thought he deserved it. John Bull was late and Padley asked him why. The answer came: 'On my way here, I dropped in to see if Mrs Padley was all right in your absence'. After a semi-cheer and laughter, nothing more was said.

One of Padley's sallies had a repercussion some thirty years later. He once began a lecture: 'Well now, Bull, when you are a judge (pause) of some obscure County Court ...' Now, John Bull was appointed a Circuit Judge in 1991 and before he settled into Guildford, as was the practice, he used to sit at different courts on the circuit. One day, I received a message that he was coming to Kingston the following week and would like to sit at the outlying court that we had at Surbiton, as the train journey there was easier for him. As the Resident Judge, I had to deal with it and we managed to accommodate him as requested. So I wrote back and told him this, adding that it was very appropriate as it was the most obscure court that I could find! I knew he would appreciate it, as over the years, we had often laughed about our lectures with Padley.

•   •   •

It really was nerve wracking to wait some time for the results of the exams to come through, but I was extremely lucky in being able to accept an invitation to become one of the delegates to the Second Atlantic Conference of Young Political Leaders. It was a most well-timed opportunity and Joy was understanding about my going. I had been to similar gatherings before in Paris and Vienna but not on this scale.

As was to be expected, this time, there was considerably greater US and Canadian participation. It was somewhat different from the first one in Paris in 1958. This time, the New World balanced the Old. There were seventy European delegates, fifty from the United States and twenty from Canada. Of the European delegates, Great Britain had nine (five Conservatives, three Labour and myself as the one Liberal). The names make interesting reading in view of the careers of some of them. The five Conservatives were: James Ackers, Edward Bowman, James Dugdale, Stratton Mills and Nicholas Scott. The Labour trio were: Maurice Foley, Richard Marsh and Shirley Williams. It is interesting to note in passing that Richard Marsh became a Conservative life peer while Shirley Williams became the leader of the Liberal Democrat Peers. A lot of the delegates were already MPs or their equivalent. Others were young lawyers who were personal assistants or researchers to MPs while some, like myself, had been or were candidates for legislatures.

I have kept a report of the conference and a list of the delegates appears at the back of it. I often wish I had shown this in recent times to somebody who could tell me what has happened to at least some of them. All I know, sadly from his obituary, was that M. J. Le Theule from Sable, became the French Minister of Defence. I have not given up and shall try and seek out some veteran from the Liberal International like Richard Moore and see if I can find out more (no pun intended!).

The conference took place in Washington, DC under the auspices of the North Atlantic Treaty Association Organization (NATO) and the delegates were divided into five commissions. The total ground covered was large but the reports that were produced were quite succinct and easily readable, especially considering the language problems. The subjects covered were:

1. Conditions for Democracy in the NATO Countries.
2. The Problems of the Alliance.
3. The Communist Challenge.
4. The West and the Underdeveloped Areas.
5. Activities in the field of Education and Information.

The reports probably got little publicity even in political circles but the important element was the benefit to those who took part and that they were able to produce the reports without serious division.

As often happens, the events outside the conference itself were important and memorable. The conference was briefed by Vice Admiral Sabin, Chief of Staff, Supreme Allied Commander, Atlantic on the military position and strategy of the NATO. Politically, the USA put on a great show for us; President Eisenhower not only sent a very warm message to the conference but he greeted the delegates personally on the lawn of the White House and made an impromptu speech of which I have the press release! Originally, he intended just to say 'welcome', but he went on to set out some very clear thoughts on a number of topics including making democracy work.

Looking at US Presidents from Franklin D. Roosevelt onwards, I suppose that Eisenhower has been the most non-partisan one. A revered war leader, he was the Republican nominee but I do not think he had any career other than being a soldier. He had to belong to one of the two great American parties in order to get elected. He was the nearest the Americans have got to having a constitutional monarch because he sought to be a unifier of the whole people. His detractors have said that he showed that America did not need to have a president but I am not one of them.

The other high-powered speakers to visit the conference were Governor Averell Harriman and the former Secretary of State, Dean Acheson. The former dealt with the economic side of NATO and its relationships with Africa and Asia while the latter dealt with issues arising from the arrival in Russia of Krushchev without Bulganin. I have a summary of his speech which, of course, is very dated indeed and makes one realise the fundamental changes that have taken place since the end of the Cold War in 1989/90. Another reminder of that was that at the end of the conference it was unanimously agreed that the western powers should stand firm on their rights in Berlin. The Berlin Airlift is another matter of past history.

One evening, I took time off and went to Maryland to see my old friend from the TV company NBC, who had been seconded to Television of Wales and the West (TWW), Bob Myers whom I mention in *Chapter Four*. I went by Greyhound bus and it was pleasant to get out into the countryside as Washington had been a very hot place. Bob Myers was at the bus station to meet me and as we drove to his house, I noticed a well-designed traditional church called, "The Taylor Z. Woodrow Baptist Chapel". I asked Bob about it and I recall his reply: "John, Taylor Z. was the most awkward cuss that ever lived in this town. He quarrelled with everybody and when he quarrelled with his minister, he said, 'Pastor, I'm going to build my own church' and that's it". I did not ask Bob if Taylor Z. was the only worshipper!

The evening was an interesting one discussing American TV and its multiplicity of channels and Bob knew a great deal about how they combined to network programmes. I could understand why, with small budgets and being dependent on advertising revenue, there were so many films and programmes with audience and public participation which would reduce costs. The other thing I began to appreciate was that with the size of the USA and far cheaper fuel than we have, people would travel considerable distances even for private engagements such as going out for an evening meal at a friend's house, when a hundred miles was nothing.

At the end of the conference, the delegates, except those from the USA, drew lots for one of the four study tours in the States lasting about three weeks. I drew that lot whose first stop was San Antonio, Texas. Before leaving, I took part in the TV programme "Today" and was interviewed by Dave Garroway. I knew that "Today" was a top nationwide programme with a large audience. I think I kept my end up in talking about the conference but with his final question, I think the interviewer tried to throw me. He either knew or guessed that it was my first visit to the States and suddenly said, "Have all your prejudices about the United States been confirmed?" I could have said that as I did not have any, the question did not arise but I expect that would have sounded rather abrupt and, perhaps, superior which the Americans would not like, so I just said, "No, but I am going to Texas tomorrow". I learned afterwards that this was a far bigger laugh than I knew because other Americans always tell jokes about Texans. When I arrived in Texas, I soon had a microphone put in front of me and I was asked what I meant by that remark. I made as bland a reply as I could saying how much I was looking forward to being in Texas and enjoying their traditionally generous hospitality.

Indeed, they had laid on a very good programme for us. We learned a good deal about Davy Crockett and the heroes of the 'Wild Frontier'. In an exciting open air rodeo there were references to the Civil War and we got to know about the 'Lone Star State' and the 'Yellow Rose of Texas'. Texans certainly like to think they are the biggest and the best. At the time we were there, Alaska and Hawaii joined the USA which then became a country of fifty States and the flag had to be redesigned. It was not too difficult to incorporate the two extra stars. The Texans were a bit upset about Alaska because of its greater size. The governor of Alaska got to know about this and sent the following cable to the governor of Texas: "If you guys down South don't shut up, I will divide Alaska in two and then you will be the third largest State!" I do not know of any reply.

As in subsequent places we visited, a good deal of the organization and hospitality was done by the local Chamber of Commerce who were also good at getting press and TV coverage. A lot more people were made aware of what NATO was all about.

We were reported as visiting military installations. We visited the Aerospace Medical Center and although I am not a scientist and have no medical training, I found what was going on there very interesting. At this time, the Russians and the USA were engaged in rival and expensive programmes about exploring space. It was an important part of the Cold War in gaining admiration, respect and perhaps awe at what could be done. At one time, the Russians appeared to have a lead and in 1957 whilst I was in South Africa they succeeded in putting a man, Yuri Gagarin, into space in what was called a Sputnik.

The Americans were determined not to be outdone and their achievement, which also caught the admiration and astonishment of the world, was to land a man on the moon. I have found an interesting quote from Dr B. Thomas the Dean of Trinity University San Antonio, which I jotted down on the back of a brochure: "The Russian Sputnik was the US educational Pearl Harbour". This certainly shows what the stakes were thought to be in the Cold War.

During our visit, we were told about and saw equipment concerning the ability of a person to survive in weightless conditions. I saw a micro-manipulator which dissected individual cells and determined their structure. It was used to study the effects of radioactive material on portions of cells. I also saw a two man space cabin and what especially fascinated me was a row of large jars about the size of those in a traditional sweet shop. They were labelled with the names of the planets and in them was, as far as was then known, the atmosphere of a planet. Particular attention seemed to being paid to Mars. References were made to Mars Jars. I thought a reference to Mars *Bars* may not have been understood!

What we saw of the Center and the people working there showed a determination of purpose the Americans can have when they are in competition, coupled with a feeling that there was no limitation on the money they needed to further the work.

Before I left San Antonio, I was appointed to the office of mayor and I suppose the other delegates were as well. I wonder how many there are of us altogether. There must be many visiting delegations and conferences each year. Still, the parchment scroll is very attractive and I was pleased to see that it begins with the traditional words: "Know ye all men by these presents".

Apart from being made mayor for life, San Antonio did have a very important effect on my lifestyle because it was there that I gave up smoking! What happened was that I took a carton of two hundred Player's cigarettes to Washington and they had all gone by the time that I arrived in San Antonio. I found a tobacconist in the main street and I said to the man there, that he would know where I came from as soon as I opened my mouth and I would like to have the mildest cigarette he had in stock. He handed me a packet of twenty which I took to try. One was enough. If the tobacco had been cured at all, it must have been in some local back garden. My mouth was sore and dry. Also, the weather was very hot. It is a strange story but I have never smoked a cigarette since. I had been a regular, though not a heavy smoker, perhaps five to seven a day since I was seventeen years old. For a time, I smoked a pipe and generally used Balkan Sobranie tobacco preferring the black to the brown coloured tin. Occasionally, I would like a cigar, especially after a good dinner, but gradually, I gave them both up and I have not smoked at all for about thirty years.

After San Antonio, the group went on to Wichita, Kansas where the highlight was a visit to the Boeing factory which employed some 17,000 people. One interesting feature was looking down on planes which were being assembled with red topped wings and tail pieces. We were told that they were for the North Polar route and the red made them more easily identifiable should they crash on snow or ice. I was able to have a one-to-one talk with the union representative. I am not sure what the others were doing but I was interested to find out about the organization of an American Union. I do not know how typical this was, but there was one union for all employees, radically different from what it would have been here. I asked about differentials and how they were decided if there was not different representation for different trades and qualifications. I was told that this was a matter of negotiation within the union. Another matter that surprised me was that there seemed to be no scheme or provision for welfare and that when an employee retired, he or she was no longer a member of the union. I wonder how far this has changed in forty years.

As usual, we met civic leaders and we also visited a farm and a new shopping centre. We went to a workshop sponsored by the Continental Oil Company which is what a local press report called "bi-partisan workshops on practical politics for employees". When the panel was asked by one of the delegates to explain for us the differences between the Democrats and the Republicans, a lively discussion followed and I hope we were better informed! As far as the Democrats, particularly, were concerned, I think it would depend on the part of the USA one was in. I have always admired the verbal ingenuity of both parties in constructing the platform for a Presidential election. We flew to St. Louis and from there, were taken to Springfield, Illinois. I think it was at St. Louis that some supporters of Senator Goldberg who was running a very right wing campaign—more than tinged with racism and colour prejudice—had a banner saying, "In your heart, you know he's right". As a TV cameraman was filming it, a man got between the camera and the banner and lifted up a placard which read, "In your guts, you know he's nuts". It was one of the best bits of instant debunking that I have ever seen

At the edge of Springfield, our coach had both a state and city police escort. Indeed, I remember that at Dallas Airport on the way to San Antonio, we had an escort of thirty six police motor bikes. America is a big country in many senses. The mayor of Springfield was a big man called Lester B. Collins and at a reception he spoke to me. I knew he had been recently elected and was the first member of his party to have been successful for many years.

Unfortunately, I cannot remember now which party he supported but for the sake of the story, I will say he was a Republican. I asked him what was the first thing he did when he arrived at the Town Hall. He put his hand on my shoulder, which went down several inches, and said: "John, I sent for a list of all the people who worked here and I fired all those I knew were Democrats!" I just hope the replacements had more to offer than party loyalty.

Springfield is the capital of Illinois. It is not a large town and in 1958 the population was estimated at 58,000. It became the state capital through the efforts of Abraham Lincoln and has become widely known through his association with it. He lived there until he became president in 1861 and he is buried there. The monument to him is most impressive as in a different way is his home. The Memorial in Washington is on a grander scale and equally impressive. As usual, we had a full programme which included a visit to the New Salem State Park. This is described as "an historic shrine". Thanks to the philanthropy of William Randolph Hearst, the village where the young Lincoln worked as a clerk in a store has been recreated as it was in the eighteen-thirties with cabins, stores and a tavern where Lincoln boarded and slept in the loft.

There was a short visit to Chicago where we were joined by some of the delegates from other tours. What I remember most is not the receptions and speeches, but going out alone one morning before breakfast and walking along by the lake. It was a memorable sight to see the layout of a great American city beside the water.

One memorable event in Illinois was quite unplanned. A good number of delegates went to see Adlai Stevenson who had just been defeated as the Democrat candidate for president. He had the Aga Khan staying with him. Stevenson had a powerful intellect and was clearly an honourable man with principles but he did not have the flamboyance or the razzmatazz that seem to be necessary during the long campaign that a candidate for president has to undertake in every state. The whole thing does seem to be increasingly superficial and very costly. I think that Hubert Humphrey was another who suffered in this way and, without being in any way partisan, I think that America was the loser by their defeats. After Stevenson spoke to us in his garden, he came over and asked Shirley Williams, Nicholas Scott and myself if we were in a hurry to go. Fortunately, we were not as we were going to leave the others and remain with Gordon Dryden, a Canadian Liberal I had met before. He had come to our flat at Buckingham Palace Road and was at the Paris conference in 1958. He was going to drive us to Canada.

When the others had gone, we went to a room and Stevenson told us that Mrs Eleanor Roosevelt had just been on the telephone. She wanted to know if he was prepared to stand for president for the third time. On the face of it, the call was rather premature but perhaps the Democrats did want to know quickly if they had to look around for another candidate. I think that he clearly wanted somebody to speak to and we happened to be there. The gist of the conversation that followed was that if the election were in Britain a candidate who had lost twice very narrowly would get a sympathy vote which might tip the scale. Americans, on the other hand, do not care for a two-time loser. Our inclination, therefore, was that Stevenson should not stand again and, in the event, he did not—but became an excellent representative for America at the United Nations. The call from Mrs Roosevelt is referred to in the biography of Stevenson by his son but our presence is not mentioned! It would be rather strange to think that we had any influence on such a momentous decision—but perhaps we were a useful sounding board.

One final thought before leaving America for the moment, and thinking of elections, is the contrast with Britain in the number of offices that are democratically elected. I suppose that a judge is the most surprising to us. I wonder what sort of High Court bench we would have in the UK if candidates were subject to election. I think the chief trouble is that very few people indeed would know anything about them and it would be strange to find them nominated by the political parties. I understand that this does not apply to all the states in the USA and some have judges made by appointment.

I used to collect cards of candidates which had mini-CVs and brief points of policy on them. I have found a number of them and apart from judge, which has given me much amusement when shown to colleagues and members of the Lord Chancellor's Department, there are ones for Marshall of the Court of Common Pleas, State Auditor, District Representative, State Governor, Clerk of the District Council and Police Magistrate. There were many more. No wonder that people often just vote for the party ticket for the lot of them!

Gordon Dryden drove us to Detroit and we went into Canada via London and Hamilton. I was interested to see the large size of the ships that were able to get from one of the Great Lakes to another. The highlight however, was to visit Niagra Falls where I was able to shoot some dramatic film. We stopped briefly at Toronto which has since greatly expanded and then on to the capital, Ottawa. We were received by the Prime Minister, John Diefenbaker and the Liberal leader, Lester Pearson. We went to the Parliament House where the chamber is quite different from ours. Each member has a desk which is useful to bang by way of applause and there was instant voting by the pressing of buttons and an immediate count. As an outsider, I thought this was much better than the Westminster system of calling a division, trooping through the lobbies, coming back into the chamber and hearing the result of the vote. A division takes about twenty minutes. I suppose it promotes the club atmosphere but that is not all important. Frequent divisions on a highly contested Bill being debated clause by clause take up a great amount of unproductive time.

From Ottawa, we went to Montreal and I remember standing above the dockside when a Canadian liberal delegate who was accompanying us pointed out a ship that he said was going to Liverpool, about 2,200 miles. When he left us, he was going to see his father who ran a restaurant in the Yukon Territory at Whitehorse on the Alaska Highway and he said this was over 3,000 miles away. It gave me some idea of the size of Canada from East to West and we were some distance from the Maritime States on the East Coast.

We went by train from Montreal to New York where all the delegates were re-united. The four tours all seemed to have been successful. Those who went South to New Orleans and cruised on the Mississippi were especially enthusiastic and certainly had a greater knowledge of jazz! We were taken to the UN. The General Assembly was not in session but it was interesting to see at first hand where – and to some extent how – the most important organization for the future of the world worked. We got no more than a glimpse of New York but the final dinner was a meaningful occasion as it put a seal on the undoubted success of the conference and the tours. I remain delighted that I was able to go and as may be obvious, I still have some very clear and enjoyable memories.

•   •   •

So back home to England and within a few days, I went off with Joy and Caroline to Seaview on the Isle of Wight where we joined by Mr and Mrs

Heward (Mears and Pop). This worked well as they stayed at the Seaview Hotel and after dinner came around to the boarding house where we were and babysat. This enabled Joy and myself to go out for an evening meal and we got to know the restaurants and hotels on the island rather well.

It was really rather nerve wracking to wait for the results of the exams. They were published on 24th June and as I was not at home I had to look through the various headings in *The Times*. I was mighty glad and relieved to find that I had passed everything. So all was set for the next important step and I was called to the Bar at Gray's Inn on 13th July, 1960. The occasion was filmed and I appeared in a photograph in the *Listener* at the actual moment of my call in white tie and tails, head bowed and shaking hands with the Treasurer, His Honour Judge Durley Grazebrook. The programme was called "The Lawyers" and attracted some seven million viewers so that it was repeated two months later which was then unusual for a documentary. My change of status was noted by *The Guardian* and I was reported as saying that there was no political significance in the fact that Dingle Foot was a Labour MP. The report added: "They are, after all, both Plymouth boys".

I kept a notebook of my earliest cases and I had an extraordinary start. Just five days after I was called, I appeared at Hendon Magistrates' Court instructed by my old firm, Amery-Parkes and Co on a traffic matter—and later the same day before the Judicial Committee of the Privy Council. It must have been some short preliminary application because the appeal itself was heard in November and lasted three days. It was a land dispute from West Africa. This appearance is not as surprising as it seems because my chambers at the time primarily did the sort of work which consisted of appeals from Commonwealth countries. For full appeals, the court consisted of five judges in lounge suits seated around a horse shoe table with the advocate standing facing them in the centre robed with wig and gown. It could be quite an alarming experience, especially if their lordships were indicating that they were against you! In the main, the court consisted of United Kingdom Law Lords who were supplemented from time to time by judges from Commonwealth countries. I recall appearing before judges from, Australia, New Zealand, Ceylon (as Sri Lanka was then known) and Trinidad. I expect there were others. Great constitutional changes had been taking place and some countries left the Privy Council as their final court of appeal on gaining their independence. This included India which was the source of considerable litigation. By these decisions, some barristers lost their practices or a good proportion of them overnight. So while the Privy Council work was interesting and sometimes rewarding, I could see that the trend would most likely be contraction rather than expansion so I tried to broaden my practice as far as I could. One trouble was that the senior clerk of chambers, Walter Butler, had been brought up on Privy Council work so this was where his knowledge and expertise lay. However, he was shrewd enough to realise where the future lay. Though he would never admit it, I think he used to get help from other clerks on the appropriate fees to charge. This was not a problem in legal aid cases where the clerk did not negotiate the fees.

When I arrived in chambers, there were two briefs on my desk. They were from Amery-Parkes and Co. and sent by Charles Brandreth. He had been a solicitor in that firm and had left and gone to the Bar. For reasons that I do not know, the transfer was not as successful as he had hoped and, indeed, deserved. He was an able advocate and so he became a solicitor again and returned to his old firm. He used to broadcast on Saturday mornings regularly on motoring matters. He doted on his son, Gyles, and was quite properly very proud when he became President of the Oxford Union and then an MP, though only for one Parliament. But the year 1997 was not a good one for a Conservative to hold his seat.

This gesture by Charles Brandreth was very kindly. I had briefed him and now he briefed *me*. In the early months, he sent me work regularly in magistrates' courts but then in September, 1960, I did my first case at The Old Bailey. It was for driving under the influence of drink and heard by the Recorder of London, Sir Gerald Dodson, He was known as 'The Wrecker" because it was said that he could wreck any defence! This time, I think he went too far. I remember him summing up to the jury; he referred to the evidence of two policemen in favourable terms and then to the medical evidence for the prosecution. Having reviewed the prosecution evidence, he said rather scathingly: "And now, I come to the Defendant". He then paused, took out a large handkerchief and made a tremendous grunt and sneeze. He briefly summarised the defence. The jury retired and returned a verdict of "not guilty". I always remember that the prosecuting counsel was Michael Self, one of the nicest men at the Bar. He came over to me and just said, "Well done". The case went over for a second day and so I was entitled to a "refresher" on my brief fee, sometimes two-thirds, often one-half. The gross total came to 29 pounds and 12 shillings and was the largest fee I had earned for a single case.

The Recorder was an interesting man. He wrote the words of the popular song "The Fishermen of England" and also one of the nineteen-thirties musical comedies. I think it was "Quaker Girl" but I may be wrong. My mother had the piano music of a lot of those shows and had taken part in some of them in the Amateur Theatrical Company in Plymouth. She gave her collection of music to Leslie Crowther who was most enthusiastic about it. He was a very talented pianist as well as being a very funny man. His death at an early age after an unexplained motor accident when his heavy Rolls-Royce turned over was a great loss to the world of entertainment. He did much hard work for charity especially during his time as president of the Lords' Taverners. There is a commemorative seat to him behind the pavilion at Lord's and when I go there, from time to time, I have a look to satisfy myself that it is being well kept and I have a silent thought about him and what he achieved.

It was Sir Gerald Dodson who, after he heard medical evidence that a defendant suffered from schizophrenia, turned to the defendant and said: "I sentence you to five years imprisonment, both of you". I do not think that today, he would get away with that. I like to think that over the years, judges have become more understanding and more polite but I shall have more to say about that later.

However, before I leave Sir Gerald Dodson, I would like to relate a story that was told about him after he retired that is so strange as to be believable. He decided to go to Paris by himself and so he caught the night train from Victoria.

This was long before the Channel Tunnel and Eurostar. The coaches were transferred on to a cross channel ferry and then put on to the rails again in France. The story goes that on reaching Folkestone, a check was made on the passengers. The railway official recognised "The Wrecker" and as he was the only passenger in the coach, he ordered it to be shunted into a siding! There the story ends and it is not known whether "The Wrecker" got to France very late or at all. I suppose that the moral of this story is, "Don't go to Paris by yourself"!

Having got to The Old Bailey, my next appearance before a jury was in September 1960 at London Sessions, now the Inner London Crown Court, at the Elephant and Castle. The case was one of driving under the influence of drink and dangerous driving. I was again instructed by Amery-Parkes and Co. and was delighted when my client was acquitted on both charges.

Between August and December, 1960, I did sixty-nine cases. For the first six months in chambers, I had to be a pupil. My pupil master was Joseph Dean. I had known him personally for some time. He was a sound common lawyer and he was familiar with Privy Council work. He did not have the best of luck in his practice. He wrote a book on libel called *Hatred, Ridicule or Contempt* which was very well reviewed but did not bring in a libel practice. That work went increasingly to specialist chambers. Then he was in one of the first cases in the newly created Restrictive Practices court but that did not lead to any further work. He was also out of tune politically with most of the rest of chambers as he was a committed Conservative and on the Westminster Council. I remember him having quite a heated argument with Dick Taverne. He was also generally out of sympathy with the movements for independence in Africa with which Dingle Foot was much involved. He was most kind and helpful to me and I learned a good deal from him about some finer points of practice at the Bar though he very seldom ventured into a criminal court. Crime was regarded as an inferior species of work to civil. I was not surprised when he changed chambers but I do not think it was the greatest success. He became a Circuit Judge in 1975 and sat in Kent. He retired in 1987 and lived, I believe, in some style in West Brabourne, Ashford. I last heard of him as being one of those totally opposed to the Channel Tunnel. I hope he did not feel too embittered when it was opened.

• • •

After the General Election of 1959, the Liberal party tried to pick itself up and in particular to improve its organization. As Mark Bonham Carter was no longer an MP, he devoted a good deal of time to this. One trouble was the considerable lack of money.

In those times, political parties were more class based. Broadly speaking the Conservatives were supported by the wealthy, businesses, the City and property owners. Labour was supported by manual workers and to a very great extent by the industrial unions. If one was taken to an unfamiliar place, you would know where the Conservative and Labour (frequently called socialist) voters would be living.

It was a strength of the Liberal party that it was not class-based but it was also a weakness in that there was no sectional interest on which it could rely and from which it could get money. Contributions had to come from those who believed in the value of having a third party in British politics based on liberal values. There were very few wealthy supporters. Some came from traditional Liberal families but there was no significant patronage to offer, unlike the days of Lloyd George in the nineteen-twenties, though the leader could nominate a very limited number of honours.

Liberals were thin on the ground in proportion to the total number of peers but they made their presence felt by being present and contributing to the debates. The only way to get money was via fund raising events, nearly always constituency based or by persuading individuals to contribute either nationally or locally. It was difficult work especially when the results of General Elections had been so disappointing. Much of the burden rested on the party treasurer, Major General W. H. Grey. Although his views were generally right wing, he was an old-style Whig quite opposed to the Tory establishment and the landed gentry. He belonged to a number of London clubs and it used to be said that you could judge the esteem in which he held you according to the club he invited you to go to! He often lunched in the National Liberal Club at the "singles" table and he always had the same meal; double club sherry, gulls eggs and brown bread. He once said to me; "The food at the National Liberal is damned good, mind you I never have anything cooked!" He took the King of the Ashanti to Boodles and when he was waiting for him to come out of the gents, a member came up to the General and commented about him bringing a black man to the club. The General who could be quite formidable when roused, replied: "It's a long time since a king came here and if you are still here when he comes out, I expect you to be standing up for Royalty!"

Once, I saw him in the foyer of the National Liberal Club and he said to me: "I've done some good work for the Liberal party today". Asked what it was, he replied: "I was coming over Waterloo Bridge and I saw the Duke of St. Albans. I pointed to the House of Lords and asked if he ever went there. When he said he did, I asked him where he sat and he replied: 'On the Liberal benches'. I said, 'It's a long time since you paid for that privilege and I should know as I am the treasurer'. So he promised me a cheque for £1,000". This would not be long before the General died in 1961. The General really worked hard for the Liberal party in memory of his son George Grey who became MP for Berwick-on-Tweed in 1941. Sadly, the son was killed in Normandy in 1944. He was replaced by Sir William Beveridge, the author of the Beveridge Report on Social Security but who lost the seat in the General Election of 1945.

However, much of his report was enacted during the next Parliament, with the return of a Labour Government. Harold Wilson and Frank Pakenham (later, Lord Longford) were two of his team. There has always been a hard core of Liberals in Berwick-on-Tweed, which enabled Alan Beith to capture the seat in a by-election in 1973 and he has held it ever since.

I cannot leave the General without emphasizing what a kind and thoughtful man he was who knew the value of encouragement. He used to send plain post cards and he sent one to Jeremy Thorpe after the 1959 General Election which read: "Glad you got in. You deserve it. W. H. Grey. " Jeremy, rightly, valued it very much. The General was very helpful to Frank Byers especially after he lost his North Dorset seat very narrowly in 1950. He was able to get him a directorship in Rio Tinto and being rather unexpectedly Chairman of Radio Luxemburg he got Frank to be the Answer Man, answering listeners' questions on a variety of subjects. The identity of Frank Byers was never revealed – but to Liberals, especially, he was a well-known voice! He was thus helped financially and I have always thought that the death of General Grey which deprived Jeremy Thorpe of such help was a great misfortune. Being a Liberal MP was an expensive business because the office, research and secretarial assistance was only publicly funded to a very limited extent. It has since been improved. The position was made more difficult when Jeremy Thorpe became leader of the party in 1967. Again, the position has changed for the better, but then, the Liberal leader had no public funding. Politics revolves around the leaders so much and this leads to expense. Inherited or self-made wealth should not be required.

I am moving some way ahead of my early days at the Bar with its mixture of appearing in magistrates' courts - sometimes doing very run of the mill motoring cases and then appearing in the Privy Council. It became a more diverse practice as some civil work came along, especially what we now call family work, then called 'divorce'. After I became a judge, Lord Denning once told me that he thought this change was important because it altered the emphasis to the importance of family matters to the family.

As far as my own family is concerned, 1961 had its sadness because in March, my mother-in-law who as I have said, was always known as Mears died. It was the same day as Sir Thomas Beecham. She was not only personally delightful and one of life's optimists but she was a capable organizer and a tower of strength as a minister's wife. When in Cambridge, on Sundays especially, their home would be full of undergraduates. She went to Cheltenham Ladies' College where being a non-conformist and coming from a Liberal family, were not assets. Her maiden name was Rawlings. Her father was a city solicitor and he stood as a Liberal candidate in the City of London in 1906 but was not elected. However, he was the first Radical Mayor of Hammersmith.

Thanks to our good friend, Dr Moya Tyson who lives in Hammersmith and is a local historian, we have got a number of press cuttings of the Rawlings and Heward families from Edwardian times. Local newspapers in those days, covered events in considerable detail and often in somewhat flowery language. Over a number of years, Mrs Heward suffered from osteo arthritis which made walking rather difficult. It was remarkable how her condition improved when she went on holiday to Grindelwald in Switzerland.

The Rawlings/Heward family had been going there since 1908, not every year but with some regularity. They stayed in the Bear Hotel until it was burnt down in the nineteen-thirties and since then, they have been going to the Belvedere Hotel run by the Hauser family. When Joy and I took our grandchildren, James and Julia Titley, they were the fourth generation to go to that hotel and we have known four generations of Hausers.

My father-in-law, Reverend Thomas Brown Heward, was a prudent northcountryman being born in Hartlepool. He was brought up as an Anglican and became a railway freight clerk in Darlington. In those days, railway employees were an elite and much respected body. Much goods traffic went by rail. Motorised commercial traffic was in its infancy. Prompt delivery was essential. There were sufficient railway companies for competition to be a spur to efficiency. In his twenties, Mr Heward felt the call to the ministry and became a Primitive Methodist. He attended Hartley Victoria College, Manchester and became very well read. In later years, he would vividly remember his Hebrew classes. In the First World War he was an army chaplain with the rank of major. He served on the Western Front and in Salonika. He did not talk much about it. The carnage was terrible in France and no doubt, he had many burials to perform and much consoling work with families.

However, he used to relate how when he was in Salonika, a popular sergeant died. An officer asked 'Pop'- he was called within the family - to go out with some others to find him and give him a decent burial. Pop explained that he was a Methodist and in those days, denomination of churches was quite important, especially the distinction between church and chapel which was often a class and political dividing line. Pop was told that being a Methodist did not matter and a group set off on horseback to find the sergeant. When he was found, a grave was dug and a short service took place.

Pop was mentioned in dispatches for his work as a chaplain. The citation was signed by Winston Churchill, who though better known for his tenure and connection with the Admiralty, had a spell at the War Office. Joy has still got the citation.

Methodist ministers were normally appointed for a period of three years, but the Heward family stayed on for nine years in Cambridge and ten years in Watford until retiring to Cambridge at the end of the Second World War.

When Mears died in 1961, the family home was sold. Pop came to live with us. Such uprootings can be difficult but in Pop's case it worked very well. He was most understanding and adaptable, and indeed very helpful after our second daughter Jenny was born in August 1962. It was full circle for him as his first church had been at Richmond.

Although it was pretty busy in court as a barrister — in my first year I did 156 cases — there were days when I was not in court and did what was called "paperwork" such as drafting pleadings and giving opinions. There was less pressure than at Goodman, Derrick and Co so I could devote more time to politics. I was particularly concerned to improve the public showing of the Liberal annual assembly knowing that the media was always ready to exploit every procedural muck up and every so called "split" in the party. It was difficult to strike the balance between innocuous and bland resolutions on which everybody would agree with a vigorous open debate on a topical subject during which some differences would emerge.

I found two very helpful supporters in Basil Wigoder and Dr Timothy Joyce. Basil had been a contemporary of mine at Oxford after the war. He became president of the Union beating Ralph Gibson, then an Independent Conservative and later, a member of the Court of Appeal, by a handful of votes. After his campaigns in Bournemouth which I have already mentioned, he was candidate for Westbury in 1959 and 1964. Basil was an outstanding criminal lawyer, taking silk in 1966 and becoming a life peer in 1974. He really enjoyed being the chief whip to Frank Byers but after Frank's untimely death his enthusiasm rather waned until Roy Jenkins became leader. Basil sadly died in Septenber 2004.

Timothy Joyce had a good sense of fun as well as a penetrating political mind. He told me that General Grey once asked him what he was a doctor of. When he replied, "Philosophy", the General said: "That's a waste of time. It has all been decided by Aristotle and Plato"! Timothy worked for J. Walter Thompson and later formed his own advertising and public relations agency an more time in New York but he fought as a Liberal candidate in Aylesbury.

Between the three of us and with the goodwill of a number of others, especially Mark Bonham Carter, we tried to take a grip on the way the assembly was run. We picked the chair of each session and adopted a system whereby every intending speaker had to fill in a card giving some personal particulars and qualifications for speaking. This was handed in to a table by the platform where there were three people who knew the party well and could mark the card if they felt there was someone outstanding who should be called. The cards were passed to the chair in advance of the debate. In this way, we discovered, for example, a delegate who had recently retired from a very high position in Rhodesia.

We also left time in the Agenda for a topical resolution. This would be done at short notice and be introduced by a party spokesman, usually an MP. We were also keen to co-operate with the media and keep them well informed about the time table. The BBC, in particular, began to send a larger number of people and John Grist often came. He was the Director of Current Affairs. Later, I got to know him well as he became a neighbour in Richmond. His wife, Jill, became a Liberal Democrat Councillor in my ward She was very good and it was sad that she had to stand down owing to failing eyesight. There were so many papers she had to read.

There was considerable goodwill towards the Liberals. Jo Grimond was very popular and, in the press office Phyllis Preston was highly rated. However, as I have already mentioned, there was some hostility which came from committed Conservative papers like the *Daily Express*, the *Daily Mail* and the *Daily Telegraph*. Under the editorship of Alastair Hetherington, the *Guardian* became less supportive while unfortunately the *News Chronicle* ceased publication.

The closure of the *News Chronicle* and its takeover by the *Daily Mail* was a sudden and sad experience. The former was highly regarded as a paper which had very talented and quality writers like Walter Layton, A. J. Cummings, Geoffrey Cox and Hubert Phillips. The latter, apart from being Lloyd George's secretary, set many fascinating puzzles. He once told me that he was on a railway journey when a family in the same compartment, somewhat noisily, tried to do his puzzles without much success. They went off for lunch and left the *Chronicle* behind. Hubert Phillips got hold of it and completed all the solutions. When they came back, he was very modest about his achievement!

As always, because I had no direct line, the calls came through the clerk's room and I am pretty sure it was Walter Butler who said I had been asked to go over to their premises at once. It was in the early evening. When I arrived, everything was at a standstill. The staff were absolutely stunned. Publication had ceased and there would be no paper the next day. A much respected crime reporter called Bishop and known as "Bish" was telephoning in from Scotland

Yard, very excited about a story he had just got. He wanted to dictate it and just could not believe it when he was told he could not. He persisted as he thought some joke was being played on him. He got in a taxi and found out the truth when he arrived.

I tried to find out what had happened and it seemed that the board of directors had decided to sell the paper as it had been losing money. I had to tell the staff that I did not think there was anything they could do about it and stop what had happened. Presumably, the directors were satisfied that they had the power to act as they did. The only thing to be done would be to negotiate the best possible terms for termination of employment without notice.

When the news got out, many people were stunned. Frank Byers tried to see if some consortium backed by the City could be set up to buy the paper but it did not get off the ground and anyway it was too late ; the deal had been done. I do not know how I got involved. Literally, I just answered the call. There was never any question of a fee.

It was, perhaps, fortunate that the political power of the newspaper was declining while that of TV was increasing. Geoffrey Cox was already in control at ITN which was separate from the programme companies. He invented the newscaster with freedom to present his own material, as opposed to the newsreader who just read out what was put in front of him. It must be by chance, because they survived on their own professional merit, that a number of the first newscasters had been Liberal candidates; people like Ludovic Kennedy, Robin Day and Huw Thomas (who was to move to Yorkshire TV).

I think that the reforms to the Liberal Assembly worked reasonably well though there were always those who would try some procedural device to get their way. Apart from assemblies, the Liberals got good publicity in the quality press for the standard of their publications. Jo Grimond was able to attract a number of academics who helped compile reports across a range of subjects such as local government, industrial affairs, consumer protection, education, transport, housing and taxation. There were series sometimes, written by people who were not members of the Liberal party but in general sympathy with its outlook. One was called "New Directions" and another the "Unservile State" while a third was "New Orbits". These thought provoking pamphlets helped the Liberal party to punch above its political weight.

With such activity, optimism began to grow about the next General Election but that did not come until October 1964. Meanwhile, the Liberals did their best to keep in the public eye but there were no by-election victories. However, there were a considerable number of successes in local government. This was good for morale as it showed that Liberals could win. It was the beginning of "pavement politics". In Richmond, we broke through in Kew, which was a particular delight to the Grimonds, and then in Town ward. It took some twenty years before control was gained of the council and that lasted for eighteen years, ending in 2002.

The party literature continued to be of high quality. A fourteen page pamphlet called "Get Britain Moving with the Liberals" was published in January 1963 with a message from Jo Grimond. There was also a song with the same name and on the back of the 45 rpm disc there was another message from the leader, this time directed to young people. The four paragraphs in the pamphlet make poignant reading today. This is not the place to set it all out but I really cannot refrain, as we await a decision on whether we should join the Euro currency, from a short quotation:

> Both Labour and the Tories failed completely to understand the great movement towards a United Europe which gained momentum in the years after the war. The country could, and indeed should, have taken a leading role in the European movement, and by so doing it could have helped positively to shape the Community to suit the needs and problems of the whole Commonwealth.

I have always supported wholeheartedly the Liberal policy of becoming a part of Europe. Joy and I were present at an early meeting of the European Movement which was held in a packed Albert Hall so that means that some 8,000 people were there. Winston Churchill was the chair and many European statesmen were on the platform including Eduard Daladier and Paul Reynaud from France and Paul Henri Spaak from Belgium who later became the Secretary General of NATO. It was Winston Churchill who began the campaign for a united Europe with memorable and rousing speeches but he was not concerned with the detail for the future. Quite understandably, he wanted, above all, a reconciliation between France and Germany but he expressed no views that I can recall on political integration. His old friend, Robert Boothby, recalled how when he mentioned the possibility of a European army to Churchill, he was aghast and said: "European Army! European Army! What shongs will they shing?!"

The absence of full British participation and leadership in the Treaty of Rome and the establishment of the European coal and steel community and the evolution of the Benelux countries shows a sorry tale of missed opportunities. I think that Anthony Eden (later Lord Avon) must take a great deal of responsibility for this. He had much experience at the Foreign Office over many years.

Perhaps it is an over-simplification, but I have often said that there is an argument for being in Europe and one for being out, but I have never understood how this country can make a success of being half in and half out.

CHAPTER 6

Life at the Bar and Another General Election

In my first year at the Bar, I was instructed by twenty-seven firms of solicitors of which fourteen were through my existing contacts. One way of getting known is through being mentioned in the Law Reports as the names of the barristers and solicitors acting in the cases that are so reported are always given. There are several series of such reports, some covering a wide range of cases while others are specialist. I was lucky in that a number of cases I was in were reported in the *Appeal Cases* reports. They were decisions of the Privy Council. The first one, from Ceylon, as it was then called (now Sri Lanka)), was in 1961. Others followed and in the 1960s there was at least one of my cases reported each year. Some were from the West Indies which was fortunate as it led to something unexpected.

We had in chambers pupils from many Commonwealth countries. They usually came for six months. With some, I remained in contact for many years. One, Sryani Nonis from Colombo, gets in touch when she comes to England as her children have been educated here. Some pupils had been called to the Bar but wanted to do a pupillage before returning to their own country. One was Tom Adams, the son of Grantley Adams the first president of the ill-fated Caribbean Federation, which was really broken by distance as well as political differences.

Tom also had a distinguished public life and became premier of Barbados. Before he joined Chambers, he had worked in the BBC World Service and continued to do some programmes while a pupil. He found out that I had done some broadcasting so he got me to go to Bush House and do a programme about the Privy Council, which seemed to go well.

I think this was in 1962 because in March of that year I became involved with Lord Rea, the leader of the Liberal peers, in a discussion about the future of the Judicial Committee of the Privy Counci and I wrote a letter to him which he kindly forwarded to the Lord Chancellor, Lord Kilmuir[1].

I pointed out that Ghana had stopped appeals from 30th June 1960, very suddenly — and a number of pending appeals were never heard. This had important implications for amendments to the new constitution. I suggested that an African judge should be appointed to the Privy Council as a matter of urgency and, "we ought to try and create a Commonwealth Court rather than retain a body which to many people is a symbol of imperial domination". I also suggested that such a court should sit in various parts of the Commonwealth.

Lord Kilmuir's reply to Lord Rea was very flattering about my letter and said that the situation was causing him a great deal of anxiety. He seemed basically in favour of trying to create a Commonwealth Court whilst pointing out "very formidable difficulties". In the event, nothing happened but, in fairness to Lord Kilmuir, within a few months he was dropped from the Government by

---

[1] Formerly Sir David Maxwell-Fyfe and known irreverently at the Bar as 'Dai Bananas'.

Harold MacMillan in the so-called 'night of the long knives' in which seven members of the cabinet lost their jobs. Lord Kilmuir was a member of Gray's Inn and it was general knowledge there that he took it very badly. The Lord Chancellor is traditionally the least party political of all state offices and no specific reason was given for his removal. He was one of the victims of a desperate political manoeuvre.[2]

None of Lord Kilmuir's successors has instigated any Privy Council reform so the Judicial Committee has continued as before with an ever shrinking jurisdiction until only the few countries now use it. For a while, some, such as Malaysia, became republics but remained in the Commonwealth, recognising the Queen as their Head and retaining appeals to the Privy Council. Unlike the House of Lords, where separate judgments (technically speeches) are given by each member, the Judicial Committeee is advising Her Majesty so only one judgment was given as it was thought inappropriate for the Sovereign to be receiving different advice at the same time! However, with a sovereign Republic, a different formula had to be adopted and, for example, the committee would report its opinion to the Head of Malaysia, the Yang di-Pertuan Agong. Once, Lord Dilhorne was finishing the judgment and could not find the note telling him what to say at the end. He was not the most patient of men and after a quick shuffle of his papers, he said, "We will advise whoever-it-is". With a gentle smile, the committee rose for the day!

The position of only having one judgment or, technically, advice, has been relaxed. I do not know the background but I suspect that some of their Lordships were uncomfortable in being associated with a decision with which they did not agree. This happens still in the Court of Appeal (Criminal Division). I remember when I was sitting in the High Court in the Strand, I was in the judges' corridor coming back from lunch when I was asked by a very senior member of the Court of Appeal if I had seen his judgment in a case in *The Times Law Reports*, that morning. I said I had and when he asked me what I thought of it. I think I replied that I was a bit surprised. He then told me that he had been to lunch on the bench table at the Inner Temple and had got an awful lot of stick from his fellow benchers. I do not know what he told them but he told me that he did not agree with a word of it — but had been outvoted by his colleagues. He was the senior of the three and gave the judgment of the court.

I do not think that a judge should be put in this position on a matter of law which must be of some importance otherwise the case would not have reached the Court of Appeal. However, I think different considerations apply to Appeals against sentence when there must often be a compromise between the three judges. Suppose, for example, that there is an appeal against a sentence of ten years' imprisonment which is dismissed. That might be the initial view of one judge; one might have thought that was a bit severe and given eight while the third might have given twelve. One could not have each judge giving his own sentence. The court has to work out a united view.

---

2 The position has, of course, been under threat. In 2002, the Labour government purported to abolish it and only later, under immense pressure from the judiciary in general, relented. Despite the scheduled creation of a Supreme Court by 2008, Lord Falconer, the present incumbent, styles himself "Secretary of State for Constitutional Affairs".

Problems of unanimity also occur in the Crown Court on appeals from magistrates' courts. The powers and jurisdiction of the magistrates' courts was reviewed by Parliament in 2003. When hearing appeals, the Crown Court judge will sit with at least two magistrates unless the parties agree on only one being present. The judge decides all matters of law but each member of the court has an equal voice in determining the facts. Sometimes, though I hope not often, the judge is outvoted. He must accept this with good grace. In fact, there is an instruction from the Lord Chancellor to do so! This followed an incident in the old London Sessions when a furious judge returned to court after retiring with the magistrates and said, "This appeal is allowed by a majority of one from which I heartily dissent". The magistrates complained.

I can only remember one appeal against conviction where I was in a minority. It was a case of careless driving and I had more sympathy with the motorist than the magistrates!

A judge has to be diplomatic and keep the magistrates on his side. This can sometimes be difficult on matters of sentence but a judge must also be careful about being led into a tricky situation. I recall one judge who was more at home doing civil rather than criminal work and had the reputation of being somewhat lenient in his sentencing. He was due to hear an appeal with two very experienced magistrates when for some reason a very inexperienced magistrate turned up for her first appeal. The number of magistrates is not laid down and she was allowed by the judge to sit as well. In fairness, she must have had three years experience as a magistrate before being put on the Crown Court list. The appeal, which was against the sentence passed in the magistrates' court was heard and the court retired. The two experienced magistrates took a clear view with which the judge disagreed. The inexperience magistrate agreed with the judge so that was two all—a highly undesirable scenario. The judge, as he was entitled to do, exercised a second and casting vote. The two who became the minority were very angry indeed.

When I got to know about this, I indicated that at Kingston Crown Court there should never be an even number of people adjudicating. In the above case, I would have allowed the inexperienced lady, if she had wished, to sit in court on the bench, but not to take part in the hearing of the case.

Another way for a barrister to get known is through press reports of the cases in which he or she is appearing. This applies more to criminal practitioners than to civil. Local papers cover their magistrates' courts and the nearest Crown Court. When the *Evening News* circulated in London, it had a feature "Courts Day by Day" and a very talented writer using the initials "J. A. J." used to describe a case before a stipendiary magistrate. They became quite well known, especially the chief magistrate who sat at Bow Street. Nowadays, I doubt if one person in a thousand would know the name of the chief magistrate. The former stipendiary magistrates are now called District Judges.

In the national press, there would be reports of contested divorce cases especially if there was any "society" name involved and again, the judge would be featured particularly if he had made some comment on a well-known person's behaviour. With the growth of the tabloids and the down-marketing of the press generally, the coverage of court cases has tended to concentrate on those involving sex and/or violence. Quite rightly, what are considered to be lenient sentences are featured.

Once thing that has annoyed me, and I took this up with Harry Woolf when he was the Lord Chief Justice, is that when a sentence of imprisonment is not passed but a community penalty is ordered the headline so often is, "Thief/abuser/cheat/thug walks free from court". This is despite, say, strict terms of a probation order or having to do a specified number of hours of unpaid work and/or pay compensation. I got so fed up with this that I used to say something like, "You are not walking free from this court and any suggestion that you are is completely wrong. If there is any trouble with you carrying out these orders, you will be brought back here and it is almost one hundred per cent certain that you will go to prison for quite a long time. Do you understand what I have said?"

I have been told that the Probation Service (now the National Probation Service (or 'NPS') and part of the National Offender Management Service (NOMs)) found this formula useful, especially as a reminder to a defendant who might be in danger of defaulting for example, by being late or failing to keep appointments.

The Times Law Reports are a good way for a new barrister to get known as they are widely looked at and not only by lawyers. I know people who regularly read them out of general interest. I was lucky in that in *The Times* of 10th March 1961 there was quite a lengthy report of a Privy Council case Jamaica called *Jetter and Others v. The Queen*. The four petitioners were members of a Rastafarian group who had formed themselves into an armed military group. They had shot one of their number as they believed he had committed "treason". I appeared for the commander of the unit. Tom Kellock represented the man who actually carried out the killing while Dick Taverne represented two others for whom the jury had made recommendations for mercy. Godfray le Quesne appeared, as he so often did, for the Crown. He was always a great debater and, like Dick Taverne, had been president of the Oxford Union. Dick went first as one of his clients was the first petitioner. He outlined the history of the Rastafarian movement. Rastafari was the title of Haile Salasse before he became Emperor of Ethiopia. My client's father, Reverend Henry, was looked upon as a modern Moses who was to lead Negroes to liberate Africa by force. Where and how they were to start this movement of liberation does not seem to have been worked out.

I thought the most interesting point was put by Tom Kellock which was that if his client had not carried out the shooting he would have been shot himself. The board and, in particular, Lord Radcliffe, were not sympathetic and pointed out that there was no evidence that anyone was forced to join this armed unit. Any person who joined was responsible in law for his acts. Duress was ruled out and indeed the jury, having been specifically asked about it, found that there was no duress. The petitions were dismissed and it is a pity that the case did not provide an opportunity for the board to consider how far duress can be a defence to murder especially in paramilitary circumstances.

Part of my desire to diversify my practice was the hope that in criminal cases I would be asked to prosecute as well as defend. In those days, it was a tradition of the Criminal Bar that one did both. I am sorry that over the years this tradition has weakened. It began with some who were politically left wing, refusing to prosecute as they did not wish to be seen to be a part of the "Establishment". Presumably, they did not wish to be a party to getting anyone convicted. I do not think the converse was wholly true. Treasury Counsel at The Old Bailey, for example – who were in a sense built-in prosecutors – used to defend, though not often. My first opportunity to prosecute came through Stanley Hopkins the clerk to the chambers then headed by Michael Havers, later to become Attorney-General and Lord Chancellor (for a very short period before he had to resign for health reasons). One curious feature was that on retirement, he received a higher pension than his predecessor, Lord Hailsham, who had two terms as Lord Chancellor totalling 12 years!

Stanley was a great friend and colleague of my clerk, Walter Butler. The chambers did almost wholly criminal work and as my criminal practice increased I was very grateful to Stanley who put work my way called "reversions" as they came to me when there was nobody available in his chambers to do it. So in 1961, I went off to the magistrates' court at Great Dunmow to prosecute for the Essex Police. It was a case of fraudulent conversion of £311. I drove there and, having found the court, there was nobody about. After a time, somebody arrived and said that half-an-hour before the time when the case was due to start, the accused had shot himself! A few more people arrived and nobody seemed to want to do anything. I think there was no other case in the list. The magistrates had been stopped from attending. I insisted that something had to be done. The court should be opened, the case called and some evidence given to record what had happened. After some persuasion, it was arranged that the nearest local magistrate should come. He was the local butcher and as he had an assistant the shop did not have to be closed. I went along, I suppose, with the clerk of the court. Nobody was there to represent the defendant!

Eventually, the court was opened and a policeman gave evidence about the shooting. I think the hearsay rules were waived! The magistrate being satisfied with the evidence, there was then a discussion on what adjudication the court should make. I said that the case should be marked 'adjourned *sine die*' which is the lawyers' phrase for without a day being fixed for the next hearing. If necessary the case would be restored to the list on another day. As far as I know, this was never required to be done. So there the matter ended.

When I got back to the Temple, I knew it was almost certain that I would find Stanley and Walter in the Feathers pub at the bottom of Bouverie Street, which I duly did. They both wanted to know how I had got on. When I said that the accused had shot himself, Stanley generously said, "Well, sir, he knew you were coming!"

I was given another opportunity in October by the Essex Police at Colchester magistrates' court when the case *was* effective and I secured convictions for careless driving. Not a great case but it was a start.

Another breakthrough case came at the beginning of 1962 when I did my first Court Martial in Germany, at Minden, when I defended, unsuccessfully, a soldier from the South Wales Borderers on a charge of grievous bodily harm.

There was a list of counsel from whom a defendant could choose. I do not know how I got on the list but four cases came within a month. I had a success in my second case, also at Minden, representing two men from the Scottish Rifles (Cameronians) known as the "poison dwarfs". I think the Army made a mistake or perhaps it could not be helped, in posting the Welsh at one end of Minden and the Scots at the other. They would meet in the town centre and I was told that when trouble broke out between them it would stop immediately if any German intervened as a Celtic alliance would instantly be formed and the Germans were jointly attacked!

However, I also defended three "poison dwarfs" charged, I think, with assault on a "bouncer" who was the West German all-in wrestling heavyweight champion, a formidable figure not least so in the witness box. It was alleged that he was attacked by the defendants who resented being told to leave a night club. They were so short and he was so big that they attacked him individually from different angles especially his private parts! The defendants pleaded self-defence and accused the "bouncer" of using excessive force in trying to evict them. When the court came to deliver the verdict through the president, it was clear that, most unfortunately, he had a severe stammer. It really was not a kindness to appoint him but being the Army he could not refuse. So the three accused having been ordered to stand up, the president commenced, "The v-v-v-verdict of the c_c_c_court is that you are each n-n-n-not, not ..." At this point, the defendants realised that they had been acquitted. Their heads just peered over the dock and then I could see them giving the thumbs up sign to me! I thought a slight smile was in order. Meanwhile, the president was continuing to announce the verdict when the Sergeant of Military Police in court shouted out, "Escort and accused: left turn, quick march!" and he marched them out of court. A large number of the defendants' friends were outside as there was a tremendous cheer. The court door closed and the court concluded its deliberations with as much dignity as it could muster. When I got outside, I was given a generous reception with much handshaking.

Another of my earliest Court Martial cases was unusual in a very different way because the defendant was a member of the Womens' Royal Army Corps (WRAC) the successor to the Auxiliary Territorial Service (ATS) in which, as I have related, my mother had served during the Second World War. The defendant was found guilty of turning a "flick knife" on three military policemen. She was ordered to be dismissed the service. Every sentence passed at a Court Martial is subject to review by a confirming authority which in this case must have taken a very different view of the evidence because the sentence was reduced to fourteen days detention which is, by comparison, a very lenient sentence.

In recent times, there have been a number of changes to Court Martial procedure as a result of rulings of the European Courts. This is not the place to go into them and discuss their merits but after some years' experience, I am of the view that the Court Martial system that I took part in was very fair both to the prosecution and to the defence. In 1965, the Attorney-General, Elwyn Jones, later to become Lord Chancellor, appointed me to the panel of four counsel who appeared on behalf of the Crown in the Courts-Martial Appeal Court. This sat in

London and consisted of three judges who sat in the Court of Appeal (Criminal Division).

I would like to make just a short comment in support of my general view. First, that in the services there must be powers for officers to deal with minor disciplinary matters such as loss of equipment and going absent. The powers of punishment have got to be clear and limited and cases dealt with very speedily. Secondly, though more serious offences are also offences under the general law, such as violence, dishonesty, driving and drugs, it is not appropriate to have them tried in ordinary courts by a jury. One cannot have offences alleged to have been committed in Germany or Cyprus or, still more so, in the Falklands or Iraq, for example, tried here in Britain as if they had happened locally. The pressures, responsibilities and discipline of service life mean that different considerations apply. A violent argument between soldiers in the same barracks can have repercussions, for example, on morale, which are far different from in civilian life.

After my first four Court Martial cases in quick succession, Walter Butler said that I ought not to continue to do so many as while I was abroad I was not available for any other work and solicitors had been enquiring about me. So I went to Germany less often, but there were still some interesting moments to come.

I was once put up at an Army Centre for Chemical Warfare. After dinner, the steward asked me if I knew their "Rainbow Cocktail". I agreed to sample it. A succession of liqueurs was poured into a long thin copita glass. They never mixed but remained one on top of the other because their specific gravities had all been carefully measured in the laboratory! I took a note of the order but, unfortunately, I no longer have it and a crude unscientific experiment could be rather wasteful! After I commended the drink to the steward, he expressed strong disapproval of our Dutch allies in NATO. He explained that a number of Dutch officers had visited the mess the previous week and had poured Advocaat on top of the Rainbow liqueurs and had ruined them all! Their nationalism was clearly misplaced.

On another occasion, I was met by an officer of the Queen's Own Hussars who had been appointed to assist the defence. He took me to the officers' mess. It was about lunch time and when we entered, everybody stood up. I realised that as I held the honorary rank of Colonel I was the senior person present. I had to react, so I just said "Carry on, gentlemen" and the Commanding Officer kindly came up and welcomed me, offering a "Black Velvet" which everybody else seemed to be drinking, so I felt I was being initiated into this rather smart regiment.

There were of course, more serious moments and in July, 1962 I was sent to do a case in Hohne which was not far from the notorious concentration camp at Belsen. On the Sunday, I decided that I would make a visit there alone, a kind of personal pilgrimage. I had been much moved by the experiences of various Jewish people. I must have gone by train because I remember walking down the road from the station to the camp which I had seen in many news cuttings and especially pictures by Richard Dimbleby and his BBC team who were among the first to arrive there after the liberation. When I arrived at the camp, I was pleased to see how sensitively it had been converted into a memorial and shrine. There were some huts remaining and photographs. I have a working knowledge of German and the words of explanation seemed hardly necessary to a person of my age but they will no doubt be helpful to younger people who did not know Nazi times and who are now the large majority.

What surprised me was the large number of people there. No organized groups, but families looking relaxed on a Sunday outing. There were a considerable number of children. Everybody was orderly, quiet and respectful. I was rather puzzled but because there was nothing untoward I was not distracted or affected by the other people. I was most probably the only English person present. I walked out of the gate, as so many had been unable to do and then returned up the hill and waited for a train. I was glad I went and have never forgotten it.

Some years later, I recalled this experience to a friend who had been in the Army, Jack Travers. In 1945, his regiment, the Worcesters, arrived in Celle, another place not very far from Belsen. He was concerned with some Germans about running the basic services of the town and when Belsen was mentioned, the Germans did not believe the concentration camp existed. So the army arranged that the Germans should be taken to Belsen by coach. When they arrived and were shown around, they did not believe what they saw and suggested that the allies had created the place in order to discredit the Germans! I was not told any more but one can only hope that with more knowledge—and the passage of time —the group came to accept, as many German people have done, the truth of what occurred in those camps.

This is not the place to argue about the legality of the Nuremburg trials in international law where the victors tried and punished the vanquished but these trials, and also the trials of many Japanese war criminals, were a way of publicly revealing the horrors that had taken place.

In August 1963, perhaps because it was the Long Vacation there, I went for the first time to a Court-Martial held in Berlin and I returned, I think, twice more. I was interested to go as it was and still is, though in a different way, a unique place. I was able to see the considerable progress since I was last there in 1953, in re-building the so-called Western sector controlled by the British, French and Americans. The Russian Eastern sector was another story, cut off by the Berlin Wall. I was taken through Checkpoint Charlie in a car driven by a British officer and I have still got two beer mats from the state brewery. The officer pointed out the spiked vertical bars that were hanging from the horizontal barrier. He said they were not there the previous week when two men in an Austin Healey drove up very fast, lowered the windscreen, ducked and got through after doing two sharp turns—and got out before the sentries could fire. It only happened once!

While we were there, two young men came up and asked if we would let them get into the boot of our car and drive them to the West. The officer had to refuse. He did not know if it was a trap and, in any event, if we were caught, there would have been considerable repercussions. For a British military car to take out escapers was a breach of the four power agreement governing Berlin.

I was allowed to be present as a passive observer at a centre where people were brought who had escaped from the East. I do not know what percentage this was because, presumably, an unknown number could have escaped and then got clean away when they reached the West. The ground rules with the Russians for those who were interrogated were that escaped criminals on a list supplied by the Russians were handed back. Others were basically allowed to remain but, in their own interests, they had to have some authority to remain in West Germany and many of them had contacts and families to whom they could go. Usually, this was a long and sometimes complicated process to unravel, especially in the context of the Cold War when there were many anxieties about the Russian KGB and the East German Stasi.

On one visit to Berlin, I sought out and found my Canadian Foreign Office contact who had been so helpful to me and the young political group on the 1953 visit. He was Mike Berenson and had continued to live in Berlin with his German wife. I never knew or asked what his exact position was but I suppose he gathered all sorts of information and reported what he thought was useful. One evening, the two of us were in his car and he pointed out a man to me and said that he was the only person to go each day from East to West and then return. His job was to check the sewage levels! Even the Cold War has to give way to the basic requirements of nature! There were also some practical difficulties in running the S-Bahn, the local railway that runs partly above ground and partly below it.

One case I did in Berlin got considerable publicity not only in Germany but also in English newspapers, especially the *Daily Mirror*. The defendant was an army chef who used one of his knives on a soldier working in the kitchen who he believed was having an affair with his wife. Typical tabloid stuff. The defendant was convicted but did not receive a particularly severe sentence by army standards.

The Courts-Martial Appeal Court did not have many cases and I only did one that was of any interest. It is in the Law Reports and the text books on criminal law.[3] The appellant was a soldier called Clarkson, and the case is known by that name. He and another soldier heard a noise coming from a room in their barracks. They were in a very drunken state, went in and watched what was going on. A German girl aged eighteen was being raped. The evidence was that Clarkson and his friend said and did nothing—not even made any gesture. They were convicted of aiding and abetting rape. They appealed on the ground that the judge-advocate had misdirected the court on the law. When I arrived at the High Court in the Strand, I was greeted by a colonel from the Army Legal Services whom I did not know. He asked me whether I thought I would be called upon. In other words, he thought that the appellants' case was so weak that it would be thrown out without my being asked to reply. I think I gave a non-committal answer. I had long ago learned that it is dangerous to be over-optimistic about any litigation.

So we went into court. Lord Justice Megaw presided. He had been an Irish Rugby international and I used to see him regularly at Richmond as he was an active president of the local rugby club and seldom missed a first team home

---

[3] The references for the lawyers are: [1971] 1 WLR 1402; [1971] 3 All ER 344 and 53 Cr. App. Rep. 445—but the case must be treated with caution as there have been later ones on the subject.

fixture. His greatest disappointment in the game was when he scored what he thought was a try against Wales which was disallowed. Fortunately, it did not affect the result of the match which Wales won but he felt strongly enough about it to mention it during a House Dinner at Gray's Inn which was given for him and Lord Edmund-Davies to mark the end of their very distinguished careers. Gray's Inn has always had a very strong Welsh element, known as the "Taffia".

The second judge was Geoffrey Lane later to become Lord Chief Justice; a straight talking ex-RAF pilot who won the Air Force Cross (AFC). Off the bench, his language and jokes could politely be described as 'colourful'. He was known by Dorothy Foot, Dingle's wife, as 'Wizard Prang' - shorthand for a direct hit.

The third judge was Ralph Kilner Brown. He and I had been Liberal colleagues for many years. He was a candidate at four general elections including 1959 and 1964 when I fought. For some years he was the president of the Birmingham Liberal Organization.

As I have said in the context of stipendiary magistrates, it is always useful to know something of the background of the judges before whom one appears. I recall one barrister making a 'howler' when he did not appreciate that the judge was Jewish and called upon him in ringing tones to exercise 'Christian charity'. Personal knowledge of the bench, of course, does not effect the merits of the case and in *Clarkson*, it was clear from an early stage that the court was against me. Geoffrey Lane, in particular, was quite caustic about the judge-advocate. What the latter did was to give a rather complicated direction about aiding and abetting an offence in general terms and then gave an analogy with a group of people who commit a robbery and play different roles, such as a driver, lookout man and so on and they were all guilty of the offence. The analogy was false because the people in the robbery were partners with a common purpose, taking part in a joint enterprise. There were other passages in the summing up which came closer to a correct statement of the law. I tried my best to convince the court that the directions given were satisfactory when looked at as a whole but the court disagreed. What had to be shown was that the appellants by their deliberate presence intentionally gave active encouragement. So I lost this case, but there were no hard feelings or repercussions from the Army Legal Services.

Apart from the necessity of participation to create a criminal offence, the case of *Clarkson*, is a clear illustration of the difference between conduct which is totally immoral but not unlawful. The young German girl was raped by three different soldiers and on each occasion four other soldiers were present, two of whom were acquitted following the appeal. In a characteristic forthright thrust, Lord Justice Megaw, an Ulster Protestant, said: "She was physically injured and her clothes were torn to shreds. To say that those who attacked her behaved like animals would be unjust to animals".

It will be interesting to see now that the European Convention on Human Rights has been incorporated into English law, whether our law will develop so that to stand by and do nothing while a human right is obviously being infringed will itself become an offence.

My practice grew steadily but not spectacularly. With the decline of the Privy Council, chambers did not have a tradition of other high class work. I was lucky, as I was the first person in chambers to be put on the "Yard List", that is on the list of counsel who prosecute for the Metropolitan Police (or "Scotland Yard"). I had appeared against their solicitors ever since I began with Amery-Parkes and Co. in 1951. They sent me work regularly but we were not a set of criminal chambers and did not have a QC who specialised in crime. I was helped by the arrival in chambers of Desmond de Silva in 1964. He had been a pupil of Felix Waley, who did nothing but criminal work. So Desmond got on the Yard List as well.

There was a feeling at the Bar and on the bench that civil work was in some way superior, that crime was rather knock-about stuff requiring a silver tongue to persuade juries and where a knowledge of everyday life was of more use than a knowledge of the law. I remember that Walter Butler once said to me, "Sir, you don't just want to become a Yard man. " I think that this attitude has changed over the years, although it has by no means disappeared.

I think it was in 1961 that I was approached by Leonard Smith to see whether I would join the Committee of the British Caribbean Association (BCA). We had met over the years in the Liberal party of which he was a lifelong member. As a young man, he had been the agent in 1929 in the General Election at Chester. The candidate was Aubrey Herbert, also a young man and a former president of the Oxford Union. He failed to win by a few hundred votes. If he had succeeded, he would have had a very different career. He was born into politics as his father was Sir Jesse Herbert who had been the chief agent of the Liberal party in their landslide victory of 1906. Despite several attempts over the years, Aubrey Herbert never got into the House of Commons but like Leonard Smith he held various appointments in the party including chief agent. Leonard never stood for Parliament or, as far as I know, for a local council. He was always the organizer behind the scenes but he had a number of other interests: Barnet Football Club, his local church, the Commonwealth Fund for the Blind, the National Liberal Club (of which he was the chair in very difficult times), and the British Caribbean Association. He was employed by Booker Brothers and knew Jock Campbell well. I think he got the job through General Grey. I often wondered how much time Leonard was able to spend at home.

I agreed to join the BCA and got interested in its work. A considerable number of West Indian people had come to the UK in the previous five years or so as well as other countries such as Uganda and to a lesser extent Kenya. The UK had a traditional "open door" policy but continuing immigration presented problems, as did the freer movement of people in the countries of western Europe. Pressure began for some control. As Dingle Foot and others pointed out, there were particular problems for those with British passports. To turn them away was a constitutional innovation. After fiercely contested debates, the Conservative Government decided to pass restrictive legislation which, among other things, gave powers of deportation to the Home Secretary. The courts were given power after conviction to make recommendations for deportation. At a BCA meeting, I suggested that no recommendation should be made unless a defendant had prior notice of it and been given an opportunity to make representations to the court concerned. A meeting of Commonwealth High Commissioners was called which I attended. It was held in the office of the Jamaican High Commissioner as he was the most senior. There was no dispute, and it was important that unanimity was shown to the Government. After representations were made to the Home Office, a clause was put into the Bill adopting my proposals. Although there has been much legislation since 1962, the provisions have remained and still apply.

Nineteen-sixty-two was an eventful year for me, in a number of ways. In March there was the sensational by-election result at Orpington where Eric Lubbock, subsequently Lord Avebury, won for the Liberals by a majority of nearly 8,000. Prior to that, it had been one of the safest Conservative seats in the country. It was a tremendous fillip. After the result, Laura Grimond was asked by Robin Day in a TV interview what the effect had been on Liberals. She replied with Asquithian superiority that she had never known Liberals drink so much champagne during Lent! Even Robin Day took longer than usual before he put his next question!

As in Orpington, progress was being made in Richmond in local elections. The breakthrough came in Kew, much to the Grimond's delight. The candidate was Richard Fiennes of the family named in the verse about Banbury Cross which is sometimes misquoted. It is not "a *fine* lady upon a white horse" but "a *Fiennes* lady".

The candidate's full name was Twisledon-Wykeham-Fiennes and this had to appear on the ballot paper. I was told that it caused confusion as some people thought there were three candidates and that they had three votes! Once the Orpington breakthrough was made, other successes came quite quickly much to the disbelief and disgust of the local Conservatives who believed that the Liberals were usurpers on "their territory". Their feelings were to remain for many years. It took the Liberals about twenty years before they got control of the council which was after the amalgamation of Twickenham, Richmond and Barnes that became the London Borough of Richmond-upon-Thames on the creation of the Greater London Council (GLC). It was a shotgun marriage across the River Thames which abolished Middlesex (except for cricket and postal addresses) and reduced the boundaries of Surrey. As far as cricket is concerned, the Oval is not in Surrey!

The breakthrough by Richard Fiennes took place in May 1960. Two years later, the Conservatives lost sixteen seats: ten to the Liberals and six to Labour. One of the losers at Central Twickenham was Kenneth Baker who was more successful in the bluer pastures of Surrey and held high office including Home Secretary during the Thatcher years, with the conventional award of a life peerage.

The reorganization of local government did the Liberals no favours and, for a time, they only had one representative on the council, Dr Stanley Rundle. He was the only non-Conservative and there used to be the farcical situation where all the Conservatives would meet in private and then the council meeting would begin with Dr. Rundle present! This was in 1969. He was a great writer and publicist. Just over a fortnight after he was elected, he called his own "pre-council meeting and over 400 people turned up. It was no surprise that in 1973, he became the Liberal candidate for the GLC and helped by a splendid record of service and well-distributed punchy literature, he won.

Much more was to happen on the Richmond political scene before that happened. It is important not to forget the Barnes part of the constituency and there were successes on the old Barnes council. Grenville Naylor, a businessman, won a ward in Sheen and was followed by Norman Mann who was the Treasurer of the Liberal Association and prominent in the League of Jewish ex - servicemen. Qn the way there were some very near misses in different parts of the constituency. I remember two wards were each lost by three votes.

I had been readopted as prospective Liberal candidate in September 1960 quite quickly after the General Election as I wanted to maintain the momentum of the increased vote. I was greatly encouraged by the local election successes as people were not only voting Liberal but showing that Liberals could actually win. I hoped that this would be repeated. Jo Grimond came to the party held after the 1962 successes and — in addition to thanking all those who had worked in the recent elections — he paid a generous tribute to me and said that Richmond could follow Orpington and return a Liberal MP. Alas! It was not to be but Jo and Laura Grimond gave me all the help they could and put their delightful house on Kew Green at the Liberals' disposal for various functions.

The activists in the Liberal party were trying very hard to get it in better shape to cope with modern political presentation. In 1962, the Constitution was revised and there continued to be a good output of literature to answer those who did not know what Liberal policy was. A very successful forty-page booklet entitled *Our Aim and Purpose,* written by Donald Wade, the MP for Huddersfield West since 1950, was published in 1961 and ran into several editions. The Liberal party was making the running on a number of important issues emphasising the need to be involved in Europe and trying to create a different atmosphere in industry by breaking down the barriers between employers and the unions and creating partnership between them. The banner above the platform at the 1963 assembly at Brighton, read "Partners in a New Britain".[4] Liberals achieved some success, mainly through Richard Wainwright, the member for Colne Valley, in getting tax relief for co-partnership schemes.

I became a bit of a trouble-shooter for the Liberal party as I was asked to help with problems that had arisen in a few constituencies. There were only a handful: Islington, Petersfield and Birmingham. The details differ but they concerned small groups of people who did not accept majority decisions and sometimes issued statements which caused embarrassment and were ammunition for local papers to say, "Liberals split". I hope I helped to smooth things over and that someone from outside the constituency was helpful in giving decisions from a completely independent viewpoint and with the wider interests of the party at heart.

---

[4] The slogan "Partners in a New Britain" at the 1963 Assembly was the title of a booklet setting out the Liberal programme. There were many bold things in this booklet though they were not new to Liberals. There was support for UNO and the Western alliance and opposition to the development of an independent British nuclear deterrent. Conventional forces should be strengthened. Greater participation in Europe continued to be emphasised and the theme of partnership should be extended to many aspects of our lives, including work and welfare.

With Sir Dingle Foot QC, MP - my head of chambers - on the occasion of his
appointment as Solicitor-General in 1964

Dingle Foot addressing the Oxford Union over an aroma of parafin in
1946 - whilst I was still studying the law. I am to the right beneath the
third row of pictures from the left, second to back row.

In the chair at the Liberal Party Conference - Brighton, 1963

On a trip to Nigeria with Sir George Baker QC, future President of the
Family Division of the High Court

An early television 'Soapbox' appearance

The author: aged 12 months

Right: Dad's Army
Idmiston 1943

Guest of honour: More friends in Nigeria

Wigged and robed

Portrait by Patricia Cain: Richmond

Sworn in as a judge at the House of Lords in 1973: with Joy and the girls. UPPA/Photoshot

Winter sports in Oxford before the days of global warming: the Arctic Winter of 1946-7
With Rudi Weisweiller on the skis (see p.29)

Just the ticket:
General Election 1964

At Plymouth College:
with compulsory headgear

Introducing Chief Clerk, Ray Foster to Her Royal Highness The Princess Royal at the
opening of the new Kingston-Upon-Thames Crown Court in 1997: with David Jacobs,
the broadcaster and Deputy Lord Lieutenant in the background (left) - and officials
from the Court Service and former Lord Chancellor's Department.

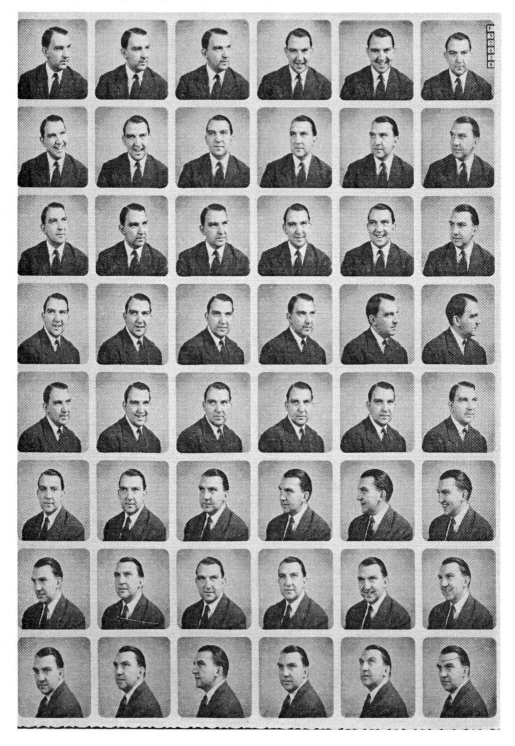

Polyfoto C 1960: what the police would call 'mugshots'

Fortunately, in Richmond and Barnes we worked together pretty well. I decided to keep away from council matters. Apart from the considerable amount of work involved in being a councillor, I thought the role of a Parliamentary candidate was different. I very much doubt if I could have taken anything else on. I had to safeguard my practice at the Bar which was in its early stages when a good reputation and also goodwill are so important—I suppose I would have had to reduce or even stop party work at national level. Others would have done so and indeed my successor but three in Richmond, Jenny Tonge, who won the seat in 1997 and held it in 2001, had been a Liberal councillor at Richmond. When one looks at the CVs of present MPs of all parties, it is surprising how many have previously been councillors and perhaps I did the wrong thing—but I was so far away from winning the Richmond seat both in 1959 and 1964 that I am sure that whatever I had done would not have made the slightest difference to the result.

I got around the constituency as much as I could, especially going to non-political functions. I was a member of the Richmond Society, the Friends of Richmond Park, the rugby club and the Concert Society. I was usually well received and there were very few snide remarks about being a Liberal. The atmosphere had considerably improved. The election was called for October 15th. I felt buoyant and enthusiastic. But I was in for a shock. It began with my adoption meeting. The guest speaker was Herbert Harris, the director general of the party and he made a very good speech. The atmosphere, however, was flat—as if we were going through the motions. During the campaign, especially in canvassing people on the doorstep, I found many people who were prepared to vote Liberal in council elections but not in a General Election. There was rather a defeatist attitude, as if I had no chance of winning in Richmond and that nationwide, the Liberals had no chance of forming a government. I did what I could to enliven the proceedings but Richmond is not a place given to razzmatazz! It is too spread out with a number of different communities. I had an excellent agent in Christopher Mott from Reading University and a number of helpers from outside like David Webster, a student of Gray's Inn who achieved some fame later as Jamie, a young police cadet in the TV series, *Dixon of Dock Green*. Returning to the law, in due course, he became His Honour D. MacLaren Webster, the resident judge at Winchester and retired in 2003.

I had a good small introductory message, one side of which was a window poster. We got this out as soon as possible after the election was called in order to show strength and it worked quite well. On it was, "If you think like a Liberal, vote like a Liberal" which was a variation of the party Manifesto which was entitled, "Think for Yourself, vote Liberal". The Liberal colour had been standardised and the literature was headlined in orange. I thought this stood out well, better than green or yellow. A lot of it was well produced: Adrian Slade, who became a Liberal GLC councillor for Richmond-upon-Thames, had a lot to do with this as well as the long-serving director of publications at headquarters, Evelyn Hill. The party owes a great debt to Evelyn who worked tirelessly on an extremely small budget She was utterly dedicated and could have earned much more money if she had gone elsewhere into commercial publishing.

A firm of local printers called Fieldwick did an excellent job on my election address using the orange colour and highlighting my name and "Liberal". There was also a good family photograph with Joy and Caroline and for the first time, Jennifer. The usual policy points were summarised and, in my letter, I undertook to do what I could to reduce aircraft noise and to fight the proposed closure of the North London line that ran from Richmond to Broad Street in the City of London. I am glad to say that the latter campaign was a success but credit must be shared by all parties. I remember a tremendous meeting in the House of Commons attended by all the mayors with stations on the line. They were indeed a most impressive "Chain Gang". The line still runs but has been extended to end at North Woolwich. It is operated by Silverlink.

One new experience in 1964 was that each candidate (as in 1959, there were only three of us) was invited in turn to Watney's brewery in Mortlake during the lunch hour. When my turn came—and I expect it was the same for the other two—I was taken to an open space near the entrance and asked to get up on a very large beer barrel. I was then given a loud hailer. A good crowd assembled, though it did not follow that all who worked there lived in the constituency. Still, they were all voters so the message was the same: to try and get them to vote Liberal.

I was listened to politely and attentively and question time was uneventful. There was no reference to 'splitting the vote', but I did have to struggle to show that it was not a waste of time to vote Liberal because the party was not going to win. I tried to show that any Liberal vote was worthwhile because the size of the vote was important for the influence that the party would have and the notice that was taken of it. At the end of question time, I was given a pint of Watney's Best and the photo opportunity was obvious as, still standing on the barrel, I raised my glass and thanked them for allowing me to come.

The other thing which each of the candidates did in turn was to visit the Star and Garter Home for Ex-servicemen at the top of Richmond Hill. This also happened in 1959. The more mobile of the residents were doing various things in the public rooms and one went over and had a short chat with them. One, who I think was playing dominoes, startled me and I think everybody else, by shouting out: "I'm a Communist!" It was soon obvious that it was a leg pull. The men were great fun and like the old soldiers that they were, they wished me luck but gave no indication of how they were going to vote. In the bedrooms upstairs, it was completely different. Some were in a very bad state, hardly conscious and just having to be turned over from time to time. One has to admire greatly those who look after them with such regular and sympathetic care. It is a side of the home that not many visitors see.

Joy, as usual, was marvellous, working hard in the committee rooms and canvassing on the doorsteps. She was a radiator of enthusiasm as well as having to look after Caroline and Jenny. She was especially good at organizing the tellers, runners and other workers on polling day. Without her experience and that of a small number of others who knew what had to be done, we should not have got our vote out as we did. One thing I did not mention at the time as I did not think it would be helpful, is that I was disappointed at the lack of leadership and support by some of the Liberal councillors and I emphasise "some". Their heart was in local government. They were concerned with their ward only and the parliamentary campaign and national issues were something else.

There were some splendid Liberal workers. One, Charles Branchini, generously guaranteed my deposit of £150 both in 1959 and 1964 and I am glad I did not have to call upon him. He is still alive at 94 and as enthusiastic for the cause as ever. He was interviewed by the BBC after the 1997 election when Jenny Tonge won Richmond for the Liberal Democrats. It was a great day for Charles who I think had taken part in every campaign in Richmond since 1945. He told the interviewer that he was glad it was the end of "false dawns" for Liberals of which there had been far too many!

I worked hard in the constituency and used every opportunity to put the Liberal case across. But, as in 1959, the result was disappointing. The figures were quite interesting compared with 1959:

1964		1959	
Royle (Con)	22, 203	Royle (Con)	27, 161
Brownjohn (Lab)	14, 053	Archibald (Lab)	12, 975
Baker (Lib)	7, 800	Baker (Lib)	7, 359
Majority	8, 150	Majority	14, 186

Thus, the Conservative vote was down by nearly 6, 000. The Labour vote was up by just over 1, 000 while I went up by precisely 441.

I hope I was a suitable candidate for Richmond. Certainly, there were no criticisms to my face and I am sure that Joy would have picked up any rumblings of dissatisfaction. It just seemed very difficult to get the campaign alight. There was much basic sympathy and agreement with Liberal policy but a great reluctance to vote for it.

The national scene was again disappointing. The target of three million votes was achieved but it resulted in only nine seats, an increase of two. It was a poor return and a great under-representation in Parliament. Arthur Holt and Donald Wade, two House of Commons Liberal stalwarts, lost their seats at Bolton and Huddersfield where the arrangements with the Conservatives ended and they had three-cornered fights. There were two good wins in Scotland while Eric Lubbock and Jeremy Thorpe held on in England with Peter Bessell being the only English win.

Post-election meetings of Liberal candidates showed the same story as Richmond. There was a great reluctance to accept three dimensional politics. The two party system, Government and Opposition, reflected in the way members sat in the House of Commons — opposite each other — was so much more straightforward and easier for the press and media to interpret. Three way swings were difficult to explain,

The country and, perhaps, especially the Liberals, had to get used to a Labour Government under Harold Wilson. It was a great change. The Conservatives had been in office for thirteen years. Labour had the advantage of trying to make a new start and Harold Wilson portrayed himself as a great moderniser and embracer of a new technological revolution. The Liberal role was straightforward. To assess everything on its merits by applying Liberal principles and policy and voting accordingly. On paper they were in a strong tactical position because the Labour majority was only five, less than the number of Liberal members.

Liberals would have been very unwise to have forced an early election. There is always general goodwill towards a new Government to see what it will do. A badly defeated opposition party, as the Conservatives were, needs time to rethink and regroup. They were tired after so many years of office. The Liberals would probably have fared badly if they had brought about another election and they had virtually no money to fund another campaign so soon. Jo Grimond played a careful role and this paid off when, after some unspectacular results, David Steel won a by-election in Roxburgh, Selkirk and Peebles in 1965. He became the youngest Member of the House of Commons at the age of 26. I went to a celebration lunch at the National Liberal Club chaired by the chair of the Scottish Liberal party, George Mackie, who won Caithness and Sutherland in 1964. This was the seat narrowly lost by Sir Archibald Sinclair in 1945. He was the leader of the Liberal party. His friendship with Winston Churchill went back to the First World War when they were soldiers together. Though in different parties, they were political colleagues during the 1930s when they fearlessly pointed out the evils and dangers of the Nazi regime in Germany. Sinclair, at least, had the comfort and support of his party but Churchill as a Conservative, was in almost total isolation.

When Churchill became Prime Minister in 1940 and formed a Coalition Government, he appointed Sinclair to the crucial post of Secretary of State for Air and he remained there throughout the War. When Sinclair lost in 1945, such was the parlous state of Liberal representation in the Commons, that no seat could be found for him. There was no safe seat anywhere. So the party had to elect what the *Daily Telegraph* called "substitute leaders" and that is how Clement Davies came to be chosen. Sinclair obtained a peerage and became Viscount Thurso but he had to wait until 1952. After his defeat, he took very little part indeed in the life of the Liberal party. I attended almost every Liberal assembly/conference from 1945 until I was appointed a judge in 1973 and I cannot remember him attending any one of them. He did once speak and that was in support of Air Vice Marshal ("Pathfinder") Bennett who was the Liberal candidate at a by-election in Croydon. I did not go to the meeting, but Joy was there and it was discovered that Archie Sinclair, as he was generally known, had left his notes in Brooks Club. Somebody had to go to London and get them extremely quickly.

After George Mackie won Caithness and Sutherland, it was held by Bob Maclennan who won the seat successively as Labour, SDP and Liberal Democrat, which I think is a record for one constituency. After the retirement of Bob, the seat reverted to the Sinclair family in another set of curious circumstances. John Sinclair, grandson of Archie, succeeded to the title in 1995. He was an active Liberal Democrat peer. He was a spokesman on tourism and knew a lot about hotel management. He had been general manager and director at Cliveden and director of the Savoy. However, he lost his right to sit in the Lords and so he stepped into the shoes of Bob Maclennan and entered the House of Commons. Others such as the Earl of Home, Lord Hailsham and Lord Stansgate (Tony Benn) have done this but they renounced their peerages voluntarily. I understand that Lord Thurso has been allowed to retain certain privileges in the Lords because he is still a peer! How W. S. Gilbert would have enjoyed this!

I digressed from David Steel to illustrate from Caithness and Sutherland what strange features there are in the history of MPs in some constituencies. I am always amazed when people say that politics is dull. It may be that some political issues and theories are dull in the abstract but when it comes to people in politics, the whole of life is there—ask Jeffrey Archer, if you can get within earshot!

David Steel continued to have youthful looks long after he entered Parliament but it also soon became apparent that he had a finely-tuned political brain. He had a good platform manner and was warm and friendly to his colleagues. The Liberal party was short of members and of talent in the House of Commons and he fulfilled a great need. He was really a professional Liberal for after he left Edinburgh University he became assistant secretary of the Scottish Liberal party until he entered Parliament. Having had no experience in any business, trade or profession does not seem to have blighted his political career in any way. The modern MP, if he or she is to do a worthwhile job in its various aspects—the constituency work, Parliamentary committees, delegations as well as be present in the chamber itself—can have little time to do anything else. The practising lawyer/MP is nowadays a rare breed. As David Steel acquired Parliamentary knowledge and political craft, it is no surprise that he became the chief whip from 1970-75 and then leader for twelve years.

When I became a judge in 1973, it meant that I had to leave party politics completely. I felt it surprising how many people outside or at the extreme edges of the law and politics, did not understand this. However, the rule is absolute and all who cherish our constitution do expect the judges to be fearlessly independent and not subject to any political pressure. I had an interesting experience of this. When the Alliance was being formed between the Liberal party and the SDP, it had to be decided which party would fight which constituency. This was resolved amicably in the vast majority of cases but there were some areas of dispute including Oxford.

David Steel wrote to me personally to know whether I would act as arbitrator in those cases. My reputation as the "trouble-shooter" still continued. I told David I would have to refer his request to the Lord Chancellor, which I did. I was gratified to receive a very full reply from Lord Hailsham. As a dedicated constitutionalist, I think he enjoyed dealing with it in his enthusiastic way. In brief, he said that no judge should do a favour for any political party and that I must decline.

In some ways, I was disappointed as I would have enjoyed re-entering the political scene, however obliquely, but having thought it over, and indeed, thinking about it again now, I am sure that Lord Hailsham was right. Suppose I had made a decision and the losing side were dissatisfied with how I had dealt with the matter and made their criticisms public. I would have had to defend what I had done and might have faced a hostile press. A judge should not be put in such a situation.

In fact, Lord Hailsham took a very narrow view of the limits of judges' work. He once told me and I expect others, that he did not think it right that Lord

Scarman should have conducted the investigation and inquiry into conditions in Brixton. I know it was politically sensitive, but sometimes there is a need for a respected and completely independent person to carry out such a task. He has nothing personally to gain from it and if friendly and approachable, as Lord Scarman was, he will not only get trust but people will talk more freely to him than to a committed politician who might be tempted, for political reasons, to "trim" his report. There is nothing so frustrating as a whitewash!

When David Steel retired in 1988 as leader of the Liberal party, he had done a stint of twelve years and was probably disappointed and frustrated, though publicly cheerful. The Liberal/SDP Alliance had not in Roy Jenkins' words "broken the mould" of British politics. It was exasperatingly close with large votes but few seats. One trouble was that the two Davids just did not hit it off. David Owen was a difficult man to work with. I do not think that basically he was a liberal man in its widest sense. A liberal man reacts in a certain way to a set of circumstances. David Owen gave the impression that politically he was authoritarian. David Steel, by contrast, was not only a liberal man but politically and in this context, ironically, he was a social democrat. He was tailor-made for the Alliance. After he got a life peerage, he became the Speaker, or more correctly the First Officer, of the Scottish Parliament. Personally, I was disappointed about this. I know what it is like to be politically neutralised (if not neutered!) and I never got to Westminster. I thought that David Steel had a valuable contribution to make in the House of Lords. However, I appreciate the lure to return to one's roots and to have a responsible role in making the Scottish Parliament - for which like other Liberals, he had long campaigned - work in an effective and efficient manner.

When Harold Wilson formed his Government in 1964, he appointed my head of chambers, Dingle Foot, as Solicitor-General. This followed a curious episode as the Prime Minister thought, not unnaturally for one who is not a lawyer, that a solicitor could be appointed to that office and it was said that he had in mind my old partner, Arnold Goodman. When the PM was told it had to be a barrister and preferably a QC he turned to Dingle Foot.

These rules have been swept away and in 1997 a solicitor, Harriet Harman, became the Solicitor-General. However, old traditions die hard and she has had to be made a QC, which again is something rather new, in order to give her rights of audience in the High Court.

In 1964, the Senior Law Officer, the Attorney-General, was Elwyn Jones who unlike Dingle Foot had been in the Labour party for a long time. He was a part of the British prosecution team at the Nuremburg trials where he would have come to the attention of Hartley Shawcross. Very much a Welshman, Elwyn used to say that his brother Idris was much better known in Wales as he had been a rugger international! Elwyn was an urbane, genial man with a generous smile and a good, light, tenor voice. When Lord Chancellor, at a Bar Musical Society Concert in the presence of the Queen Mother, he sang alternate verses with John Read of the D'Oyly Carte Company, of the Lord Chancellor's song from *Iolanthe*.

Both the new law officers were members of Gray's Inn and at a House Dinner, Dingle Foot spoke first as he was the older and more senior of the two. In fact, Walter Butler, the clerk, was disappointed that Dingle was not made the

Attorney General. He said to me, "I had hoped for the gold but only got the silver". The Attorney, though a member of the Government party in Parliament, is not a member of the Cabinet but is brought in to advise the Government on legal matters from a professional point of view. He has, however, in recent times got closer to the Government in some respects. His office was always in the Law Courts but was moved during the time of the Conservative, Patrick Mayhew (1987 to 1992) to be closer to Whitehall and Downing Street.

The law officers used to prosecute, especially the Attorney, in cases involving security and treason and certain murders and cases of great public concern. Now they only very rarely do so. One well-known instance was when in the 1950s Sir Reginald Manningham-Buller (previously referred to by Bernard Levin as "Bullying-Manner") prosecuted Dr Bodkin Adams, a number of whose lady patients in Eastbourne had died and he had benefited in their wills. Geoffrey Lawrence QC defended and the doctor was acquitted. The judge was Mr Justice Devlin, a brilliant man who rose to be a Law Lord. Most unusually, he wrote a book about the trial. I recall Lord Hailsham once asking me if I had read it. I had not. He then declaimed furiously, "He ought never to have written it". He then changed his expression to a mischievous grin and said, "But, it's a jolly good read!" - and burst into loud laughter.

Shortly after the doctor's acquittal, I was doing a case at Lewes and, with another member of the Bar after the day's work was done, caught a train which started at Eastbourne. We went into the restaurant car and there at a table opposite was Dr Bodkin Adams with a smartly dressed elderly lady with the traditional twin set and pearls, but not, I think, a blue rinse. He was very attentive to her and rather curiously poured the tea himself. I watched very carefully as the sugar went in! Of course, there was nothing to be done about it but I thought it was an interesting observation.

A number of uncomplimentary stories circulated in the Temple about the Attorney, but I was present in the court of the Lord Chief Justice, Lord Goddard, when the Attorney was before him and two other judges one of whom asked a question. The Attorney answered and Lord Goddard, who was getting deaf and tended to shout a bit, turned to his colleague and said in a voice that went all round the court, "You know, Reggie's not as bad as many people are saying".

There was a curious system about the briefing of counsel for a number of Government departments. They were known as "nominations" and were in the gift of the Attorney. It was said that it stemmed from the time that the Attorney received a salary and was not paid fees. It was really to compensate his clerk for the loss of a high fee earner, who would usually have been the head of chambers. Not surprisingly, the clerk would do what he could to see that the members of his own chambers benefited from this patronage. There was a nominations list of counsel kept in a book. Who got on it was shrouded in some mystery. My clerk, as clerk to the Solicitor-General, insisted that when the Attorney's clerk was away (and he was vigilant to find out when this was) the book came to him. I was, therefore, pleased to receive some work for the Department of Health and Social Security (DHSS) and to go to court for an order making a person a vexatious litigant that required the approval of the Attorney to institute.

I did not think that Dingle Foot was happy as Solicitor-General. One of the tasks of the Solicitor-General is to be a member of the Government team which works on the annual Finance Bill and gets it through the Commons. It is lengthy and complicated work. Dingle was no economist and as far as I know had never done a tax case at the Bar. Sometimes, often late at night, he had to get up and explain the legislation. Then there was an adjournment debate about a man called Hamilton and it involved the provisions for extradition concerning Ireland and, of course, there are different provisions for citizens of Eire and of Ulster. With his Commonwealth experience, extradition was more Dingle's territory than the Finance Bill but I understand that he put up an embarrassing performance. He was reappointed after the General Election of 1966, but it was no surprise to close observers of the political scene when he was dropped from the Government in 1967.

While Dingle was Solicitor-General, his place as head of chambers was taken by E. F. Noel Gratiaen QC. He had been a judge in Sri Lanka and had acted as chief justice but he was of Portuguese extraction and that did not appeal to the Prime Minister, Madam Bandaranaike, and her Nationalist Government. How far Noel, as we always called him, was forced to leave Sri Lanka, I do not know but life was clearly not comfortable for him and Dingle, who was a kind and compassionate man, took him into chambers. He soon built up a busy practice but it was nearly all Privy Council appeals, especially from Sri Lanka. Unfortunately, this was not good for the future of chambers from the work point of view. Noel was a very big man and became president of the Blackheath Rugby Club — always called "Club" in Rugby circles. It is one of the oldest clubs. The sight of him and Walter Butler who was rather a small, slim man, leaving chambers and slowly moving up to El Vino's Bar in Fleet Street was one of David and Goliath. Because of his friendliness, Noel created a good atmosphere in chambers. He had died by the time I was appointed a Circuit Judge in 1973 and I have always been glad that his widow let me have his full-bottom wig and box. When I retired I sold it to Nicholas Blake, QC.

When Dingle came back to the Bar and resumed as head of chambers, he was like a liberated man. He also enjoyed being a backbencher and sometimes being a bit rebellious, especially on a personal liberty question. In addition, in 1968 he became Treasurer of Gray's Inn. Each Inn of Court appoints for one year one of the benchers to be its Treasurer. To the outsider, the name is rather a misnomer for he or she does not just deal with the finances but runs the show and is the figurehead for all special occasions. It is the peak of a career in the Inn. Each year, Gray's Inn has a garden party. At one time, it was free for the members, but now they have to pay. The Treasurer is the host and with his wife, receives everybody. The Treasurer is allowed to invite a certain number of guests in addition to those who are traditionally invited such as the Lord Chancellor and the Treasurers of the other Inns. Both Dingle and Dorothy were generous hosts and were well known for giving parties both at their flat in Westminster and in chambers. Many people from Commonwealth countries would be invited. On the occasion of the Gray's Inn Reception, they themselves invited a large number of people without keeping the Inn informed and, perhaps, without telling each other. On a warm summer's day, it was not surprising that the drink ran out rather early. I remember that by a long white cloth covered table in the marquee, Lord Edmund Davies was standing in a white jacket. No drink was there and an irate and not very senior member of the Inn came up and said; "Can't you do something about it?" The Law Lord was very calm and collected. He took no offence and diplomatically said that he thought that something was being done. I am not sure he was right, but the people there made the Reception an enjoyable occasion.

Dingle's Treasurership had another misfortune which was featured in the *Daily Express* of 29th November, 1968, under the heading, "People and Places". The Treasurer often reads a lesson during a service in Gray's Inn Chapel on Sundays. Dingle read from the wrong chapter of the First Book of Corinthians which contained the following, amongst other passages in the same vein: "I actually hear reports of sexual immorality among you, immorality such as even pagans do not tolerate"!

It was not difficult for Dingle to resume his practice at the Bar including cases in Commonwealth countries. On 11th June 1967, in a series on top figures of the Bar in the *Evening Standard,* Edgar Lustgarten referred to "Dingle Foot, the most travelled QC of them all". Once, after he had finished a case in Singapore, Walter Butler arranged for him to go to a VIP room at Heathrow. It was a Wednesday, Walter explained that we (always "we") were in the Court of Appeal on Friday and he had brought the papers with him. Dingle was duly grateful and said that he would go to his flat and begin to work on the papers. Walter then explained that he had not made it clear that the case was in the West African Court of Appeal sitting in Lagos. The plane was waiting. There were no formalities to be done as Dingle was in transit! When Dingle looked aghast, Walter replied, according to what Dingle told me later, "Sir, I do not think that Lady Foot will be pleased with us"!

Walter died in 1970 and Dingle wrote quite a long tribute in *The Times* of 12th February. He recorded that Walter joined chambers in 1923 and became chief clerk in 1937. He never moved chambers. Walter frequently travelled with Dingle and sometimes, though not very often, with other members of chambers. He was well-known in legal circles in many Commonwealth countries. Dingle recalled what he described as Walter's "finest moment". A telegram arrived from Northern Nigeria just addressed "Butler, London". There were thirty-one Butlers in *Who's Who* including the Chancellor of the Exchequer, but the telegram was delivered to 2 Paper Buildings, Temple.

After Walter died, Dingle declined. This was no fault of Walter's successor, Gordon Breadmore who had been in chambers for some years as second clerk. He was a steady, conscientious man but essentially a 'backroom boy'. He had not been able to travel abroad and there was the difficult matter of building up the work of chambers apart from the Privy Council. Dingle increased his fondness for Irish whiskey and spent convivial times in the Garrick Club. In the General Election of 1966, he retained his seat at Ipswich by 6,873 votes. In 1970, he thought he was in again and on the Monday, before Polling Day on the Thursday, he sent a telegram to chambers saying, "It's in the bag". There was a last minute swing to the Conservatives and Dingle lost by just thirteen votes. The Conservative victor was Ernle Money, an unusual Tory, who had a great knowledge and love of the arts. He had the advantage of having served in the Suffolk Regiment and his local connections served him well because Dingle had been dubbed "The Member for Africa". Dingle was a very disappointed man. He had been in Parliament since 1935 with a break from 1945 to 1957. He loved and respected the House of Commons. I never got to know why he did not go to the House of Lords. Some said that he was still at heart a Liberal and certain Labour people thought he might leave them, as indeed some did including George Brown when the SDP was created.

One thing is certain, that Dorothy would have loved it. After all, two of Dingle's brothers, Hugh and John were life peers and she was only the wife of a knight!

When I decided to apply for the Circuit Bench, Dingle was more than helpful, as always. I remember driving him from the Temple to Westminster and, in the privacy of my car, having a frank talk about this change of life and him asking me to be sure that it was what I wanted to do. The Circuit Judge was a new judicial creature created by the Courts Act 1971. He thought it would be a good job for me. I was appointed in March 1973. Chambers gave me a dinner. Dingle presided and I remember he kept asking me if we had had the Loyal Toast!

Dingle had a sad death in 1978. He went to Hong Kong with Nigel Murray as his junior. Nigel was a stalwart of chambers who in 1984 agreed to go to Botswana as a Judge. It was a considerable uprooting for him and his wife Shirley. They had roots in London and in Ireland. Nigel liked the social life. He was a member of the Garrick Club and fond of riding and golf. After three years, he was not appointed Chief Justice there basically on the ground that it was right to have a native person and not an expatriate. This was understandable having regard to the mood of the time and the change to independence throughout the African continent. The Murrays, therefore, returned to England and Nigel to 2 Paper Buildings. In 1982, that is before he went to Botswana, he was appointed an assistant recorder. He resumed practice and was asked to sit with some regularity on the Western Circuit. He must have done well, otherwise he would not have been in the demand that he was. There seems no reason why he should not have been appointed a Circuit Judge but in 1991 he became a Queen's Bench Master sitting in the Strand at the Royal Courts of Justice. Perhaps he preferred that life but in 1994 he was appointed a recorder though continuing as a master. He was a big man who ate and drank well. In November 2000, he went into King's College Hospital for a liver transplant. Joy and I went to see him. He was a shadow of his former self with his face fallen in but he was cheerful as usual, sustained by his devoted wife, Shirley who brought the food he needed every day from their flat in the Temple. Shirley told us that the financial food allowance at the hospital was less than one pound per day. A liver had been found for the transplant and Nigel was facing the operation stoically. He sent me a card after our visit saying he would keep his promise to write my obituary! It was not to be. The liver was found not to be right for Nigel so another one was sought but while this was being done, he deteriorated and died. It was a terrible shock when Shirley rang me up. She was very brave. Fortunately, their son,

Simon, had just started at the Bar and was in good Western Circuit chambers, just below the Murrays' flat in King's Bench Walk.

I referred to the death of Nigel Murray in the context of him going to Hong Kong with Dingle Foot in 1978. After they arrived, they had a conference with their clients. After a time, this became concerned with a technical aspect of the case with which Dingle was not involved. He, therefore, left the conference and went back to his hotel. He ordered some sandwiches which were brought to his room. When the conference ended, Nigel went to find Dingle. He did. He was dead in his room, having choked on a sandwich. It must have been a terrible experience for Nigel.

Joy and I heard the news in the 8 a.m. bulletin on the radio. Dorothy was bereft. They were a devoted couple who had been married for many years but had no children. Because we were abroad, Joy and I did not go either to the funeral or the memorial service. We felt rather badly about it. However, I pay my respects to Dingle whenever I go to St. Margaret's Church, Westminster because there is a stone in Dartmoor granite which Dorothy had put up in his memory. I stand in front of it and say a silent prayer in gratitude for his life and for the chance that he gave me to go to the Bar.

• • •

On 17th August 1962 our second daughter was born. We called her Jennifer Katharine. I got rather in the dog house because I had been told by the nursing home at Wimbledon that nothing was expected to happen that day — but, to my astonishment, when I got back to chambers in the late afternoon, my junior clerk, Gordon Breadmore, told me that I was the father of another girl! So I went off to Wimbledon as fast as I could and found a healthy girl with lots of black hair ,which she has never lost.

Jenny was very competitive with her sister but they got on well. They went to the same schools and Jenny also got to Newnham College, Cambridge. She is musical but in a different way from Caroline. She played the flute well but but her main interest has been in singing and this still plays a large part in her life. She has been in a number of high class choirs including the Philharmonia Chorus. She would have liked to have continued with them but the commitment continued to increase to several days per week when they were recording as well as giving concerts and it became too much. She sang with some of the greatest soloists and conductors. In recent years, she has sung at St. Luke's Church, Chelsea and their choir form the basis of the Naylor Singers who sing in cathedrals when the regular choir has a break. I know that this has taken her to Canterbury, York, Westminster Abbey, Ripon, Worcester Peterborough, Gloucester, Exeter and Cork. There may have been other places that I have not remembered, but the list is long enough to show what opportunities there have been to visit historic churches.

Jenny has always been a good organizer and when quite young at school, she got together singing groups especially at Christmas time, to go out and sing for charity. She once put on a concert at our local church, St. Matthias, Richmond and through sheer hard work and personally urging contacts to come, she got together such a large audience that it greatly surprised the church activists including the vicar, Canon John Oates, who later became the Rector of the journalists' church in Fleet Street, St. Bride's. He and his wife Sylvia became good friends and John was most helpful to Jenny. He was one of those gifted preachers who did not use a note. It always seems to sound more sincere and heartfelt than when it is obviously read out.

Jenny's organizing ability has been reflected in the jobs she has had. While working at Sotheby's, other positions there became vacant and she was surprised to be told that the Chairman, Lord Gowrie, wanted her to become his PA. This was a happy time for her as apart from the work itself she met many interesting people. Unfortunately, when Lord Gowrie's time as chair ended and he became chair of the Arts Council, there was a reorganization of Sotheby's and some Americans moved in — with disastrous results, including much publicised criminal proceedings. Jenny was made redundant and went off on a memorable and satisfying visit to China

She has had a number of ups and downs in life and not enjoyed the best of health. Sadly, her first marriage ended in divorce. It was a difficult time for her and for Joy and myself. In the circumstances, it was fortunate that there were no children. She has now remarried. Joy and I are delighted about it. Her husband is Richard Hedley, a barrister whose practice has grown very much, in the Midlands. They met in the choir at St. Luke's, Chelsea, so he being a tenor and she a soprano, they now have many opportunities to sing in harmony! To the delight of the whole family, a son, Jonathan was born in September 2004.

Having progressed from the magistrates' courts to Quarter Sessions, I made my first appearance in an Assize case before a High Court judge at Kingston in March 1962. I was instructed by a local firm of solicitors, Sherwood, Cobbing, who became a regular client. The judge was Mr Justice Lawton who had been appointed the previous January along with seven other QCs. It was a glittering array that included John Megaw and Leslie Scarman, both of whom went to the Court of Appeal. The latter got to the House of Lords and John Megaw was the unlucky one. Richard Wilberforce never went to the Court of Appeal but, most unusually, straight from the High Court to the House of Lords. He is rivalled only by Lord Radcliffe, who went from the Bar to the House. This was even more unusual and the reason was said to be that he had been involved in a divorce and was not suitable to sit on the bench! Lord Denning once told me that the Law Lords were not judges but members of Parliament who had judicial functions. It is a nice distinction and certainly helped Lord Radcliffe! Others in the eight were John Widgery, who later became Lord Chief Justice, and G. G. (Scottie) Baker with whom I went to Nigeria, as I related in *Chapter Four*.

Mr Justice Lawton was known to everybody as "Fred". He was an outstanding advocate who did not specialise. He did civil work including libel as well as criminal work. He was the son of a prison governor and went to Battersea Grammar School. He was a great enthusiast about the law and the legal profession. He never seemed to mind who heard his forthright views, even in a railway carriage. He too, was unlucky not to go to the House of Lords. He had hopes when Margaret Thatcher became Prime Minister because she had been a pupil in his chambers. These were the ones clerked by Stanley Hopkins to whom

I have already referred. Michael Havers succeeded Fred as Head of them. Others there who pursued successful careers in other field were Robin Day and Airey Neave, who was killed at the House of Commons by a bomb under his car.

The case I did at Kingston was a plea of guilty to robbery with violence of a bank official of £164 and theft of a bicycle, for which the defendant received fifteen months and three months consecutive. The day was not remarkable for that but waiting with a lot of other barristers to come on I realised that there was a sudden exit of my colleagues. I did not appreciate why. I could not move as my solicitor was talking to me from behind, having tugged my gown in the traditional way. I heard the judge say, "That will be Mr Baker". I stood up and learned that the defendant had applied for a dock brief and the vanishing barristers were not keen to take it on.

I went to see my new client who told me that he had been charged with unlawful sexual intercourse. The girl was under age. The defendant had only been in the country for a few months and did not know the relevant law, but that, of course, is no excuse. It had to be a plea of guilty. The prosecution presented the case very fairly. It seemed that the girl was a willing partner. I said what I could in mitigation and Fred imposed a fine of £25 with two months to pay. I thought it was a reasonable result but when I went to see my client afterwards I found him in considerable distress. He was alone and did not seem to have anyone with him at court. When I asked what the trouble was, he replied, "Sir, I did not realise how expensive pleasure was in this country"! I did what I could to comfort him and only hope he kept away from too young girls in future.

Another different experience was appearing before the benchers of Lincoln's Inn for a Nigerian student accused of cheating in the paper on criminal law in the Bar examinations. I had a silent role at the hearing as I was led by Edward Gardner QC, MP – "Ted", as he was known, had a distinguished career in the Navy during the Second World War and was a reporter with the *Bolton Evening News* before coming to the Bar. He never forgot his shorthand which I envied as he could get down any part of the proceedings verbatim unless, of course, he was on his feet speaking. He tried to combine the law and politics as had been done before with considerable success including by my head of chambers, Dingle Foot. However, it became progressively more difficult. QCs were expected to attend throughout their cases and the demands of attendance in the House of Commons made it increasingly a full-time occupation. Apart from being a Parliamentary Private Secretary, Ted never held office – though he was an influential backbencher becoming chair of the Select Committee on Home Affairs. He never got a judicial appointment, though I am not sure whether he wanted one. It was rather a similar story with Petre Crowther QC, MP who often sat as a recorder and when he retired as an MP he applied to be a Circuit Judge, but he was refused by Lord Hailsham. He made no secret of his disappointment.

One other interesting lawyer/legislator is His Honour Judge The Viscount Colville of Culross who was appointed a Circuit Judge in 1993, having been a recorder for three years. He has spoken in the House of Lords on matters of law reform proposals and one only hopes that what he says is listened to because so many proposals are initiated by those who do not have to carry them out. He is one of the few remaining hereditary peers who continue to sit in the House of Lords – at least for the time being.

To return to the benchers of Lincoln's Inn, there were twenty-six of them sitting in a semi-circle each with a pad and an examination paper in front of them. Christopher Slade, later a Lord Justice of Appeal, appeared for the Inn and was, in reality, the prosecutor. In the middle of the room was a small table for the use of the advocates. When he was called upon, Christopher Slade gave Ted Gardner and myself a large wink, approached the table and said, "I would be grateful if the Masters of the Bench would turn to question 4(a) in the examination paper in front of you". Whereupon Lord Justice Harman who, I think, was presiding, turned to another Chancery Judge and said in a loud voice, "I bet you do not know the answer". The bencher remained impassive.

The defence was that the sheet of paper that was discovered by the invigilator was not brought in as a crib but that when the examination commenced, the candidate wrote down what he remembered on a sheet of paper, in case it was useful when answering the questions! He did not seem to know very much, which is not surprising as he had failed the paper nine times before. The rules have been changed and a paper can only be taken three times. The benchers retired and decided that the charge had not been proved to their satisfaction, so it was dismissed. Unfortunately, the case had a sad ending because very soon after it was heard the candidate was taken ill during a spell of severe cold weather, caught pneumonia and died – so he never had another attempt to pass the examination.

I do not want this book, or even a part of it, to become a recital of cases in which I appeared but I will recount one experience which was most unusual.

It concerns an ordinary case of dangerous driving. There was some dispute on the facts about how the accident was caused. At the luncheon adjournment a man came up to me and said he had been driving the car following the defendant whom he knew as a colleague in a business of running pin-tables in Wardour Street, Soho. He said that after the accident, he had taken some photgraphs which he showed me. The photos were so sharp and clear that I asked him whether he was a professional photographer which he denied. Because it was obvious to me that they would resolve some of the disputed points, I asked if he was prepared to give evidence at 2 p.m. when the court resumed. He agreed to do this. I explained the position to the chair of the London Sessions (now the Inner London Crown Court), Mr Reginald Seaton, known as "Reggie" and he agreed that the witness could be called to produce the photos. I always remember that in order to see them, Reggie took off his glasses. He too was very impressed and thanked the witness for coming forward.

About a month later, the witness was arrested. He was Gordon Lonsdale, the Russian spy. I am not surprised he was such a good photographer! He had assumed a Canadian identity but, recalling him now, he did have rather heavy Slavonic features. His English was good and his manners were impeccable. This is not the place to consider what is known about his activities in the West but he was often called a "master" spy, whatever that may mean. He was exchanged for Greville Wynne in Berlin. Wynne ran a mobile train exhibition in Eastern Europe and was said to be spying against Russia. The British authorities rather played down his role as a passer-on of information and it was suggested that the Russians had driven a hard bargain and that it was not an exchange of equals. I have always been rather sceptical of this. It is wise for any intelligence activity to be minimised so as to reveal as little as possible. Over the years, I have come to know a little about intelligence and under cover activity and the first thing to appreciate is that, when necessary, truth goes out of the window.

In the late nineteen-sixties, the law and politics occupied a good deal of my time and I was also interested in going to concerts and watching rugger, as well as having a full family life with a wife and two children. I was able to earn enough at the Bar to keep going but payments by some solicitors were often very late. I used to mention this to Walter Butler but he was most reluctant to do anything beyond a formal reminder and, perhaps, a phone call on the line that he wanted to get the books up to date: "We don't want to upset them, sir, they are very good friends of chambers". Some of the delays were a disgrace. I think there was one payment some three years after I became a judge. I tried to promote a scheme whereby, after a second reminder, a final reminder would be accompanied by a copy sent to the Law Society with a note of the previous bills. In this way, the Law Society would have found out which firms were the principal offenders. Nothing happened, as the Bar Council was reluctant to initiate any scheme and the barristers' clerks were opposed to it.

Over many years, one of the planks of Liberal policy had been to create a system of industrial partnership between employers and the workforce. The Conservatives were basically the party of capital and the bosses while Labour drew its strength from the trade unions. Politics was very much on a class basis. The Liberals campaigned to end this warfare which, like all types of war, was destructive and, in this case, led to bitter labour disputes and strikes. While there was much support and sympathy with the Liberal outlook, there were anxieties about how it would work in practice. If company profits were to be shared with the workers, what happened when there were losses was one question that was frequently asked. what was the role of shareholders? Would workers get shares in the company for which they worked and what rights and powers should these shareholders have? How would this work alongside outside shareholders who had invested in the company? Should workers have representatives on the board of directors and, if so, should their voting power be limited? If there was not a closed shop, should those who were not union members receive benefits which had been obtained by union negotiation?

It was obvious that there were no easy and brief answers to such questions. With some optimism, in 1965, the Liberal party council set up a Standing Industrial Policy Committee whose immediate function was to produce a practicable co-ownership policy. It was also asked to submit slogans, hand out leaflets and more detailed publications on co-ownership to the publications department. As if that was not enough, long-term functions included:

> the study of all forms of co-ownership and co-partnership being practised: the provision of an information service to assist those willing to start similar schemes, and the study of the various economic and social factors involved in co-ownership.

George Goyder was appointed chair and the committee had eight members which included David Steel, Christopher Layton and Professor Michael Fogarty. While the members had varied experiences in industry, there was no director of a multi-national company or any representative of one of the big trade unions. The committee met regularly and successfully submitted a resolution to the 1966 Assembly at Brighton. This called for employee participation on the boards of nationalised industries and in the private sector, a mandatory system of profit and capital increase sharing, as well as voting rights. It also called for works councils for every industrial unit with over fifty employees. For reasons I do not recall, the committee was enlarged in 1967 and I was brought in as chair. The former chair remained on the committee. As I found out, he was a man of strong views and perhaps, this is why he no longer continued as chair. George Goyder was the managing director of British Industrial Paper Ltd, from 1935 to 1971 and during the whole of the Second World War, he was responsible for the procurement, supply and rationing of newsprint to the British Press — a very high powered and responsible job indeed.

Christopher Layton also remained on the committee and edited the final report which was called *Partners at Work* and was published in September, 1968. Christopher had been with the chemicals company ICI and the Economist Intelligence Unit before becoming economic adviser to the Liberal party from 1962 to 1969. He failed to get into the House of Commons at Chippenham. In 1966, he lost by just 694 votes. The Labour candidate, Giles Radice, got over 10,000 votes but, in those days, tactical voting was little known or practised.

Among the newcomers to the committee was Ian Steers, who had been my best man in 1954. Since then he had enjoyed a very successful career in the City, specialising in Canadian securities and banking. It was clear that my rôle was to try and get the members to achieve a unanimous report. In this, I failed and in the end, George Goyder and Elizabeth Abraham made dissenting notes. George was against the committee's proposals for profit sharing but it was a narrow difference because he was in favour of a company setting up from profits a trust fund held on behalf of employees as practised by the American Company, Sears Roebuck, for over fifty years. The dissent of Elizabeth Abraham was put in more general terms, that the committee had not recommended a fundamental restructuring as between "management" and "work". She seemed to incline towards "self management".

I do not think that these differences fundamentally affected the value of the work of the committee but rather they illustrated the many ways in which agreed principles of industrial relations could be achieved. When our report briefly reviewed the work of a number of Liberal committees that had sat since the publication of the Liberal Yellow Book in 1928, we wrote:

> Since then, various Liberal committees have presented a variety of schemes but all have been inspired by the same basic philosophy, the need to bring to an end the separation between worker, owner and employer.

We went into some detail about the election and function of works councils and – anticipating the growth of companies and multi-national diversification – we recommended that:

> In addition to setting up works councils at the level of the individual workplace, central councils should be set up in companies containing more than one plant.

When it came to what we called "The Seat of Power", we noted that in large companies, ownership had often become largely divorced from managerial power; as an example, we recorded: "No member of the Board of ICI, for instance, owns more than one per cent of its shares".

What turned out to be a minority of the committee argued for a two tier system with a supervisory board which would have overall responsibility for financial policy and company strategy generally and the executive board which would be responsible for day-to-day management. This system has been practised in Holland and in Germany and, indeed, was suggested in the Liberal Yellow Book of 1928. The majority felt that in practice many British boards acted in this way and that they were capable of evolving to include employee and consumer representation.

We made a number of detailed recommendations concerning employee representation at board meetings and acquisition of shares and considered various schemes. We then recommended one as a norm and not as a straightjacket – and I think that it was because of this that the recommended scheme was not passed in a resolution to the Liberal Assembly, 1969. A resolution in general terms in line with the work of the committee was carried. Briefly, the crux of our recommendation was that after an initial period of five years, shareholders should receive five per cent of the profits and that any residue was to be shared fifty-fifty between employees and shareholders. There was a certain amount of flexibility which had to be detailed and technical so I understood how this was not able to be adequately presented at a party Assembly. We also dealt with management consulting with the workforce before important decisions were taken and, in our conclusions, looked forward to a new society where the workers were not alienated from the place where they worked but were partners in the enterprise whether public or private. We looked forward to the development of a European company law which would incorporate our thinking.

I learned a lot from the work of the committee and I think it was worthwhile not just for me but as a contribution to the knowledge and thinking on a very important subject. The Liberal party itself was grateful for what had been done.

The other area in which I helped the Liberal party was broadcasting. It began in 1960 with the setting by the Postmaster General of a committee with very wide terms of reference: "to consider the future of the broadcasting services of the United Kingdom".

The chair was Sir Harry Pilkington from whom the committee took its name. Its members were widely drawn and included Joyce Grenfell and Richard Hoggert as well as, for a time, Sir Peter Hall and Sir Jock Campbell. It did its work thoroughly and its report was not published until June, 1962. It was unanimous. The background was that Independent or Commercial Television was created by the Television Act 1954 which expired after ten years. There had been a bitter fight to break the monopoly of broadcasting held by the BBC whose standards of public broadcasting were highly regarded throughout the world. They were bolstered by the reputation it had for accuracy, truth and integrity in its news programmes that had been much enhanced during the Second World War by its reports from correspondents led by Richard Dimbleby.

The experience of commercial broadcasting in the USA with its desire to maximise viewers and listeners to attract advertising and thus put on programmes with the widest appeal, led many to hope that it would not be introduced here. Liberals had always opposed monopoly institutions unless they could be clearly shown to be in the public interest, for example, in those days, there was no contest about the monopoly of the Post Office but industry with its cartels and restrictive practices was another matter. Though in a minority, there were some staunch Liberal defenders of the monopoly of the BBC including Lady Violet Bonham Carter and Lord Beveridge. Lady Violet was a Governor of the BBC and took her duties very seriously, especially when she thought that programmes were unfair to the Liberals and did not give their view. She must have been an avid viewer because she used to ring up, generally at lunchtime, the Director of Current Affairs of the BBC, John Grist, with considerable frequency if she had an adverse comment on a programme shown the previous evening. Very often she would be demanding a further programme to redress the balance. Though little known, this work by Lady Violet was of considerable importance in keeping the small but hopefully influential Liberal party in the public eye. Jo Grimond was her son-in-law but that did not prevent some differences of opinion arising, though they were very much in agreement on the big issues of the time and the need for an independent Liberal party. Jo invited me to chair a committee which would brief him on broadcasting matters. It was unofficial in that the Liberal Party Organization was not involved. Jo often worked that way. He was not a party organization man. He was personally shy, though always charming, but unlike Jeremy Thorpe, Jo did not relish going off and cheering up the troops. He once told me that he was no good at being introduced to the oldest Liberal in Wales as he did not know what to say!

It seemed to me that what I had to do was to avoid reopening the controversies of the creation of Independent Television as it was not going to be scrapped after such a short existence but to ask the views of those involved with broadcasting professionally for their comments on the present situation how they saw the future and how they would like TV to develop. The committee never was a committee in the sense that it never met—but I would write to people and sometimes see them, collate their views and pass them on to Jo.

Nothing was ever published. People in the BBC especially had to be circumspect and would not want criticisms attributed to them. A number of broadcasters were not employees but self-employed, earning fees from their engagements. They too, did not want to jeopardise their careers. Four well-known broadcasters had been Liberal parliamentary candidates, Robin Day, John Arlott, Ludovic Kennedy and George Scott. I got considerable help from them.

Robin was something of an exception because he was prepared to speak out and write about the future of broadcasting. I doubt whether it did him any harm but, in himself, he was a disappointed man. He used to say that he had failed at the Bar — but he was a great success as an interviewer, especially of politicians. He fought the Hereford constituency for the Liberals in 1959. He was close to success and his efforts to obtain an important administrative post in broadcasting also failed. It was really rather sad. I recall that when I was chair of the Liberal party and held a press conference on the eve of a party Assembly, Robin, who was covering the conference for the BBC, said to me afterwards, rather late at night, "I am a leech on the body politic". That he was wholly wrong about himself was clearly shown when the Temple Church was crowded for his memorial service in 2000. It was held there at his own request, perhaps showing that the law really was his true love. He was an Honorary master of the bench of the Middle Temple. His debating skills were first seen at the Oxford Union and he used to refer to the post-war years there as the "golden age". He valued the company, over the years, of his Oxford contemporaries and it was therefore appropriate that at the service the three readings were by William Rees-Mogg, Ludovic Kennedy and Keith Kyle, while the first address was given by Dick Taverne QC.

For the committee, I corresponded with the Viewers and Listeners Association and also, the Screen Writers Guild. There were strict rules curbing what could be broadcast which irritated and frustrated writers and others. The guild pointed out that as a result of the Television Act 1954, the restrictions were greater on ITV than on BBC. ITV was not allowed to broadcast a satirical programme called "What the Public Wants" as a rival to the BBC's very successful "That Was the Week that Was".

Some research was done on party Political Broadcasts and the allocations of time. I got some figures for four years. The broadcasts went out at different times on both BBC and ITV. The allocations were based on figures at the previous General ~Election. For reasons I never knew, the Liberals were getting twelve and a half per cent of sound broadcasts but only eight per cent of TV time. All this seemed to be decided in a rather hole and corner way. I was asked by Jo Grimond to go along with him to a meeting at the House of Commons chaired by Iain MacLeod as Leader of the House. Each party was represented together with the BBC and ITV. Jo made a strong complaint and I think he was helped because Liberals had been doing rather well at recent by-elections. He got a better proportion but how this came to be decided through the "usual channels", I never found out. My feeling is that the Whips' Offices wanted to be influential. They did not like what they called "maverick" MPs building up a reputation and following resulting from TV appearances. Both Bob Boothby and Michael Foot were fearlessly independent-minded and very successful "on the box".

Another thing we did was to have a survey completed of local programmes on ITV for each region. What we knew was happening was that companies were taking programmes off each other, often American films and what was called "networking" them. The figures were quite startling for local programmes based on a sixty hour weekly showing. The Welsh were top but only with fourteen per cent while Ulster was lowest with nine per cent. I think that some representations were made to the Independent Broadcasting Authority about this. I know that John Arlott, a Hampshire man like Lord Denning, felt strongly about it. Getting programmes from somebody else and not making them oneself was a way of saving money.

The general thrust of our views was for a very limited expansion of channels for both the BBC and the ITV. To start a channel whether financed publicly or privately, was a very expensive operation. The days of satellite, digital, on-line and cable facilities were far off. What was done had to be financially successful.

The Pilkington committee was much more restrictive in its conclusions. While it believed that the BBC "should be authorised as soon as possible to provide a second programme of television", it called for a fundamental reconstruction and reorganization of independent television with the Authority planning programmes and selling advertising time. "The programme companies would produce and sell to the Authority programme items for inclusion in the schedules planned by the Authority". This would have strangled the regions and put programme power into a few national hands. Fortunately, it has not come about so that the consequential recommendation that, until this change had been achieved, independent television should not provide any additional television services, became academic. The committee rejected proposals for a service of subscription, pay-as-you- view television.

On sound radio the committee was even more restrictive. It believed that there should only be one local broadcasting system provided by the BBC and financed from licence revenue. Again, this proposal was never adopted. Our approach could be summarised in an extract of comments I prepared after a memorandum circulated by the BBC on the future of broadcasting which I described as "cautious and sceptical". I was referring to Pay-as you-view:

> A more positive approach would seem to be that if there is an organization prepared to risk its finance on such a project, it is in the interests not only of a free economy but also of the consumers, that it should be permitted to do so. It would only attract artists and technicians away from other forms of TV if the programmes were drawing sufficient viewers to be a financial success".

I think that this comment has stood the test of time. The only modification I would make is that a most powerful organization like the one led by Rupert Murdoch might be prepared to accept losses in a particular sector, say sport, in order to weaken the competition and put forward bids for events which they could not.

I believe that the work of the committee was useful and constructive: certainly, Jo Grimond expressed his gratitude for it. I do not know what happened to it after Jo ceased to be the leader of the party in January, 1967. Jeremy Thorpe had some TV experience in current affairs programmes apart from party broadcasts and he, no doubt, used his own contacts. I have no recollection of him getting in touch with me and no papers to show that he did. I did not mind as I had much else to do and so had Jeremy.

About this time, I was busy doing a number of talks on the English Legal System on the World Service of the BBC I have got scripts of twenty-three of them. They went to various countries including Russia, Rumania and East Africa.

I do not recall how they came about. It may have been after my broadcasts to the West Indies with Tom Adams. I tried to illustrate the principles of English Law and Procedure by making up simple cases. After a few broadcasts to Russia, I asked the producer whether there had been any listener reaction. Although listening to foreign broadcasts was officially banned in Russia, there must have been some listeners otherwise, the broadcasts were not worthwhile. With a wry smile, the producer told me that there had been a letter from a white Russian exile who said that what I had described bore no relation to his experience in Scunthorpe magistrates' court! Some months after the Russian broadcasts had finished, I was very pleased to be told out of the blue that they had been repeated and I got another cheque for one half of my fee!

The Rumanian broadcasts produced a surprise of a different sort. Just before the start of one of these, the producer put before me a piece of paper saying he would like me to do an extract in Rumanian. I had no time to practise but I did my best and afterwards, he was very pleased with what I had done, which was a relief. The broadcasts are an example of how one thing follows another.

One day in Richmond, I think it was on The Green, I was talking to a man I knew slightly called Speight. He was at the Foreign Office and in charge of the Cultural Exchange Programme with Eastern Europe. He told me that the Russians had, in recent years, only been granting visas to those scientists whose brains they wanted to pick. They had been given an ultimatum and a list of occupations. It was to be all or nothing. The Russians opted for all and I was asked if I would like to be the lawyer. I agreed and was given the choice of Czechoslovakia, Hungary or Rumania. I chose the last of these because it had been showing some signs of political independence which was unusual in the then-called Soviet bloc.

I was briefed by the Foreign Office before I went but when I arrived in Bucharest there was considerable mystery about who I was. Some people seemed to think I was coming from an English University. Anyway, it was soon apparent that my escort—or "minder"—was a man called Murescanu. He was a teacher of English at Bucharest University. I was never quite sure of his status so I called him "the Professor". He spoke remarkably good English considering that he had never been out of Rumania and I know that he was helped by listening to radio programmes in English. He was a nice friendly man whose wife came from Transylvania and spoke German, which was also helpful. The Professor had made a study of the English Romantic poets such as Byron, Wordsworth, Coleridge, Keats and Shelley. Fortunately, I had studied some of their works with Jim Parsons at Wellington School. Prompted by The Professor, it was surprising what I could remember and, indeed, recite. He had written a basic English-Rumanian conversation book and gave me a copy which though published in Bucharest, had a label on the back saying, "Collet's, 45, Museum Street, London, WC1". I found this book most useful and learned some basic phrases which I used in the hotel and to greet people. I have tried to do this in a number of languages when I have been abroad and find that it does create good will. Speaking Czech I got an extra pillow for Joy when we were in Prague but there was a very unexpected consequence after we had visited Turkey.

I was sitting at The Old Bailey and when I came into court, I noticed there were two people in the dock who were chatting away. According to the court list, there was only one defendant. The clerk explained that the second man was the interpreter. I have always been a bit suspicious of interpreters and wondered how much some, a very small minority, help witnesses. I once had an exchange about this with a French interpreter. When the interpreter at The Old Bailey came forward, he took the interpreters' oath and then looked at me and said in a loud clipped voice, "The language: it is Turkish". I looked straight at his fierce brown eyes and said, "Teşekkür ederim" which means, "Thank you very much". He was astonished and neither he nor the defendant knew how much or how little Turkish I understood.

In the hotel in Bucharest where I was on the Cultural Exchange Programme, I noticed that the room opposite was not occupied. It faced the street so I asked if I could change into it. I was refused and then realized that mine must be bugged. I found out that it was by making comments such as, "I need more soap" or, "This room needs dusting" — and there was always the correct response. It happened enough times to make me believe that it was not a coincidence, but I never said anything and took as much care as possible with my papers and other possessions.

It is sensible not to be too adventurous in trying to counter bugging. This did not happen in Bucharest but there was once a high-powered civil servant on a mission abroad who thought his room was bugged. In searching around he found a box under the bed with a nut which he started to unscrew. After a short time, there was a loud crash. The chandelier in the room below had come down!

Shortly after I arrived in Bucharest, I was taken to the British Embassy and noticed that on either side of the entrance gates there were two soldiers. I was told that they kept a careful watch on who came in and out. My arrival enabled the ambassador, called Glass, to invite a number of Rumanian lawyers to the Embassy. This was the first time it had been done. Some knew some English and, from what I could find out, the only English lawyers they had heard of were D. N. Pritt QC and John Platts-Mills. They were two well known left wingers who had been expelled from the Labour party. Both had been MPs.

I was taken around the courts. My visits were informal and this enabled The Professor to whisper to me what was going on. I think the programme was carefully arranged because, one day, he and I were walking along and I asked what a certain building was. He told me it was the equivalent of the local magistrates' court. I said I would like to go in. He said it was not on the programme. I went in and he followed. I hope he did not get into trouble for it. I never heard that he did. What was taking place was a real mixture of cases — some criminal, some domestic. All were quite short. Some were just applications for court orders. Like other courts, this was a court of three. In all courts, the chair was legally qualified and sat with two "peoples' assessors". They were the lay representatives of the people and in the English translation of the constitution which was approved in August, 1965 they are referred to as the "peoples' jurors", though this function is very different from members of a British jury. An assessor is elected for two years by his or her local authority (peoples' council) and is paid but has no training. The result is a loyal party member. From what I saw, he or she clearly influences the verdict and also the punishment.

I was told that about one-third of the members of the legal profession in Rumania were women and occupied important positions, not only at the Bar but also in the judiciary. This was illustrated when I went to the international port of Constanta on the Black Sea. The legal adviser to the Port Authority was a woman in her early forties. One interesting thing that she told me was that in the previous year there had been three disputes with the Russians on maritime matters in the Black Sea and they had each been referred to the City of London for a decision by agreement. It was interesting because it demonstrated firstly, by the esteem and respect in which the City was held and secondly, that the Russians did not always lord it over the so-called Eastern European satellites.

The Professor and I went to Constanta by train. We were in coach with a central corridor and I was asked by a passer-by whether I was the American Big Band leader Woody Herman! I smiled and denied it. In fact, I was taken to Woody Herman's concert in Bucharest and thoroughly enjoyed it. It had a very warm reception and showed that everything was not barred that was American. The thaw was beginning. Tourists were being encouraged. This was evident when we went to the coastal resort of Mamaia. There were great blocks of apartments and some hotels. Free holidays were given to champion workers, based, I think, on output. There were awards to factories and to individuals. There was a carefully manicured, artificial beach. A man told me he could tell which country people came from by when they were prepared to swim in the sea. The Scandanavians came first, then the British and then people from the Mediterranean countries. All I know is that The Professor had to try very hard to get me to swim, but he did and I found it very cold indeed.

From Mamaia, we went to the Bulgarian frontier which was probably the least open of the Eastern European countries and the most backward economically. We met quite a strong armed presence and turned around. It was some twenty years later when I was active in the Medico-Legal Society that I went to a meeting with Joy on the Georgy Markov case. Markov was a broadcaster from Bulgaria in the BBC World Service. He was walking along Waterloo Bridge going to his place of work at Bush House, Aldwych when he was jabbed in the thigh by the end of an umbrella. Poison had been injected into him and he died. There was a similar incident in Paris which failed. The lecturer told us how the umbrella worked and that the bullet had two holes of different sizes to create a spraying effect. After the lecture was over, the chair asked for questions and comments and a man seated immediately behind Joy and myself stood up. He identified himself as a police inspector who had been on the case and said that before coming to the meeting, he had been to the Metropolitan Police Laboratory and got the bullet. He then produced a small case and Joy and I were the first to see it. It really was no bigger than a pellet. Georgy Markov's widow was very courageous and spent much time, I think without success, trying to find out who the killer was and who was behind the murder. I understand that it took place because Markov was a very effective broadcaster who was very well informed about the principal members of the Bulgarian regime. The authorities had somehow got wind of the fact that Markov had obtained considerable information about corruption and could name names. He therefore, had to be disposed of - and he was - in a most calculated and shameful way. There was an alleged confession by a man living abroad in 2005.

In Rumania the only other place I was taken was the former Royal Palace at Sinaia which had been converted into a Peoples' Centre for Cultural Activities. It was gothic or rather mock gothic in style and might have been the setting for the musical comedy, "White Horse Inn" - though in fact that was in Austria at Durnstein. I thought that the countryside setting was better than the building itself but unfortunately, on the day I went, the visibility was not good.

Back in Bucharest, I could have caused an international incident. The Shah of Persia was visiting Rumania at the time and there was a state procession which passed the hotel. I went to the room opposite mine which I knew was empty and stood on the balcony. The Shah and Ceausescu came by in an open car. I was not too high up and if I had had a brick or two I could have dropped them on their heads! There were none available.

When I returned to London, I made a report to the Foreign Office about my visit. It was, of course, a serious and, I hope, helpful document and I did not include the above incident! I also wrote a twenty page pamphlet for the British Society of International Understanding (BSIU), not just on my visit but on the history and politics of the country. I did this with the help of material supplied by the Foreign Office Library who were most helpful. Re-reading it for present purposes, I have been surprised at my knowledge!

The chair of the BSIU was Instructor Rear Admiral Sir Arthur Hall, the chief "schoolie" of the Navy. He and his family were old friends of the Heward family and, as I have mentioned, he proposed the health of Joy and myself at our wedding. The families still remain in touch through his son, Commander Tim Hall and his daughter, Joan Pearson; with grandchildren, this is a friendship that has gone on now for nearly one hundred years. The Governors of the BSIU were high ranking servicemen and, being forward looking, Admiral Hall, known as Peter, recruited three young politicians, one from each party: Stratton Mills, Richard Marsh (now Lord Marsh) and myself. The BSIU, under the editorship of John Eppstein, produced two pamphlets each month. There was a main series and a popular series. The contents were either on a particular country or a contemporary issue. The essential requirement was that they had to be objective. I always thought that the most valuable thing was the distribution to schools in the hope that pupils would be made aware of and become interested in what was going on in the world. Used imaginatively, and perhaps with visual aids, they could be of considerable help to teachers. I do not know what has become of the society now or whether it still exists. Like other people I know, I have become rather sad about the downgrading of history in our schools but some TV programmes have stimulated interest in a creative way. The fact that well over a million votes were cast by viewers to decide who is the greatest Briton does show that interest can be aroused.

I have never been back to Rumania. I was hoping to go to Constanta again in 2001 when on a Swan Hellenic cruise around the Black Sea but it was not on the itinerary. The only repercussion from my visit apart from BBC talks came some two or three years later when my erstwhile minder, The Professor, told me that he had got an appointment at a University in Tucson, Arizona and was passing through London. Joy and I met him and his wife and gave them a brief tour of London. They were most surprised that we could walk into 12, Downing Street and I was able to show them where the Judicial Committee of the Privy Council did its work. They had been able to bring out only a very little money though they did have some jewellery which they could sell if necessary. Sadly, they were not allowed to bring their children out of Rumania. They had to remain with grandparents. I suppose this was some kind of security against unacceptable behaviour whilst outside Rumania. We exchanged letters and Christmas cards but they fell off after a time so I do not know what happened to them.

After Rumania, I started to become more active again in the Liberal party and was elected chair of the Candidates' Association. This was somewhat curious as I had not fought the 1966 General Election, but, as I have already recounted, I had fought the two previous ones. The next important event in the Liberal party was in January 1967 when Jo Grimond resigned as leader. There had been hints and speculations about his going from political columnists. He was known to feel that ten years was enough and that he was disappointed at the party's lack of progress. It still only had twelve MPs. True it was twice as many as when he started but it was still only about two per cent of the membership of the House of Commons. After the announcement, everything moved with great speed. In those days, the Leader was elected by the MPs only. They met and held an election. Six votes were cast for Jeremy Thorpe who — as he was entitled to — voted for himself. Eric Lubbock and Emlyn Hooson each got three votes so there was no bottom candidate to be eliminated. The three men met. Eric and Emlyn agreed to withdraw. Then all twelve MPs met and Jeremy was elected unanimously. It was all over in 24 hours. There was considerable disquiet in the party at what had happened so quickly and without consultation. I was quoted on the front page of the *Daily Telegraph* as saying, "I tried to get in touch last night with a number of Liberal candidates and it was clear that there was no obvious successor to Mr Grimond. In these circumstances, it is clear that the Liberal candidates ought to have had some opportunity to consider the matter".

Deliberately, I did not query the result. I personally, thought that Jeremy was the best candidate but of course, I did not know and could not forsee the disastrous personal matters that were to end his leadership.[5]

---

[5] It was a bit of a farce that only the twelve Liberal MPs were entitled to vote. The justification for it was said to be that it was the leader of the Parliamentary party that was being elected and there would be many problems if an extended electorate chose an MP that the others did not want. This reasoning could not survive the democratic process because in reality, the leader was the leader of the whole party. So after Jeremy Thorpe resigned, there was a contest between David Steel and John Pardoe on a one party member-one vote basis. It became rather a bitter fight descending into the personal arena with references to whether John Pardoe had a toupée. It always surprises me how strongly the Democrats and the Republicans fight the campaign for their Presidential candidate in the USA. Many unhelpful things are said but once the candidate has been chosen the erstwhile rivals fall in behind and fight for him and their party. John Pardoe, however, was unexpectedly defeated in North Cornwall in 1979 and after that, he faded away from the political scene, which was a pity. He worked hard as party Treasurer and was an effective Parliamentary spokesman on Treasury matters. He and Denis Healey had quite an abrasive relationship.

Jeremy Thorpe was much liked in the Liberal party. His enthusiasm was infectious. I remember that when my daughter, Caroline, was chair of the Cambridge University Liberal Club, he visited them and they went around the Cambridge market. Caroline told me that Jeremy had a considerable knowledge of fruit and vegetables and their prices! This impressed the stallholders. Jeremy complained to me, and most probably others, that Jo Grimond did not encourage and support him and Jeremy thought Grimond disliked him. I do not think this was so. In fact, I told Jeremy that we had a meeting in Richmond very soon after he was elected leader and Jo publicly said that he thought that Jeremy would be very good. I was sorry this did not get to Jeremy's ears earlier.

Some people got thought it demonstrated that Jeremy was lightweight and a showman. This was a harsh verdict as he was a first class political campaigner. He worked out which seats were winnable and created a fund to help them. This was sensible but he kept control of the money.

This caused concern to the party treasurers who did not know what the position was. People such as Jack Hayward, who was anxious about the future of Lundy Island which was in Jeremy's constituency, gave money to him. In public, Jeremy continued to do well. His first speech as leader at the Blackpool Assembly in September, 1967 was described in *The Guardian* as "able, witty and incisive". He was considered to be a worthy successor to Jo Grimond. It is interesting to recall how much coverage by the press there was of political events. The *Guardian* report on the Assembly contained reports on the debates with comments and feature articles by their political staff. There were fifty-two pages. Cause and effect are sometimes difficult to disentangle. Complaints are often made about the decline of interest in politics and that for young people, in particular, they are a turn off. If there were to be more imaginative and challenging reporting, then perhaps public interest would increase.

Apart from the winnable constituencies drive, efforts were being made to consider the next General Election under Jeremy's leadership. Could more seats, at last, be won? I continued to be active in the higher regions of the party and became chair of the Executive in 1969. The party was in more financial trouble than usual and according to the *Daily Telegraph* (not the friendliest source for Liberals) on 20th October, 1969, it was going to be £1 million in debt at the end of the year. The president elected at the Assembly the previous month in Brighton was Lord Beaumont who was said to be on the verge of resignation unless given assurances by Jeremy Thorpe about boosting income. The president took the chair for the quarterly meetings of the Party Council. In October, after just a month in office, a motion of no confidence in Lord Beaumont was tabled. I had to take the chair while it was debated. It was lost by thirty-seven votes to fifty-two. Tim Beaumont carried on but the vote must have come as quite a blow. He was a rich man and supported the Party generously.

The Liberal party had to fight the forthcoming General Election on as wide a front as possible. It was clear that there would be little financial help coming from headquarters. They had to concentrate on broadcasts, publications and the party manifesto. Campaign money would have to be almost wholly raised in the constituencies themselves. I had to decide what to do myself. My health was not causing any problems and I thought that as chair of the party I had to set an example and seek a constituency to fight. I did not want to be far from London and Richmond. I had to keep my Bar practice going although as a candidate I would have to spend the last two to three weeks before Polling Day campaigning full-time. So I was glad to be selected for Dorking.

There were about ten candidates initially. I thought this was encouraging. It was quite a high number to come forward to contest a seat with a Conservative majority of over ten thousand. I had little time to prepare because I was selected in April. It was thought most likely that the election would be in the autumn but it was called for June 18th 1970. The constituency was an interesting one as apart from Dorking itself, it contained a number of villages such as Shere, Gomshall, Charlwood (very close to Gatwick airport), East and West Horsley and Abinger Common. Fortunately, there seemed to be a small number of Liberals in each place and I got a good reception when I went around. However, there were the usual pessimists (nearly always Tories) who said I could not win and there was still some talk about "splitting the vote". The Conservative member was Sir George Sinclair who had been in the Colonial Service. He was an unusually moderate Tory which made him a more difficult opponent. He refused to share a platform with the other candidates. In the end there were only three of us. The Labour candidate was John Fahy. At the previous General Election in 1966, the gap between Labour and the Liberal was 12,201 to 7,629 which was quite large but I did hope to make inroads into this as the Labour Government under Harold Wilson, like most governments, had been a disappointment, especially in getting the economy going.

Our chambers got some publicity because we had three candidates. Dingle Foot (Labour) lost Ipswich by thirteen votes while Charles Fletcher-Cooke (Conservative) retained Darwen and greatly increased his majority from 1,735 to 9,094. The national swing to the Conservatives was not so great as that but they did get an overall majority of over thirty - so, enter Edward Heath as Prime Minister and the road to Europe. In Dorking, the campaign was steady but not spectacular. There were good attendances at village meetings but the result was once again, for me, a disappointment. Sir George Sinclair increased his majority to nearly 15,000. The Labour vote went down to 10,500 but the Liberal vote also went down from 7,629 to 7,103, about the same as my earlier totals in Richmond. I remember that when Joy and I got home rather late after the count, my mother who was looking after the children, asked if it was worth it. I kept up a brave face. That it was worthwhile in those difficult days is shown by what has now happened. While the Liberal Democrats have not yet won in Dorking, Liberal candidates in 1970 in Sutton, Carshalton, Richmond and Twickenham all came third and none had 7,000 votes. They are now Liberal Democrat seats and further examples can be given from other parts of the country.

For the Liberal party as a whole there were losses, so that the Parliamentary party was reduced to single figures. It was a somewhat shaken Jeremy Thorpe who was returned for North Devon with a majority of just 369. I was in a car with him and as we stopped outside the National Liberal Club, he told me that it had been a pretty rough fight and that rumours were being spread that he was homosexual. I said nothing but I was surprised. I had known him for some twenty years and I had not ever seen him act in any way as to suggest that he was that way inclined. While he did not openly go around with girlfriends, neither did he obviously keep the company of men.

Jeremy had married Caroline Allpass in 1968 and they had one son, Rupert, who became a photographer and is now married and lives in California. Though he later suffered severely from Parkinson's disease, Jeremy did the long journey to see him on two occasions that I know of. As if things politically were not difficult for him after the 1970 General Election, he suffered a severe personal blow when Caroline was killed in a car crash eleven days later driving to London from North Devon on 29th June, 1970. There seemed to be no explanation for the accident. Why it happened is pure conjecture, for nobody knows how tired she was or whether she had any worries that were troubling her. It seemed such a short time since Joy and I had been at their very large wedding reception at the Royal Academy. Everybody used to say what a lovely person Caroline was, obviously intelligent and a very good foil for Jeremy. There was wonderful music at her funeral service in St. Margaret's Westminster, including a most moving rendering of the slow movement of Bach's double violin concerto played by Yehudi Menuhin and Robert Masters.

Jeremy's love of music is shown by his choice of Marion Harewood three years later as his second wife. She was formerly married to the Queen's cousin. Jeremy, with typical panache and excellent mimicry, told me that when the engagement was announced, a stalwart North Devon supporter exclaimed, "Is our Jeremy in line for the throne, then?"Marion was a concert pianist and much involved in the Aldeburgh Festival. The Thorpes had a house at nearby Thorpeness and, again with Jeremy's flair for the memorable, they had a Christmas card of themselves which said, "The Thorpes at Thorpeness".

Marion was a stranger to the political scene so there was a mixture of musicians and politicians at another glittering wedding reception which was held at Covent Garden. It was in 1973, quite shortly after I was appointed a judge. When Joy and I came to be introduced, Jeremy said to Marion, "He's just been made a judge so we cannot get him either to the Commons or to the Lords". Goodness knows what Marion made of this.

Then the stormclouds began to gather around Jeremy and Marion must have wondered what on earth she had let herself in for. For over thirty years she has behaved quite wonderfully towards Jeremy. Going to court with the greatest regularity both at Minehead Magistrates' Court and The Old Bailey must have been an enormous strain culminating, with waiting for the verdict and the relief of the acquittal. I was present on a rare occasion when she intervened. It was during a press conference which Jeremy called at the National Liberal Club before he was prosecuted. A reporter suggested, in essence, that Marion had put up money to pay off a blackmailer. She stood up and was visibly angry in her complete denial.

Shortly after Jeremy was acquitted of conspiracy to murder, we had him and Marion down to our house at Richmond for a quiet dinner which I hope they enjoyed as a complete change from all that they had been through. It also showed that they had some friends. The strain on Marion and Jeremy was not confined to the trial itself. Once, when Joy and I went to their Devon home whilst I was sitting at the Plymouth Crown Court, Marion told me how it had been besieged by reporters and cameramen during a visit by the former Speaker, George Thomas. One of the problems is if a remark is overheard and then reported out of context. As far as I know, Marion has never put a foot wrong and has refused to write a book.

After the trial, Jeremy tried to make a comeback outside Parliament. It seems that difficulties were put in his way by certain people, for example when he tried to get a job with Amnesty International. He did succeed however in working for the United Nations Association and he also had his own agency to help bring about business with Third World countries. He had been away too long to return to the Bar.

Joy and I kept in touch and I was able to help on two occasions. The first concerned an author called Michael Bloch. He wanted to write a book about Jeremy which was going to be very frank. He saw him and a number of other people including me. This was always on the understanding that the book would not be published until after Jeremy's death. Eight years passed and then, towards the end of 2001 Michael Bloch, having changed publishers, decided to publish. The *New Statesman* said that Jeremy had lived too long for Bloch's purposes! Jeremy, and others like me, felt betrayed. At Jeremy's request, and I was quite willing to do this, I wrote to Bloch and quickly got a conciliatory reply. The publishers agreed to keep to the original understanding. The *Evening Standard* 'Londoners' Diary' wrote quite a feature about it which flatteringly — and incorrectly of course — referred to me as a former High Court Judge. This occurred again in *The Times* after I was one of the signatories to a letter in 2002 concerning a TV programme on Jeremy's trial and the events leading up to it.

It is true that I sat in the High Court with some regularity so perhaps that is how it came about. I have noted that the newspapers often refer to persons as judges when strictly speaking, they are not but have sat, say as an assistant recorder or deputy and are thus carrying out judicial functions. I remember once being fooled by a newspaper headline placard which said, "Judge convicted of gross indecency". Of course, I bought the paper, only to find out that the "judge" was the judge of a flower show!

The letter to *The Times* made a number of points and asked that Jeremy should be left in peace and queried whether there was any possible interest served by the programme after such a long time. Richard Ingrams in the *Observer* thought that the letter had only drawn attention to the programme and as a result, had increased the viewing figures. The programme was shown and afterwards Jeremy delivered a scathing attack on it, likening it to trial by television and comparing it with show trials in Eastern Europe. What I disliked was the considerable amount of time given to Norman Scott setting out his version of events. His version of events was rejected by the jury and Jeremy denied his allegations from the outset. He made a complaint to the Broadcasting Standards Commission which was not upheld.

• • •

After the General Election of 1970, it was time to resume practice at the Bar. Briefs came in regularly and I was able to pay my way with the education of two daughters at St. Paul's Girls' School. I did some interesting and varied cases, mainly in the criminal courts because as I explained earlier, the Privy Council work was declining though Dingle Foot after his General Election defeat at Ipswich, was able to resume his practice there pretty quickly—and get a good proportion of the work that was going.

It was at this time that I got to know better the Liberal party Treasurer, Sir Frank Medlicott. He was a solicitor and briefed me as a barrister. He also had the difficult task of tackling Jeremy about the money that he had raised and not put into the party account. Apart from the 'winnable seats' money, there was other money that was raised during the General Election.

There was an echo of this during the hearing of the committal proceedings against Jeremy at Minehead Magistrates' Court when the late Sir David Napley cross-examined the prosecution witnesses at considerable length. I was one of those who doubted whether this was wise for it did seem that there was a case to answer which is what the magistrates had to decide. If a witness was open to criticism he might be able to rectify it when he gave evidence at the trial. Apart from that, there was further publicity on a considerable scale and the possibility for springing surprises at the trial, for which the late George Carman QC became well known, was considerably reduced. In fairness to Sir David, whom I knew for many years when we debated at the Hampstead Parliament, I will say no more—except that during the proceedings I had to write to him as I had seen a report in the *Evening Standard* that when he cross-examined Jack Hayward, he suggested that I was a trustee of the money donated to the Liberal party. I said that this must refer to the money given by Jack Hayward during the 1970 General Election when I was chair of the Executive and a member of the Finance and Administration Board. I made it clear that I did not know of Mr Hayward's donation nor was I a party to the discussions between Sir Frank Medlicott and Jeremy Thorpe on what should be transferred to Sir Frank as party Treasurer. I am glad I have kept my letter because it has reminded me that my belief then was that £60,000 out of £75,000 was transferred into the account of the Liberal Party Organization. I got a reply from Christopher Murray, Sir David's assistant, who had not been able to get hold of a copy of the *Evening Standard* but he had checked the depositions made by the clerk of the court and could find no reference to me being the Trustee of the Hayward donation. However, he did remember that my name had been mentioned—but he could not elaborate. He promised to write again when he had found out more, but there was nothing further from him.

It is sometimes curious how peoples' paths cross. It was not until January 2002 that we again had contact, when Christopher Murray came to a Conference at St. Antony's College, Oxford, representing the Law Society's Criminal Law committee. The Conference was organized by the Liberal Democrat Lawyers Association and the purpose was to consider the report on the criminal justice system by Lord Justice Auld. As I had retired and was free from judicial restraints, I felt I could go and I thoroughly enjoyed it, especially being able to take part in the discussions. Christopher Murray revealed that his first contact with the Liberal party was when it fell to him to tell David Steel that Jeremy

Thorpe had been arrested! I did not raise the matter of our subsequent, unfinished correspondence.

Sir Frank Medlicott sent me a number of civil cases for which I was grateful but my practice grew more on the criminal side. Thanks to prosecutions for the Metropolitan Police Service and defence solicitors like Jeffrey Gordon, I was seldom out of work and there were some absorbing cases. I will pick out two but after such a long time, I will not name names.

The first concerns a seventeen-year-old grammar school boy who, after a holiday in Greece, thought that life at school was rather dull and humdrum. So, he played truant and cycled to Littlehampton. After sleeping on the beach, he got aboard a five and a half ton cabin cruiser and sailed it to Boulogne. He then decided to go to another port where there was less chance of being recognised. However, he ran aground — but was able to limp back to Boulogne where he was taken to the British consul.

At Littlehampton magistrates' court, he was charged with stealing the boat. I represented him and pleaded not guilty on the basis that he had no intention of depriving the owner permanently of the boat. The magistrates dismissed the case. The interesting legal point is that under the Theft Act 1968 there would have been an offence of taking a conveyance without the owner's consent to which there would have been no defence. However, this case was heard in July, 1967 before the Act came into force. As is the normal rule with criminal legislation, it was not retrospective. At the hearing, the matter of compensation was raised but the magistrates had no power to deal with that as there had been no conviction. I never heard if there were any civil proceedings or any payment by way of settlement. It would have been difficult to resist such a claim as clearly the boat had been damaged while in the possession of the schoolboy. Whether he had any money to pay is another matter but perhaps the boat was insured to cover an unauthorised taking.

The second case occurred in 1972 at The Old Bailey just after I had been appointed a recorder. My role at the trial as junior counsel was a silent one as I was led by Sir Charles Fletcher-Cooke QC, MP. I had, however, appeared at the committal proceedings some weeks before at the Marylebone Magistrates' Court and succeeded in getting some evidence excluded on the ground that it was hearsay. The point was not re-argued at the trial which was helpful to at least one of the defendants. The case concerned a robbery on a bank in Baker Street, London in which property worth well over £1 million was taken over a weekend. It was very well planned and Robert Harman, who prosecuted, reminded the jury that it happened in a way that was very similar to the Sherlock Holmes story, "The Red-Headed League" - in that a tunnel was dug into the bank from a neighbouring property. In the fictional story, the thieves were met at the bank by detectives but, in the real-life episode, they were not caught like that. The raid was only discovered when the staff arrived for work on the Monday morning. The tunnel did not run from the adjacent premises, which were a restaurant, but under that, starting from the next premises which were a handbag shop, the lease of which had been acquired by one of the defendants.

The tunnel was forty feet long and was so expertly dug that it did not need any supports. It came out in the safe deposit room of the bank where one of the team rented a safe box. When he went there, he always had an umbrella so that he could measure the room to make sure the tunnel came out in a place which was not blocked. There were many valuables in the boxes after the robbery was discovered but a number of them were not claimed, presumably to avoid questions being asked by the police.

There were some other features that made this an extraordinary case. While the robbery was being carried out, two way walkie-talkie conversations took place and they were overheard by an amateur radio enthusiast, a dentist from Wimpole Street. He dialled the police and gave them as much information as he could. Unfortunately, at first, the call was not taken seriously. It seems to have been considered a Saturday night hoax, so the Post Office was not alerted in time to locate the calls. Moreover, when the police did call at the bank while the raid was taking place they did not see anything wrong from the outside and nothing was done.

Our clients, however, were not those who took part in the raid but were two people accused of receiving £32,000 in money that came from the bank. They pleaded not guilty on the basis that they did not know where the money came from and were therefore not dishonest. They were businessmen who did a lot of transactions in cash. They were acquitted.

CHAPTER 7

Starting on the Bench

In 1971, I had to decide what course my future career would take. I had tried to get into the House of Commons three times and the prospects for the Liberal party did not look any brighter than when I began in 1945. This did not mean that my loyalty to the party had weakened. I still believed in the need for it and in its policies especially for Europe and for a new system of industrial relations. I also had to consider what was happening in chambers. I could see no long term future there. Tom Kellock, also a Liberal candidate several times, had come back from the Commonwealth Secretariat. He took silk and also, like me, became a Circuit Judge.

I decided to try and go along the judicial road and applied to be a recorder. This was a new type of judicial post resulting from the fundamental reforms introduced by the Courts Act 1971 which came into operation on 1st January, 1972. I dealt with some of this in my Presidential Address to the Medico-Legal Society in 1987 on "The Work and Life of a Circuit Judge". I still think it is a fascinating story: how this country works and changes are made in its traditional institutions.

It begins long ago with the ending of regional government in England which followed the Norman Conquest. The kings of England were anxious to preserve their authority and maintain the peace. It was thus necessary to have a system of law and hopefully justice, controlled by the King's Judges coming out of London regularly for their sittings or assizes. They went out by different routes to the county or shire towns and established the various circuits of the Bar. They went with the King's commission or command to hear and determine (*oyer et terminer*) and to have appear before them those who were detained awaiting trial (gaol delivery). The latter requirement was the beginning of the writ of *habeas corpus* which still remains an important weapon in the armoury of those seeking the liberty of the subject.

It is often difficult to say with precision when institutions were first established with any firmness or certainty, but it seems generally accepted that it was in the reign of Henry II (1154-1189) that the royal judges regularly went on their assizes. This system which survived for so long was only altered by changes from time-to-time in the assize towns, particularly by additions in the north of England at the time of the Industrial Revolution in the nineteenth century.

It must have been obvious that the itinerant judges could only deal with the important cases. There were magistrates to deal with local matters. They had judicial as well as administrative powers and this was confirmed by an enactment of 1344 in the reign of Edward III. However, there was a gap between matters suitable to be dealt with summarily by local magistrates and major matters dealt with by the judges on assize. The gap was filled by Quarter Sessions (meeting quarterly) based on the county or borough. To them went matters not only of crime but for example, relating to highways. To the Quarter

Sessions a professional element was introduced so the Borough Quarter Sessions would be presided over by a recorder who was a member of the Bar – and where the County Quarter Sessions had such a legally qualified chair, it had an extended jurisdiction.

The continuous increase of population and its transfer from the countryside to towns meant that the system of assizes could not cope in dealing with cases with reasonable or acceptable expedition. After the Second World War, the problem was accentuated by the building of the so-called New Towns, so while there were no assizes at Stevenage or Harlow, for example, they could still be found at Huntingdon and Oakham. If there was no work for the judge to do, he would be presented with a pair of white gloves to symbolise the purity and clean living of the population!

In this country, the pace of reform is often exasperatingly slow and only seldom does law reform bring political benefit to MPs, so it was not until 1966 that a Royal Commission on Assizes and Quarter Sessions was set up under the chairship of Lord Beeching, a former chairman of ICI but more importantly for this purpose, he had been the chair of a commission that led to the emasculation of British Railways, from which it can be argued that it has never recovered. Perhaps the deepest effect was the almost total destruction of the branch lines which were the arteries of rural life. The equally fundamental reorganization of the English Courts of Law did not have such drastic repercussions though over the years, many of the smaller courts have closed and are continuing to do so.

I do not know how far the Legal Commission was dominated by the personality of its chair, but I venture to suggest that the thinking behind the proposals for the reorganization of the Law Courts bears a considerable similarity to the thinking behind the proposals for the reorganization of the railways (though a good deal of this originated from the Nationalisation Act 1947). To put it briefly, power and control were to be gathered into the centre, hence the considerable expansion of the Lord Chancellor's Department (now the Department of Constituional Affairs (DCA)) and the creation of a British Railways Board. Any delegation of powers from the centre was on efficiency and managerial grounds with accountability to the centre. The Railway Companies became regions while the law circuits became administrative units each with its circuit administrator accountable to the Lord Chancellor. The list of assize Towns proposed to be abolished is a catalogue reminiscent of the stations in the Flanders and Swann song, "The Slow Train".

It was against this background that Beeching proposed the creation of Crown Courts with full-time Circuit Judges and part-time recorders. The latter would no longer be attached to specific places. The Beeching Committee reported in 1969 and by accepting the thrust and basis of that report, the Government committed itself to a considerable building programme for the new courts. The necessary legislation dramatically illustrates the absolute power of Parliament, for section 1(2) of the Courts Act, 1971 states, "courts of assize are hereby abolished"; (3), "Courts of quarter sessions are hereby abolished"; (4), "There shall be a Crown Court in England and Wales which shall be a superior court of record". Would that all legislation could be so clear and precise!

With all this going on, together with the reforms which changed the basis for divorce that resulted in much more family work being done in the county courts, it seemed that my application to become a new-style recorder was well-timed. I was not disappointed. Quite shortly afterwards, I was asked to sit as a deputy judge at Kingston County Court. I had no training of any kind and I had no papers sent to me in advance of the hearing. So I arrived in some trepidation of what was in store for me except that I did know from a phone call that I would be dealing with a number of short cases.

So I arrived and when I entered court and everybody stood up, I realised what a lonely place the judge's seat was. There were a considerable number of people including robed barristers and solicitors. I could not see the clerk until he stood up. My general memory is of trying to speed things along so as to finish the list and I have a particular memory of only one of the cases. It concerned a fatal accident. Liability had been admitted but there was no agreement about damages. One of the counsel was Adrian Hamilton, QC who was most experienced in this type of case. He said to me, "I am sure that the court [meaning me] is familiar with the recent guidance given by the Court of Appeal for the amounts to be awarded under the Law Reform (Miscellaneous Provisions) Act of 1934. " I think I remained silent, having helpfully been given the range between which I should operate.

At the end of the day, a man came up to me and said he was observing on behalf of the Lord Chancellor's Department. I had no idea this was being done. He said that he expected I would like to know that he thought I had done well. I do not know who he was but I was pleased and relieved.

A few weeks later, again to my surprise, I was asked to sit at The Old Bailey but I did not have to go there. In view of the number of cases outstanding, some Old Bailey cases were being held in the Law Courts in the Strand. This was helpful to His Honour Judge Edward Clarke QC as it enabled him to go to lunch at Lincoln's Inn in his year as Treasurer. Off the bench, he had a good deal of charm but in court, he was a most difficult judge to appear before, especially for a defence counsel. He would try and take over the whole case and frequently interrupted with rather sarcastic remarks. This was most unfair to young counsel who were trying to do their best and did not have the experience to stand up to him.

However, I was present in court when he had his comeuppance in a very unexpected way. A defendant with many previous convictions went into the witness box. The usher was not present so the judge took over and said, "Take the Oath. You know what to do". Realising that he might have revealed that the defendant was not a man of good character, he quickly added, "You've seen the other witnesses in this case do it. Take the card in your hand and read the words aloud". The man took the card and hesitated. Edward Clarke then said, "Go on. Can't you read?"

"Yes, I can."

"Well read it". After further hesitation, he began to read the oath which the usher swears when the jury retire to consider their verdict, "I swear by Almighty God, that I will keep this jury in some quiet and convenient place ...". There was a verbal eruption from the bench. "You will do no such thing! Put that card down". There were smiles in court but no loud laughter as Edward Clarke was upset that the dignity of his court had been disturbed in this way.

As at Kingston, I had to deal with a number of short matters and fortunately, they turned out to be straightforward. Nobody from the Lord Chancellor's Department approached me but I did have the satisfaction of being told that evening in El Vino's bar by Julian Bevan, a most experienced practitioner in the criminal courts, that the Bar thought I had done all right.

So I had to wait and see what happened to my application. I was soon to hear. I got a letter from Hume Boggis-Rolfe of the Lord Chancellor's Department saying that the Queen had been pleased to appoint me a recorder from 1st January, 1972. I was thus in the first batch appointed under the Courts Act 1971. The Warrant of Appointment, dated 1st December, 1971 was signed by the Queen and Lord Hailsham. I was glad to know that I was "trusty and well beloved". On the South Eastern Circuit, there were twenty-seven appointments of whom four were solicitors. We were sworn in before Mr Justice Eveleigh, a presiding judge of the circuit. I had rather a long wait as it was done individually in order of call to the Bar and my years as a solicitor did not count! I remember I was the last but one. Arnold Russell Vick was the last.

We then had some training, which today, I expect would be regarded as very inadequate. It was before the days of the Judicial Studies Board, and residential seminars were unknown. We had two half days. One consisted of sentencing exercises conducted by Lord Chief Justice Widgery. Like me, he had been a solicitor before becoming a barrister but he also taught with the "crammers", Gibson and Weldon. He was quite school-masterish. When he introduced sentencing exercises for the High Court Judges, there was some opposition. Mr Justice Melford Stevenson, for example, once said in his forthright way, "You sentence off the top of your head. If the man's a shit, down he goes. If there's something to be said for him, you do your best not to put him inside." For the purpose of these exercises, the judges were divided into syndicates and the senior one would be the spokesperson. Melford Stevenson and John Widgery were different personalities. Melford was very impish, often with a straight face. When asked how his syndicate had got on in one case, he replied in a booming voice, "There was a strong minority of one, thinking of twelve years or so. Somebody mentioned probation but he was soon silenced. The remainder were for between three and five years, so we had a British compromise of four. However, out of deference for the minority I mentioned initially, it was agreed that this defendant should suffer an extra punishment, namely, that he should be visited once a week in his cell by Lord Longford". I am sure that the light relief on a serious occasion was very welcome.

The other half-day of our training consisted of lectures. There was one on summing up by Fred Lawton (Lord Justice Lawton) and the other on sentencing by Gerald Hines who was the senior judge at what had become the Inner London Crown Court. He was very knowledgable on criminal law and procedure but made a very bad mistake when he put it around that he was going to be made a High Court Judge. Such things are meant to be kept confidential – or they were in those days. Word gets about, especially in and around the Temple and the London Law Courts, and the appointment was never made.

Thus trained, I was called upon to sit which I did at various county court and Crown Courts on the circuit. I had to sit for a minimum of twenty and a maximum of fifty days per year. I was, therefore, surprised to see from a cutting from a local newspaper in April that I had been sitting in Sutton for three weeks.

A barrister's relationship with the chambers' clerk is almost bound to change when it is known that someone is interested in a judicial appointment—because if the clerk thinks the barrister is likely to get it, the barrister is not a long-term prospect as far as the clerk is concerned. The clerk is therefore, unlikely to push you, especially at the expense of others of similar seniority who are likely to remain in chambers. However, I had no difficulty with Gordon Breadmore and we seemed to carry on much as usual. The only restriction was that I could not appear as an advocate in a court where I had recently sat as a recorder.

I am not sure that I would have benefited from further training, except perhaps, on the civil side where something about the Rent Acts and other property legislation and also about the new divorce legislation would probably have been of help. The jurisdiction of the county court is quite wide. I remember once going to Guildford county court to find out that I was going to try a case covered by the Agricultural Holdings Acts. This was quite new territory for me. Fortunately, I had competent counsel on both sides and the law was straightforward once I had made certain findings of fact.

I soon learned that I must not worry about the cases I had dealt with. Some years later, when I had become the resident judge at the Kingston Crown Court, each year I had to swear in the new magistrates. After this had been done, I would give them a short talk in which I referred to trying not to worry about their last case. If they were doing that, they would not be concentrating on their next case. Magistrates have the advantage over trial judges in that they are not sitting alone and the retiring room provides a great opportunity to clear one's mind.

All the time I sat as a judge, which was over twenty-five years, there was concern about the delays in bringing cases to court for hearing, especially criminal cases where defendants were on remand in custody. A number of times I have been asked for my views and I used to say with as much emphasis as I could muster, that the first thing that was required was a survey of all the courts to find out how often they were used. I knew that some county courts were underused while some Crown Courts had ever increasing waiting times. I suggested for example, that some Crown Court work such as licensing appeals (which did not require a jury or security presence), could be heard in a county court. I ran into a brick wall. The county courts and the Crown Courts were separately administered and got their budgets via the Lord Chancellor's Department whilst the Home Office had certain funding and other vague responsibilities with regard to the magistrates' court matters, until everything was placed under the Lord Chancellor's Department in 1994.

It is not easy to know of one's own reputation. I do not think I was regarded as a "soft touch" but there were times when I was prepared to give people a chance. This was always on the understanding, which I spelt out in open court, that if they let me down and committed further offences they would not get another chance and would be severely punished. I tried to see that a note to this effect was put on the file An example of this was of a prostitute who took drugs and stole prescription forms from a doctor's surgery. She had a bad record of convictions but a headmaster and his wife came from a long distance away to say that they had known the defendant from childhood and were prepared to give her a home. I allowed her to go with them and only hope that she kept out of trouble and was helped with her drug problems. I never heard any more and trust that it worked.

One of the most satisfying things that I found as a judge was to receive letters from people and, sometimes, from a parent telling me how they had got on and were grateful for what I had done. Quite often they were too shy to write or felt they could not write a suitable letter and I would hear about them from a probation officer. There was the other side of the coin and occasionally I would get a letter of protest about a sentence I had passed. I used to acknowledge all the letters I received but only shortly and I would never enter into a debate about what I had done.

I was only once taken to task in the press about a sentence I had passed. It was in the *Western Evening Herald* on 28th September, 1995 under the heading, "Judge Failed the People". I was sitting in the Plymouth Crown Court and I had put a drug addict on probation for threatening another boy if he gave information to the police. I ordered compensation of £100. The article pointed out that he had been on probation before. I appreciated that, but in my view it was important to try and continue the rehabilitation treatment and get the defendant off drugs. The probation service must have been willing to do this otherwise I would not have been able to make the fresh order.

What is important is to have a wide judicial discretion so that the punishment is right for the particular case, balancing the crime, the offender and the victim. It is sometimes a difficult task and that is why a Court of Appeal is important to look again at cases where criticism can legitimately be made of a sentence. It is because cases are so different that I am all against minimum sentences and such matters as "three strikes" and then it's gaol. Take a case I had of a man who had two previous convictions for residential burglary some time ago. He goes out and returns rather drunk. By mistake, he goes into the flat next door, sees something he likes, I think it was an ashtray, and takes it. A few days later, the loser sees it in the defendant's flat. They are not on good terms and the matter is reported to the police. Goodness knows why, but perhaps on the insistence of the loser, a prosecution is brought. As it is a residential burglary, it comes to the Crown Court. I forget what I did, but I expect the matter would have been dealt with either by a fine or a conditional discharge with a payment towards the costs.

The situation is now quite different since section 4 Crime (Sentences) Act 1997 was brought into force in 1999. This provides for a minimum of three years for a third conviction of domestic burglary. The result is so absurd. In the example I have given, a judge would invoke the escape clause that it would be unjust to pass such a sentence "in all the circumstances". These circumstances have to be stated in open court which I hope would not be difficult.

Being a recorder was an excellent opportunity to help decide whether I would like to apply for a full-time appointment. I found I liked doing the work although at times it was stressful. I was less familiar with the civil work except for running down actions, where my experience with Amery-Parkes and Co. was most useful. I found the family work sometimes quite fraught, with embittered husbands and wives. I tried to create a "round table" atmosphere and did as much as I could in the privacy of my chambers. It was easier when there were children as then I could say that whatever their differences as husband and wife were, they were and would remain father and mother – and we had to work out what was best for the children when they went their separate ways.

In civil work too I was a "settler" and tried to get a solution which would avoid the expense and possible acrimony of a court hearing. If the usher told me that the parties were talking, I used to send him back to them with a message of encouragement and that I was on call to help if they thought I could be of any use. In matters of negotiation, I had learned a lot from Arnold Goodman.

In criminal matters, a recorder was under more restraint than a judge but I can conveniently jump ahead to say that – when I was a judge – I was not in sympathy with the guidance that was given about only seeing counsel in private in exceptional cases. Some judges refused to see counsel outside of the courtroom at all. Whenever I was asked to see counsel, I did so to find out what it was about. If I could not help, I soon said so, but sometimes it was useful, for example, to be told that a witness was in an emotional state owing to a recent bereavement.

Unlike some judges, I was prepared if asked by counsel to give an indication about sentence in the event of a plea of guilty, sometimes, to only some of the charges. I would look through the papers and see the defendant's antecedents and any reports. Then I would ask counsel to see me in my room with the shorthand writer present. I did not want there to be any misunderstanding on what was said, particularly by me. If I felt I could, I would say that *on the information before me* (which I would emphasise) I had in mind a certain sentence on a plea of guilty. I would not enter into any bargaining about it. I would then also emphasise that if a plea of guilty was not forthcoming, and the case went for trial, I was not in any way bound by the indication I had given. Then, the sentence would depend on all the evidence and other matters that had emerged during the trial. I knew that there had been some trouble in the Court of Appeal when some judges had not protected themselves in this way. I am glad to say that I was never taken to the Court of Appeal over seeing counsel.

I believed I saved much time, trouble and also anxiety for witnesses. I was told of one case at The Old Bailey where an old lag asked his counsel to see the judge and if he indicated he would give four years or less he would plead guilty, otherwise he would give it a go and plead not guilty. A High Court Judge was dealing with the matter and he refused to see counsel about anything. So a trial took place lasting two-and-a-half weeks. The defendant was convicted and received a sentence of four years. I hope the judge was told how much his refusal to see counsel had cost in time and money.

My practice at the Bar kept jogging along but the quality work was not coming into chambers. I became increasingly sure that I would like to be appointed a Circuit Judge. My appointment as a recorder was for three years from 1st January 1972. I did not know what was going to happen and then I had a letter in 1973, from the Lord Chancellor's Office saying that the Lord Chancellor "had it in mind" to recommend me to the Queen for appointment to the circuit bench. I had to decide whether to accept. I was forty-seven which was rather young and I loved the work at the Bar with its friendships as I did the political scene. However, I remembered one barrister who was offered a judgeship. He asked if it could be deferred for three years or so. He was never asked again. I do not know the circumstances. Perhaps, the Lord Chancellor had changed or a note was not made on the file. I regarded this as a cautionary tale. I discussed it, of course, with Joy. The salary was then £9,750 but there were favourable pension provisions, some books and a health insurance scheme with BUPA. I was expected to sit for 200 to 210 days each year and possibly more. Despite the prospects of earning considerably more at the Bar, Joy and I agreed that I should accept, which I did. I had to move fast as I was asked to sit from 2nd April. So, having told Dingle Foot and Gordon Breadmore, the clerk of chambers, off I went to the robe and wig makers to get kitted up.

I had made one of the most important decisions of my life and I can truly say that I never regretted it. In the widest sense of the word, I enjoyed life on the bench but at the beginning, I missed life at the Bar, especially the discussion of cases with other members of chambers and their experiences with judges and other barristers. We were helpful to each other. The bench was quite different. You were in sole control of your court when it was sitting. To a great extent, you created the atmosphere and the pace of the proceedings. The new judge must feel a sense of some loneliness and that it why I enjoyed going to the larger courts where I found lunch with the other judges most valuable. Problems could be talked over. The senior judge could make announcements about something that was going to happen or had happened. In and around London, I knew which judges were approachable and, sometimes, I would ask about something that had caused me anxiety. I was never rebuffed.

The county court was different. Often, there were two judges sitting in one place; sometimes, I was by myself. Some county court judges would do their best to finish their list by lunchtime and they often succeeded. The golfers were particularly good at this. Most played fair and would offer to help the other judge if his or her list was going slowly. Some did not. A certain Judge, Judge A, was well known for getting away and leaving the other judge, who varied, to carry on. One day, Judge B had a long case with QCs on each side – which was unusual in the county court. As soon as he saw the names of the parties, Judge B realised that he knew one of them and could not do the case, so he suggested that he and Judge A exchange their lists. There was considerable opposition but the QCs could not be turned away, neither could the parties, so the exchange was carried out with some ill will.

Judge B did not know all the local people like Judge A did, so his list went rather slowly. When he rose for lunch, he asked his usher to see how Judge A was getting on. The usher returned and said that everybody had gone home. Judge A knew the QCs, had them in his room and the case was settled by 11.00 a.m.! I was told this story by Judge B who thought it was not his lucky day!

It was an important day for me when I was sworn in by the Lord Chancellor, Lord Hailsham, in his room at the House of Lords. I went together with Joy, our two daughters and Gordon Breadmore. It was a short ceremony in which I took the judicial oath. The Lord Chancellor gave brief congratulations, had a friendly word with everyone and that was it. We went back to lunch at the National Liberal Club. There were some nice photographs in the local press and I was encouraged by the number of letters I received, wishing me well. It was particularly good to hear from people with whom I had lost touch over the years.

I found that when I was first appointed, I was like a travelling reserve around the circuit. I quite enjoyed this as it enabled me to see how other courts worked and to learn from experienced judges. I did not often have to be away from home though once I sat for a week at Ipswich. I was able to see Joan and Trevor Knott who lived at Felixstowe. Joan had been a Liberal candidate in East Anglia and represented that part of the country on the Party Executive when I was chair. Trevor had an interesting job designing and marketing protective glasses for industrial use. It is good for a judge to meet people with different occupations and interests. I was always a bit worried about Joan when she was a candidate as she had to drive many miles alone at night after the political work was done. There were no mobile phones in those days but I suppose that the roads were safer then and there were fewer high-jackings and muggings. Anyway, she never had any trouble.

My talks with Trevor Knott and others made me realise how wrong is the suggestion that judges live in ivory towers divorced and sheltered from what goes on in the world. Of course, in my time, many judges had served in World War II or done National Service. That apart, judges—and especially circuit judges—really are concerned with life in nearly all its aspects. All sorts of people appear in court from highly educated, sophisticated fraudsters (not excluding Old Etonians!) to very poor and illiterate people who got engaged in awful, sometimes perverted, violence. Language has to be unrestrained in order to recreate past events as accurately as possible. This sometimes shocks people coming to the courts for the first time.

I found that I enjoyed the drama of the criminal courts, although the civil courts are more intellectually stretching, and generally more likely to involve a decision on some point of law. I liked to have the mixture of work and it was fortunate that I had enjoyed a mixed practice at the Bar. I was given more criminal work and in 1975, I was asked to sit regularly at the Inner London Crown Court. I quite welcomed this as I knew the other judges and the staff. It was not a bad journey to Newington Causeway, not far from the Elephant and Castle—though all journeys whether by car or public transport in and around London got worse as the years went by. As at the Bar, you could not be late. I was only late twice during my time on the bench. Once by about ten minutes at the Law Courts in the Strand when traffic around Parliament Square had come to a complete standstill and once by about half an hour when going to Woodford when there was a recent accident and no traffic diversion in operation.

•   •   •

At Inner London, I got great help from the judges and not just in court matters. Henry Elam invited me to go to a Dining Club called Our Society. This met at the

Piccadilly Hotel. After the hotel changed hands, the society moved to the Imperial Hotel, Russell Square where it has remained, largely due to one of the directors, Richard Walduck, who is a justice of the peace and keen on the legal matters that we have at our meetings. Our society has an alternative unofficial name of "The Crimes Club". It is not used officially as it might lead to misunderstandings! The membership is limited to seventy-five and consists mainly of lawyers, doctors and writers. A dinner is followed by a speaker. Sometimes a recent case is discussed. The proceedings are private. The Society was founded in 1903. One of the earliest members was Sir Arthur Conan Doyle. Of the present members, the oldest is His Honour Alan King Hamilton QC who is now over 100 years old. He attends regularly and is generally the first to ask a question! He once got up and said something like, "I remember this case, I was there throughout as I was the judge's Marshall". I think it was some sixty years ago and he was able to amplify, though fortunately not contradict, a number of points that the speaker made, who was not at the trial but had done a good deal of research.

Then, Judge Paul Layton asked if I would be interested in joining the Medico-Legal Society. He invited me to a meeting at the Royal Society of Medicine which I must have found interesting as I decided to join. After that, I regularly attended and learned a lot, especially from the doctors. I much admired the patience and skill of the forensic doctors who do so much to solve crime. One remarkable character was Doctor Julius Grant, a forensic scientist independent of everybody, who had his own laboratory. After graduating in chemistry at Queen Mary College, London, he was one of the first qualified scientists to be employed in the British paper industry by the firm, John Dickinson. This was in 1931, but it stood him in very good stead over fifty years later because in 1983 he was asked to examine what were claimed to be the Hitler Diaries. Despite the contrary views of historians and publishers, he had little difficulty in declaring them to be forgeries. The paper used was not available at the time of the entries! Less well known, is that earlier, in 1967, he came to a similar conclusion about diaries said to have been made by Mussolini.

Julius Grant was very kind to me. I think he liked to talk to someone who wanted to hear and learn from what he said. He had a long and active life, dying at the age of 89. I felt flattered at being asked to give the address at his thanksgiving service in Gray's Inn Chapel in 1991. I was somewhat hesitant because I had not been professionally associated with him and only knew him during his latter years. However, his wife, "Michael", was very insistent and I felt I had to do it. What I did not include was that once I was told about a piece of wood that was an exhibit in court. Examination revealed that it had 109 coats of paint on it. Before I could get any further, Julius Grant said, "A piece of theatre scenery" — and he was absolutely right!

Unlike Our Society, the Medico-Legal Society does publish, in the *Medico-Legal Journal* (excellently edited for many years by Diana Brahams), an account of its proceedings as approved by the lecturer. I have already referred to one dramatic incident when an account was given of the death of the Bulgarian, Georgy Markov on Waterloo Bridge. There were many other interesting meetings. I was elected to the council of the society in 1977. The president is elected for a two year term with the two professions alternating. In 1985, the president was Professor Hugh Johnson from Guy's Hospital, but he sadly died the following year and I was asked to succeed him. I was not sure about a judge taking this on, though I knew that some had done so but not for some time. I also knew that Lord Hailsham had strong views on what judges should and should not do, so I wrote and got clearance. The first meeting was called "Up in Smoke-The Psychology of Arson", which passed off without any untoward incident! A varied programme had been set up including a "Top Cop" (Geoffrey Dear) on "Public Order" and a "Top Silk" (Robin Simpson QC) on "Confessions: Their Reliability". I got some praise from some older members who were pleased that they could hear me when I took the meetings. I took particular care to ensure that the questions from the floor were heard and if necessary, I would repeat them which meant that the speaker had a little more time to consider his answer!

I had one other dining club that I enjoyed taking part in and still do. It is the Whitefriars, which claims to be the oldest surviving dining club in Britain. It was founded in 1868 by a group of journalists and limited to forty people, who have a weekly dinner on Fridays. Guest speakers began to address the club in 1896 and that tradition has continued unbroken. In 1880, a veteran operatic tenor called Donald King was elected. As a boy, he had sung at the coronation of George IV in 1822! Winston Churchill was a member and, as a young man, took the chair for Lady Randolph Churchill who was the Guest of Honour at a Ladies' Night. Other members were Thomas Hardy and H. M. Stanley while Mark Twain was an honorary member. The members are known as Priors and the dinner chairman (who varies) is known as "The Prior of the Day". After the loyal toast, he proposes the club toast which commemorates "The Whitefriars of old". It also refers to those "Who, broken by fortune, dwell in Alsatia". This often puzzles guests. Alsatia was a haven for down-and-outs between the Temple and Blackfriars. I was first taken to the club by my pupil master Joseph Dean. It used to meet in the Cock Tavern in Fleet Street but after the newspaper industry moved away, its dinners have been held in various London clubs including the Athenaeum, the Arts Club and the Saville. Like all clubs, the Whitefriars has had its ups and downs but it is now on the up again with a new committee and chair, a solicitor, Brian Lincoln, and secretary, Mary Baum, who have succeeded in getting good and interesting speakers which is the key to success.

I have been very lucky in that Joy with her knowledge and keenness for politics and the law has frequently been with me at the functions of all three these dining clubs.

• • •

After a year, mainly at Inner London Crown Court, I was asked by Judge Richard Vick whether I would like to sit at Kingston-on-Thames on a regular basis. I had always liked Kingston, it had a good bar mess and the food at County Hall was rated some of the best and reasonably priced around the London courts. I am sure this helped to create a good atmosphere. County Hall could only accommodate two courts and an occasional third in a rather small room. Opposite was Weston House where the court was held in the conservatory. This was closed after having been visited by Harry Woolf when he was a presiding judge of the South Eastern Circuit. Four new courts had recently been opened in Kingston in a building in Canbury Park road conveniently near the railway and bus stations. It was a disused warehouse and its main claim to fame was that it had belonged to the Hawker aircraft company and parts for the famous Hawker Hurricane fighter plane in World War II had been made there. Hawkers had a big factory nearby at Ham. With the completion of the new courts, more judges were needed and that is why Richard Vick spoke to me.

Apart from anything else, Kingston was only some five miles from Richmond and it was a convenient journey for me through Richmond Park, apart from winter evenings when it was closed. In 1976, Kingston Crown Court extended to Guildford where there were two courts. There was also a court at Surbiton. This arrangement was not easy to administer and sometimes a lot of people were in transit. It was always a risk to transfer a case from one venue to another when the defendant was on bail!

The arrangement lasted until 1986 when a new four court building at Guildford was opened by the Duke of Kent who was—and still is—the Chancellor of Surrey University. I was by then the resident or senior judge at Kingston and invited to go to the opening in that capacity. Lord Hailsham was in his second term as Lord Chancellor. The judges, in full ceremonial kit, were lined up in quite a small room to be presented to the Duke and Lord Chancellor. The Duke was first and asked me, I thought rather surprisingly, if Kingston would continue now that Guildford had been built. I wonder if anybody had briefed him because he could have had no idea of the backlog of cases and the necessity to have a considerable building programme to try and cope with it. When Lord Hailsham got to me, aided by his walking sticks, he asked where I was sitting and when I told him it was Kingston he said that it was there that he had his greatest humiliation in court. He was determined to tell me and anybody else in earshot all about it. He began by asking me if I knew Lord Justice Singleton. I said I did. Lord Hailsham then said it was Surrey assizes and he was prosecuting a case of gross indecency. When he had finished his opening address to the jury, Singleton shouted out from the bench, "Mr Hogg, where's your corroboration?" Answer, "I have not got any". The judge, "Well, that's the end of this case. The defendant is found 'Not Guilty'". At this point, Lord Hailsham burst out into loud laughter. Meanwhile, the Duke of Kent had long since got to the end of the line and was beside a wall unable to go anywhere until the Lord Chancellor moved. He did, after a time, quite impervious to anything else that was going on.

Years later, at a Surrey Law Society dinner in Chancery Lane, I found myself sitting next to Lord Hailsham, who told me the same story again and he enjoyed it just as much. It was a bit embarrassing because he kept turning and talking to me and taking virtually no notice of the president of the society on his other side, whose great evening it was. I think I was the only person there whom he knew, but when his turn came he gave an excellent hard-hitting speech. I always remember one remark, "The difference between a professional man and a tradesman is that the former has sometimes to give unpalatable advice while the latter never denigrates his wares in the market place".

I thought it was unfortunate that the resident judge at Kingston, Richard Vick, usually sat at Guildford. It suited him as he lived at Godalming but although he was always helpful when asked he could not easily keep in regular touch with the other judges and have a united policy. There were also problems between Surrey and Greater London. We had some Surrey police cases and some from the Metropolitan police. The magistrates' courts were also divided in this way. Many of the difficulties were eased when the separate Guildford courts began to operate but there were still some difficulties as the police and county boundaries did not coincide.

The police are very conscious of their own "patch" and any vehicle from another force entering it was supposed to give information about itself. This could result in strange and unforeseen incidents. A great supporter of the police was the comedian, Tommy Trinder, who was a favourite speaker at police functions at which he would usually be given a present. He told me he had thirty-nine truncheons! He was asked to go to the one-hundredth anniversary of the Met at the Festival Hall. He accepted on condition that he did not get another truncheon! He was assured that as it was a special occasion, he would get something different. In due course, he was presented with a sword. At the end of the proceedings, he said to some police that he could not go to Waterloo Station carrying a sword. They agreed to take him home. He lived at Walton-on-Thames just beyond the boundary of the Met with Surrey. So, with the sword in his hand he got into the police car. Two policemen were in the front seats but when they crossed the boundary, they did nothing. The car was spotted by a Surrey Police patrol car which stopped them: "Hello, hello, what have we here?"

"Tommy Trinder and a sword."

"Oh, yes? Let's have a look."

Tommy then got out and was instantly recognised. He got home without any further trouble. He was a great supporter of Fulham Football Club and I remember having a long chat with him about old players some of whom like Bobby Robson and Jimmy Hill have had distinguished careers in the game after their playing days were over. Tommy knew a lot about the players whom I remembered and what had happened to them. He was genuinely interested in the club. I do not think he would be best pleased to know that it is now controlled by Mohammed Al-Fayed and that the ground may be sold for development into flats. The site by the river near Putney Bridge must be extremely valuable and desirable. There has been talk of Fulham sharing Stamford Bridge with Chelsea. I hope this does not come about for the sake of both clubs.

I got on well with the other judges at Kingston but it was soon apparent that the new courts at Canbury Park Road did not suit me. There was no natural light and they had an air conditioning system which often failed. One end of the building would be hot and the other cold with a strong draught blowing throughout. By the afternoon, I would be parched and get a headache or migraine. I was not the only one. Judge Arthur Mildon QC was another sufferer. I felt I could not continue like this. For one thing, a judge has to concentrate and hear every word of the proceedings. So I sought help and got myself transferred to the old assize and Quarter Sessions court at County Hall. It was built in 1893 and was very impressive. It was closed after the new courts were opened in 1997 and is now used for filming legal TV series such as "Cavanagh QC " and "The Bill". It is owned by Surrey County Council and as it is a Grade I listed building I do not think it can be used for anything else. One sad thing is that the splendid Royal Arms which were behind the judge's chair have been stolen. Of course enquiries have been made but nobody knows anything about it and no clues have emerged. I wonder if and when and indeed where it will turn up! I think this should be a treasonable offence!

I was lucky in that when I arrived at Kingston, the chief clerk (now known as the court manager) was Fred Treasure. I first came across him when he was with the Metropolitan Police Solicitors' Department. I used to see him around the London courts, especially Inner London and The Old Bailey. When that department was wound up with the creation of the Crown Prosecution Service, Fred joined the Lord Chancellor's Department. I hope they realised how lucky they were to get him. However, the trend was not to have people with legal experience but to have experienced administrators from other Government departments. I have already mentioned Judge Edward Clarke QC sitting at the Law Courts in the Strand. One Monday, when he arrived, there was a clerk to greet him who said he was new. "Where have you come from?" asked the judge, expectinq to hear the name of some other court, but the answer was, "From the Ministry of Agriculture and Fisheries". So, an increasing number of the staff were not legally qualified or had legal training except for courses within the department. To create a similar working set up to other Government departments was, in my view, mistaken. It was clear that the judges did not fit into it. This was bound to cause friction because they were given no control over how the courts were run. The size and allocation of the staff was not their responsibility. The administrative functions of the county court registrars, for example, were removed and they retained only judicial duties. They were later called District Judges (County Court). Fred Treasure once told me that he had no authority to order pencils and paper!

What I did not like was the downgrading of the court within the system. I always regarded the clerk of the court as the "eyes and ears" on whom I could rely to help put on an efficient show. Soon a judge was to have no regular clerk and after the court started in the morning they wanted to leave and do bills of costs, known as "taxation". I used to stop them doing this without my permission and I wanted to be satisfied that, if they left the courtroom, an experienced usher would remain. This was coupled over the years, with a considerably reduced police presence and the privatisation of the prison delivery and dock service. Meetings of judges made protests and I know that successive Lord Chief Justices made representations about it, but to no avail. The hand of the Treasury was not far away. It was sadly, therefore, no surprise to us when one day a man leapt forward at The Old Bailey and attacked Judge Ann Goddard. She was very brave about it but it must have been most frightening. It was after I retired and I only hope that security has improved—but that should have been done long ago.

One of the first private firms to transport prisoners to court was Group 4. Unfortunately, there were some escapes which got publicity. I wrote a letter to

The Times asking what had happened to Groups 1, 2 and 3. I was sent a reply saying that they had never existed because the name was the result of an amalgamation of four companies. Apart from escapes, there were problems with late arrivals at court. The vans had to make calls at a number of different courts around London and the journeys were often during the hours of heaviest traffic. Kingston did not fare well. Once, two defendants were put in a cell at Canbury Park Road. They were not collected at the end of the day and were forgotten. The van arrived very late to find the whole building locked up. The fire brigade was called and the men were released to be taken to Wandsworth Prison

All this was witnessed by a court reporter who heard a commotion when he was in a nearby pub and — being a keen reporter — went to see what was going on. He did very well out of it. He was retained by a local paper but when he got anything in the nationals he was paid "lineage" that is, so much for every line that was printed. I knew that the *Daily Mirror* made a big "splash" out of the story. I never heard that the prisoners claimed anything for wrongful detention but people were less litigious in those days.

Having been active politically, I was conscious of the press when I was on the bench. I knew what havoc they could do in reporting an unguarded remark. I also knew that they could be helpful in reporting comments of general public interest. A judge can call for things to be investigated or put right. I always knew when there was a reporter in my court as it did affect what I would say — or not say!.

There was an occasion when the press greatly disappointed me. About twelve reporters from national newspapers came to report a case where a scoutmaster was accused of acts of indecency with some of the scouts for whom he was responsible. Rather run-of-the-mill stuff in the *News of the World*, I would have thought. The first business of the day was an award I had made, I think of £100 each, to a married middle-aged couple who had behaved with great courage. Looking out of their front window, they saw a group of youths trying to seize a mountain bike from a young boy. They went outside and remonstrated with them. After a few moments, the wife returned to her home and rang the police who came very quickly. The youths ran off leaving the bike behind. Some, but not all, were caught. I thought this was worthy of a press story as an example of taking a deliberate risk to prevent crime. For all the couple knew, the youths or some of them, may have had concealed weapons. I told my clerk to alert the press about what was going to happen. None of them came into court until the scoutmaster's case began. I expressed some disappointment but I had the last laugh. As the case was concerned with events in Kingston had already had some recent local publicity, I allowed an application that it should be tried at Guildford with a Jury drawn from that part of the county. Meanwhile, I ordered that there should be no further publicity about it. The press were not exactly best pleased but I was sure that I had acted in a way that would ensure the fairest possible trial.

I took the view that judges should be prepared to enter the public arena and not be figures of sanctimonious mystery. This was not shared by the older judges at Kingston such as "Bertie" Wakley and John Ellison. The former, very politely, asked me if I thought it was right to address Richmond Rotary on "The Life and

Work of a Circuit Judge". I did it knowing that the press would not be present and a press report approved by me would be issued. The Rotarians were pleased with my visit and asked a lot of questions about how judges were appointed, and my views about criminal cases, on juries' verdicts, the role of a barrister and so on. I got useful feedback from some people who had done jury service. The waiting about seemed to be the strongest complaint. Thus encouraged, I later spoke to the West Thames Branch of the Institute of Directors. However, these were rare occasions and more often, I would be asked to speak at functions for those more directly concerned with the law, such as magistrates.

John Ellison did not engage with the press at all nor was he concerned by it. I once told him of a report in a newspaper of a case he had tried but he was quite indifferent to it. He was a forthright man who said exactly what he believed. He lived at Egham and dealt with a number of cases concerning the women at Greenham Common who mounted a lengthy protest against the storage of nuclear missiles at the USA air base there. He had no sympathy with the protest and once addressed a protester by saying, "Madam, when you got to the top of the perimeter fence, instead of climbing down and getting into the base where you had no right to be, it would have been in the public interest if you had fallen backwards and then, you would have landed in the river Kennet". One of the Sunday papers had the headline, "Judge Tells Protesting Woman to Fall into the River". The trouble is that an indifferent attitude can lead to unfortunate remarks made on the spur of the moment getting reported and showing the judiciary in a bad light. This is especially true of remarks made to or about women in sex cases and sometimes they can cause great anger and distress.

Another judge who was very much his own man and usually sat at Knightsbridge, was Sir Harold Cassel. He described himself as "the world's worst judge". Once he gave bail over the lunch adjournment and said, "Don't let me down or I shall look a proper Charlie". The man absconded and a headline the next day was, "Judge — A Proper Charlie!".

I tried to learn from these episodes and to praise people when I could, such as a 17-year-old shop assistant who was very vigilant when three men came in who turned out to have bad criminal records. She cleverly stalled until the manager came after she had been presented with a stolen cheque card. The police were called and they were arrested.

I was very worried when a severely mentally impaired man had to spend six months in prison because a hospital bed could not be found for him. His condition had deteriorated while in prison which did not have the facilities to cope with him. There was also the effect on the other prisoners. I remembered the advice I had been given by Lord Rea when I wrote to the Lord Chancellor, Lord Kilmuir, about the state of the Privy Council Judicial Committee, namely, "Go to the top". So I wrote to the Health Secretary, Virginia Bottomley whom I had met, most urgently and said, "It is quite clear that he should not be in Wandsworth prison any longer". I knew that she had been a psychiatric social worker and chair of the Lambeth Juvenile Court. I am glad to say that she did intervene and the defendant was assessed by a psychiatrist and sent to a hospital for an indefinite period after having been found unfit to plead. A press report helpfully added that the case had highlighted the shortage of beds for mentally ill patients in London. Apparently, two patients were often competing for one bed.

In a rather different way, I was able to draw attention about alarms on sale to the public to use when they were personally attacked or about to be. I was dealing with a case of a serious indecent assault on a student coming home from a party about 3 a.m. She had a personal alarm which went off — but it sounded like a car alarm so people who heard it did nothing. I suggested that the police should consult with manufacturers on a way to make the alarms sound different. I did have a letter from a manufacturer so I was glad that some notice had been taken of what I had said.

Another matter of violence was the attacks that were being made on cash-point customers of banks and building societies. I suggested that special cubicles should be provided rather than that the customers be on the street. Of course, nothing can be completely safe but if the transaction is made in a cubicle at least the money can be put away before leaving. The *Sunday Express* carried a feature article and a report for ICL Financial Services revealed considerable public anxiety about street transactions. Some of the reactions from the banks and building societies, I thought, were rather lacking in understanding for the victims. They indicated it was a small problem. That may be true numerically, but I am sure that they would have commented differently had they been in court to listen to the suffering that some of their customers had been through.

Perhaps the most serious case I dealt with of danger to the public concerned a man who broke into a signal box near Clapham Junction railway station which could not have been manned. He started switching signals between red and green and according to the prosecutor, the railway network was brought to a virtual standstill for four hours. Very fortunately, there were no accidents or damage but what might have happened was almost too appalling to contemplate. It may be that the fortunate outcome was due to the fact that the defendant rang Waterloo control headquarters and said, "I have control of the trains. I am playing at creating a major disaster". I praised two telephonists at Waterloo and awarded them £100 each for taking the call calmly and keeping him on the line until he had been located.

It was no excuse that the man had been drinking heavily and had a history of depression. Not surprisingly, I took a very serious view of what had happened and the great potential danger to the travelling public. I passed a sentence of five years' imprisonment. However, I had made a mistake. I had exceeded my powers. This was not pointed out to me at the time. The charges were of endangering the safety of railway passengers, which had a maximum of two years, and of causing small scale criminal damage to the signal box. The defence lawyers checked the position and brought the case back to me for the sentence to be varied. This can be done within 28 days. So I had to make a reduction to a total of 30 months which I thought was quite inadequate. No judge can keep all the maximum sentences in his head, but I should have checked it myself and, if I may say so, counsel were not on the ball either.

One of the troubles is that our criminal law is now almost wholly statutory and is "all over the place". The Law Commission began to draft a criminal code which it added to from time-to-time but nothing has been done to enact it, although the present Government has mentioned creating such a code, so additional Acts are passed piecemeal with considerable frequency. These days, we seem to have a Criminal Justice Bill every year—sometimes several times a year!

The variety of cases in the Crown Court is very great but, for the moment, I want to concentrate on violence. There has been a great change over the years. I know it can be simplistic to talk in generalities but people do seem to have shorter fuses and less sense of humour and fun. I have known serious violence take place over whether the victim was trying to jump his turn at a bar or whether he or she had looked rather fondly at another person's partner. One trouble has been that far too often it has not deteriorated into fisticuffs but a knife has been produced. This was happening so often that in 1994 I gave what the *Evening Standard* called a "chilly warning" after dealing with a case at Kingston where a man had armed himself with a meat cleaver. I said, "South London cannot become an armed camp of people going around arming themselves. Those who carry weapons are often tempted to use them. Warnings have gone out in a number of courts, including this one, over a number of years that people must not arm themselves with weapons."

I did not do this lightly but I did not want it to be felt that I had overstepped the mark and I wrote to the then Lord Chief Justice, Lord Taylor, expressing my concern at what was happening. I was glad to have had an understanding reply and assurance that the Court of Appeal was aware of the seriousness of the use of weapons.

It is said, with perhaps just a touch of truth, that the attitude of a Circuit Judge to the Court of Appeal changes over time. At first, he is anxious and respectful, then he is indifferent and finally he believes he was right and they were wrong! I remember that during my first year, Fred Lawton (Lord Justice Lawton) asked me how I was getting on. I told him I had been knocked down on sentence a couple of times. He told me not to worry. What they were worried about was "that shadowy judicial figure, the under sentencer". In those days, the prosecutor had no right of appeal against sentence. Now, under the Criminal Justice Act, 1988, the Attorney-General can refer certain serious cases to the Court of Appeal if he considers that the sentence was "unduly lenient" and the range of cases was considerably extended in 2003. This happened to me once when sitting at The Old Bailey. I passed a sentence of eight years on a man for buggery and indecent assault. He pleaded guilty thus saving the witnesses the ordeal of giving evidence. The Court of Appeal increased it to eleven years. I wonder what they would have given if the case had been contested. They must have been thinking in terms of fifteen years. I was not convinced I was wrong!

Circuit Judges are often a bit annoyed when their sentences are reduced by small amounts. The Court of Appeal has very often said that it only reduces a sentence when it is considered to be "manifestly excessive". What happens in practice is often rather different and I expect it results from the compromises that are bound to happen from time-to-time with an appeal court of three judges. What was being done was known as "tinkering". I remember once being a bit upset when a sentence I had passed of eight years was reduced to seven. I told the then recorder of London, Jimmy Miskin, about it during the pre-lunch drink and asked what I should do if I had a similar case again. He put his hand on my shoulder and said, "Dear boy, next time, you give him nine years, the Court of Appeal will reduce it to eight and that's what it should have been in the first place! " I was duly comforted and, perhaps, learned not to take myself too seriously.

However, I do remember why I felt as I did. It was one of those cases that are remembered because it contains facts that are unusual. The defendant was an experienced airline pilot and after he had landed at Heathrow, he had a rendezvous with another man to whom he handed a bag. They had been under surveillance, presumably, to use the time-honoured phrase, "as a result of information received", otherwise known as a tip-off. The bag contained about ten kilograms of heroin. The pilot pleaded guilty to possessing a controlled drug with intent to supply. This was on the basis that he believed that what he was bringing in was cannabis. I heard him give evidence about this and it emerged that he was going to receive about £7,000 for agreeing to act as a courier. I took the view that nobody would be paid that amount for bringing in around ten kilograms of cannabis but it did make sense for that quantity of heroin. I was able to weigh up all he said and I disbelieved him. As I was entitled to, I tried this issue myself without a jury. I thought that for a pilot to do this was very serious and gave him eight years. The Court of Appeal upheld the manner in which I had dealt with the case but said that they did not think I had given enough credit for the plea of guilty and that the defendant had given evidence for the prosecution in the trial of the other man, which I knew and took into account. Putting these two factors together, the Court of Appeal thought that seven years was the appropriate length. There was no mention of eight years being "manifestly excessive"!

There seem to be two approaches depending on the composition of the Court of Appeal. One is not to interfere unless it is thought that the sentence was beyond the range of what was appropriate even if the sentence was a severe one; the other is to see what is thought to be appropriate. I have one transcript which refers to "longer than was necessary". In that case, four years were reduced to three. A similar result occurred in another case where the defendant was thought to have been "slightly over-sentenced". This can be contrasted with a case where four years was upheld. "Four years in this case was at the top of the bracket. Other judges might have given a lesser sentence. But we certainly cannot say there was anything wrong in principle in the sentence and it is not so high that we ought to interfere". Perhaps, I may, at the risk of "gilding the lily", include another quotation, "On the one hand, the sentence is not manifestly excessive or wrong in principle. Putting it in the context of sentences which have been imposed in similar cases, it appears to be in line with them". They then said there was some personal mitigation and reduced the sentence from two years to eighteen months!

There was considerable pressure by the Home Office for sentences to be reduced because of overcrowding in the prisons. Lord Lane and his deputy, Tasker Watkins, always denied that this was the reason for what the Court of Appeal were doing.

Unless Circuit Judges are quite impervious to these things, it is good for morale when they get approval from the Court of Appeal judges, who do examine cases with the greatest thoroughness and care. Counsel will make every criticism they can of a judge's summing up to try and persuade that court that the cumulative effect is that the conviction should be quashed. In my day, the test was whether there had been a "material irregularity". It has been changed to "unsafe". Another change which I regret is the abolition of what was called the "proviso". This meant that the Court of Appeal, if it found that there was a material irregularity, did not have to quash the conviction if it felt that notwithstanding the irregularity there was satisfactory evidence to justify the conviction. This meant that it had the power to look at the matter broadly and come to what it thought was a just solution. It can, however, order a re-trial but I am not an enthusiast for this. The witnesses have to come to court again, usually many months later and then often be questioned on the basis, "Do you remember the last time, you said so and so? I have got the transcript here, why have you changed your evidence now?"

I am glad to say that it was only very occasionally that I had convictions quashed because I had made a mistake. I was not lucky with cases concerning animals. Apart from a budgerigar which my younger daughter once had, we have never kept animals: no dog, no cat and I have very rarely ridden a horse or shot at anything. I had a case where a man on opening the door to a policeman, said to his dog, "Kill that man!" or words to that effect. The dog rushed at the policeman, knocked him over and bit him. The prosecution case was that this was done deliberately. The defendant denied any criminal act or behaviour. At the end of the evidence, I discussed with counsel whether there was another way to put the case, namely, that the defendant had been reckless. The Court of Appeal were doubtful whether I should have intervened in this way but, having done so, they were not satisfied that I had explained sufficiently to the jury what being reckless involved — and so the conviction was quashed.

The other case was a civil one. A horse had jumped over a gate and got on to an adjoining road near Heathrow Airport causing an accident to passing traffic. I held that the keeper of a number of stables near the road was liable for negligence. When the matter went to the Court of Appeal, it soon became apparent where its sympathies lay. They were all with the keeper of the horse: "What more could he do?", "The gate was padlocked", etc., etc. So the appeal succeeded.

However, I did succeed in getting another animal case half-right. Again, it was a civil case and in the High Court. It concerned a horse that had bolted during the carnival at Birchington, Kent. The horse was pulling a wagonette and the two occupants were injured. The driver was the first defendant and he accepted my finding of negligence against him. Two floats behind was a Wild West Association group who let off a cannon. This disturbed the horse but he calmed down and was able to start with the procession. Unfortunately, a cadet drum and bugle band struck up from an adjacent street. They got nearer the horse which reared up and bolted. The second defendants were the organizers of the carnival. I held that they were also negligent and were thirty per cent to blame. The driver, in my view, had to bear the main responsibility and this was not disputed on appeal. I felt that the organizers were at fault in not finding out what the bands were doing, where they were going and when they were going to start to play. The bandmasters were not given any instructions.

The Court of Appeal held that the band had started playing before they had joined the procession and the main organizer, who was very experienced, had not known this happen before. They also held that he had given adequate instructions to the Wild West Show and the letting off of the cannon was in contravention of them. So the result was that the organizers were absolved from blame and the driver of the wagonette became one hundred per cent responsible for the claim. I do not know how much that was as I only dealt with liability.

I had another case which involved a horse and whether I got that right will never be known. It was an appeal from the Richmond magistrates' court to the Kingston Crown Court and there was no further appeal which would have been limited to a point of law. The case attracted considerable publicity.

The offence alleged was "wilfully riding a horse at a pace greater than a hand canter". The events took place in Richmond Park. In the magistrates' court, it was alleged that the horse had galloped up a hill at 30 m.p.h. A press report was seen by a Mr Charles Harris, aged 75, who was a graduate of the Spanish Riding School at Vienna. He had a lifetime's experience of horses. He was amazed at the speed alleged and thought there must be a "miracle horse" so he went out see it and the hill it went up. He thought the horse could probably do only about five miles an hour because it would not be able to get its legs in sequence to do a gallop up the hill. It was not suggested that Mr Harris had any connection with the defendant. I thought it was very impressive that he came forward and gave evidence.

From the moment that I knew that I was going to hear this appeal. I thought it was wise in view of my almost total ignorance of equestrian matters to do a little homework. It was obvious that the expression "hand canter" would be discussed. I knew it was a pace between a trot and a gallop. The prosecution described it as a pace which was "sedate and collected". What I found out which was interesting, though I do not think it was of any practical use, was that the word "canter" was short for "Canterbury trot" – the speed at which pilgrims were supposed to proceed towards Canterbury. The appeal was allowed.

There was a curious sequel. The defendant went off with a number of press reporters and photographers to Richmond Park to provide a "photo opportunity". After doing a couple of canters and starting a third, the horse got fed up, started moving quickly and was pursued by a dog. Two police officers in a Land Rover followed and stopped her for speeding! I do not know what was said but she was cautioned and the matter went no further. In court, I described the law as "archaic" and recommended that it should be changed. When I was writing this book, I went to the notice board at the Richmond Gate of the Park and found the Royal Parks and Other Open Spaces Regulations 1997 displayed, but owing to condensation, they were largely unreadable! A very nice man called Joe Scrivener, arrived in a Land Rover. He had recently started working in the park, having been at Kew Gardens and offered to help and find out how fast a horse could be ridden in the park. He established that it was still at "a hand canter", so my efforts to bring about a change here have not been successful.

At first, I was a bit of a judicial "Jack-of-all-trades". I did not mind that, although it meant that there was quite a bit of reading to do to keep up-to-date. Parliament was particularly active in changing the law of divorce. There were many lengthy debates in both Houses. The Roman Catholics, of course, held strong views against what they considered to be further relaxation of the sanctity of marriage and family bonds. Others wanted to move more rapidly towards divorce by mutual consent regardless of blame and behaviour. As might be expected, in the end, the Divorce Reform Act 1969 was a compromise between these views. In one way, there was a radical shift in that there was only one basis for divorce, which was that the marriage had broken down "irretrievably", but this could be shown in five ways of which only two were completely new. Adultery and desertion were familiar grounds to the courts while "unreasonable behaviour" was in reality a diluted form of cruelty. The new grounds were, continuous separation for two years with the respondent consenting to the divorce or five years' separation when consent was not required. The law was moving away from matrimonial fault. Once one of the five grounds was proved, the court concentrated on the division of property and the future of the children.

Property matters were often successfully negotiated by solicitors though sometimes there could be bitter disputes, but the judge had full control over matters concerning children. He had to have a statement about the proposed arrangements for them and be satisfied about these or that they were "the best that could be devised in the circumstances". Often, happily, the parties would present joint proposals for custody and access and the approach of the judge would be to agree with them if he could. One parent, usually, the petitioner, would attend the hearing which would be in chambers. In a minority of cases, there would be no agreement and the judge would have to hear and determine the matter. Often, these cases were bitterly contested between the parties, though sometimes wealthy parents would seem to be competing in their generosity towards their children. Care had to be taken to explore all matters such as remarriage, accommodation, health, education and the dangers of splitting children between parents.

In nearly all contested cases it was necessary to have a report of a divorce court welfare officer. He, or often she, would be specially trained and hopefully experienced in exploring all aspects and presenting a report with recommendations. I was acutely aware of not appearing to rubber stamp the recommendations, though to differ from them required very close and careful reasoning. I found that the difficulty was that these reports were bound to take some time. A number of people had to be seen and fully interviewed. When to see children and what to say to them was particularly difficult.

I found that the welfare officers were hard pressed. Some had an excessive case load. It is an example of where Parliament and the courts had provided a course of action to be taken but adequate resources were not available. The situation is one that has impressed itself upon me most strongly and I am going to give other examples of this which are not exhaustive.

I have referred to court staff and security arrangements but other matters also stem directly from the work of the courts. There has been great controversy in recent years over whether prison "works". I have always felt that generalised arguments about this were not helpful. "Works" for whom? Who should be in prison? What should happen in prison? These are just three of the many questions that could be asked. It is not for me to examine these questions — at any rate in this book — but over the years, I have visited a number of prisons and institutions for young people. What has struck me is that much more should be done to provide work for prisoners. When I made enquiries, I used to be told that there were objections from trade unions. I can appreciate anxiety about forced labour but to work and to have payments made on release or to go to prisoners' families seems to me to be far better than confining people to a cell to vegetate for many hours in the day.

I have twice visited Coldingley prison, a so-called industrial prison, in Surrey. Of course, the prisoners have to be carefully selected. I saw one workshop where metal signs were being made. If any quarrel or tension had broken out, some tools could have caused severe damage. Another group was working in the automated laundry where quick movement and control were needed. On one visit, I asked the governor if any prisoner had tried to get out of Coldingley and he told me that nobody had tried but added this amusing story.

The laundry takes linen from hospitals including ones for mental patients. One day, the Governor was approached by a prisoner running across a courtyard and asking him to come at once as something very serious had happened. He then added, "Somebody has tried to break into our prison!" The Governor went to investigate and found that, when the incoming laundry baskets were being unloaded, one was very heavy indeed. It was opened up and inside was one of the patients from a mental hospital! He was detained until the return journey was made but not, I hope, in a laundry basket with clean linen!

The prisoners were well-behaved because they did not want to go back to where they had come from. When I talked to a group of them, the main grouse was about the decisions concerning parole. They were made without any reasons being given. There was strong feeling that some had got parole who did not deserve it and the reverse also applied. I believe that this situation has now improved and the law has been clarified about eligibility for parole depending on the length of sentence. There is less discretion.

One other improvement is the regime for those prisoners who are coming to the end of long sentences. They are allowed out for home visits and to seek jobs if they have not got one for when they are released. It is a position of trust and discipline to return when the leave is over. There have been some abuses, including a man I had to deal with who read adverts by prostitutes whom he then visited and was violent to. In addition to being punished for any new offence, he would have to serve the balance of the old one.

The treatment of young offenders has caused much anxiety and differences of opinion. Over twenty years ago, William Whitelaw, Home Secretary, introduced the "short, sharp, shock". This was a short sentence of, say, two months where there was rigorous physical exercise which was done in the style of army "square bashing". The difficulty was that the muscularly strong came out stronger while the timid and weak became worse. I always favoured the Borstal ethic which focused more on training. I remember once going to

Huntercombe and seeing a group of lads being taught how to build a brick wall. Sometimes, they could get a City and Guilds qualification.

I have been told that the discipline and concentration of music is a good therapy. However, it was in an adult prison, Wandsworth, that I once saw a group walking along with musical instruments. The assistant governor told me that they had a class once a week. After a few moments, I heard a most terrible rendering on the trumpet of "Oh, Come All Ye Faithful'. It was nowhere near Christmas so I suppose that the message was thought to be of general application to Wandsworth Prison!

The difficulty with providing training is that it costs money. There have to be the facilities and the teachers. Such money as there is has to deal with the continuous problem of overcrowding and being able to provide basic facilities starting with accommodation and reducing the sharing of cells.

It is the same story with what is now the National Probation Service. After I became the resident judge at Kingston, in 1982, I became a member of what was then the probation committee for South West London and served until my retirement in 1998. Throughout that time, I was struck and impressed by the ability and conscientiousness of probation officers, especially those in the field dealing with their clients. They were grossly overworked and understaffed. The result was that often they were not able to make contact frequently enough. The work requires understanding and much patience. Some people on probation[1] try and see how far they can go without being taken back to court, for example by missing appointments and failing to get work. This is particularly important with people who are on probation with a condition of treatment for drug addiction. They may get in a mood when they just cannot be bothered. Then they get desperate for money.

The lack of funding of the Probation Service is a serious matter if alternatives to prison are to be viable and successful. I will give one example. Some years ago, a dedicated probation officer tried to help young tearaways who had been put on probation and were dotty about cars. He got hold of some old bangers that worked, taught the lads how they functioned and how to drive safely and sensibly. I was told that this scheme was a considerable success. However, it had to close through lack of money.

The time of probation officers was often taken up with having to prepare reports for the court and to go to court to help with the decision of whether a probation order should be made in a particular case. When I first started, it was done most informally. The judge would see that the duty officer was in court and ask him or her to see the defendant. He would come back later in the day and have a discussion with the judge. Sometimes, further inquiries would have to be made but often a probation order was made on the day. Then, it was thought that the matter should be dealt with more thoroughly so the case would be adjourned, usually for three weeks for a written report. This was often several pages long giving lots of family background and explanations for behaviour.

---

[1]   The former probation order and similar orders such as that concerning drug treatment which I mention are now replaced by and subsumed with a new-style 'generic community sentence'.

At one time, they often contained sociological jargon which was rather fashionable but wordy and, I think, sometimes American-inspired. I remember once reading, "William is the epitome of the sibling deprivation syndrome". This meant that he has suffered a bit from being an only child! I am glad to say that this trend had declined by the time I retired. I admired the thoroughness of these reports but they must have taken hours to compile and I did wonder how this fitted in with the shortage of staff.

A considerable pressure on the resources of the Probation Service came about with the introduction of community service orders (CSOs) by the Powers of Criminal Courts Act 1973. Very briefly, a court could make an order for a defendant to do unpaid work in his or her spare time for a minimum of 40 hours and a maximum of 240. He or she had to consent. The reason for this, Gerald Hines explained in an answer to a question from me at his introductory lecture after my appointment, was that, otherwise, there would be a breach of the laws of slavery! I was an admirer of this scheme. For many offenders, custody was not the answer, a person doing the work would have to turn up on time and do the work properly. This is a useful discipline and the work would be something of use to the community. [2]

So the Probation Service had to find what work there was in the locality, then it had to see whether a defendant was suitable for work and if so, what work and how he would fit in with others. It needed a great deal of organization to set this up. Special training was required for selected probation officers. I used to go to the local community service centre and also visit some of the projects. I recall going to a scout hut at Kew which was being very well refurbished. The floor especially, was excellently done. Apparently, one member of the team was very good at doing this but his order was due to expire before the work could he finished. There was some anxiety whether he might commit another offence and get some more hours to do! However, to his considerable credit, he came back voluntarily to complete it. I have been told that this is by no means uncommon

I had to take part in some discussions which I thought were rather unnecessary but some magistrates, in particular, regarded as important which was whether community service was an "alternative to custody" or whether it was a sentence in its own right. The issue went to the seriousness of the offence and the history of the offender which had to be considered before an order could be made. My approach was not so analytical and I suppose I invoked something of Melford Stephenson's principle of sentencing off the top of one's head, but not quite. If prison or detention was not inevitable and a fine was not adequate punishment, then it seemed to me to be proper to consider community service. I always gave a pretty severe warning about the consequences of failing to comply with the order and that custody would follow a breach unless there were quite exceptional circumstances. I hoped that this would remain in the defendant's mind and, indeed, that a probation officer would remind him of it when there was any problem such as lateness without excuse.

---

[2] CSOs are also now part of the generic community sentence: see last footnote. A "unpaid work requirement" can now be ordered for up to 300 hours, similarly curfews, electronic tagging etc.

Yet more responsibilities came to the Probation Service with the introduction of curfew orders and electronic tagging. There have also been considerable organizational changes involving centralisation and at one stage even some threats of working to rule. The prisons are overcrowded and the number of custodial sentences that the courts pass increases every year. If this trend is going to be reversed, then community penalties must be seen to work and not be regarded as a soft option.

•   •   •

After I had been on the bench for six years, I sent the Lord Chancellor's Permanent Secretary, Derek Oulton, a memo on my work and experience as a circuit judge. He was a very approachable man whom I first got to know as a fellow parent at St. Paul's Girls' School. He was appreciative and certainly understood the problems of the backlog of cases and how the Crown Court was burdened with cases of the utmost triviality. One of the factors that contributed to this was the extensive right of electing trial by jury on matters of dishonesty, including as once happened in Court One at The Old Bailey, of theft of one can of shandy! I wrote again in 1983 after ten years of the Courts Act and made a number of similar points. I did have a written reply and also a full talk at the House of Lords. Certainly, there were some improvements in reducing the backlog of cases and Lord Lane initiated what he called "the blitz". The experiment was made at The Old Bailey to have extra sittings starting, I think at 5 p.m. but it did not work and was later tried in other courts, especially magistrates' courts, with the same result. It often takes a lot of people to get together to start a court and London is an increasingly difficult place to get into and across but I shall refrain from commenting about the Congestion Charge!

I have written about some of my experiences with the Lord Chancellor's Department as a result of referring to the shortage of Divorce court Welfare officers and others who have an important role in the work of the courts such as probation officers. I was particularly worried about the lack of resources for family work. At Kingston, there was a centre where access visits could take place. It was very important for children to keep in touch with the parent who did not have day-to-day control. It was used when there was no other suitable place for these visits. There were great difficulties in keeping it going and providing the necessary furniture and equipment in order to make the visits take place in reasonable surroundings and atmosphere.

When I began, the family work was rather different from now as regards the hearing of divorce petitions, because in nearly all cases, the petitioner had to attend and give oral evidence to prove the ground for divorce. Sometimes, this was an ordeal, especially in cases of "unreasonable behaviour". Often, there was a long history of abuse and violence. I tried to cut this sort of distressing evidence to a minimum and briefly take over from counsel with a comprehensive question and then say that I was satisfied. Nobody ever objected. The names of the cases were published and the press kept an eye on the lists, especially in the Law Courts in the Strand. Often photographs were taken of well-known people or their spouses as they arrived or left court.

The cases did not take long though judges varied considerably in the speed with which they dealt with them. I tried to be quick but also courteous and help as best as I could when people began to get upset. However, the number of hearings was dramatically reduced by the introduction of the so-called "special procedure". What happened was that the papers would be looked at by the registrar. If there was no defence or admissions had been made, he had to see whether the petition had made out a ground for divorce. If so, he would give his certificate. The case would be put in the judge's list and the names of the parties would all be read out in open court. The judge of the clerk would indicate that these were cases to which the special procedure applied and ask if there was anyone who wished to be heard apart from on children's and property matters — which would be dealt with later in chambers. Very occasionally, there would be such a person. The most usual reason was an objection to paying costs. The judge would make some inquiries and if he could deal with matter on the spot, he would. Otherwise, the petitioner would have to be notified and an appointment made for another date. Once a man put up his hand and when I asked him what he wanted to raise, he replied, "I turned up for my wedding and I think I ought to turn up for my divorce". I think I said that he was quite entitled to do that. Once anything had been dealt with, the judge pronounced decrees of divorce or annulment but they were not final until all matters were concluded.

The special procedure was known as the "quickie divorce". I must say that I have had doubts about it. If marriage is a solemn and important event, I think it should only be ended with some formality that shows the importance of the occasion. If a judge is understanding and courteous, I believe that the party who is asking for the marriage to end should come to court. If there are children, he or she has to come anyway and the two things can be done on the same day. I hope I dealt with children's appointments in a helpful way. I was always willing to see a child in my room without a parent but usually with the welfare officer present. I remember one bright boy of about ten telling me that everybody else had been asked about his future and he would like me to hear what he thought about it. He was not precocious but thoughtful and I was very glad he wanted to come. I am sure I did my best to help him.

I would like to mention just one curious experience that I had in the Family Division. In the days when oral evidence had to be given by the petitioner, I came to the Law Courts and when I looked at the list of cases in my court, to my astonishment, I found that one of the names was that of a tutor I had at Oxford! I resisted the temptation to look at the papers and told the clerk that the case should be transferred to the judge in the adjoining court and I would take one of his. I thus denied myself the opportunity to tell anyone interested in my activities at Oxford that I was an undergraduate who had divorced his tutor!

In one sense, I did not enjoy doing family work because of its emotions and I had not myself had an upbringing with both my natural parents, but I believed that I could do the work in a satisfactory way. I think I was only once overruled by the Court of Appeal and they kindly stressed that the circumstances had changed after I had dealt with the case.

I was, therefore, a bit disappointed to receive, out of the, blue, in July 1991, a letter from Mrs Justice Bracewell, who had been appointed a judge of the Family

Division the previous year, having been a circuit judge since 1983, which told me that my name was not among those sent to the Lord Chancellor to do family work. The explanation was that the Children Act 1989 was due to come into force in the following October and that cases would "be dealt with by judiciary who by reason of their experience and training are specialists in family work".

In my reply, I told her that I had been doing this work since 1972 but was doing less and could not regard myself as a specialist. I therefore, resigned from the Family Courts Committee for South West London and said that as there was often only one judge sitting in a county court, I would no longer do any county court work. It would be quite impractical to be absent on the days when family work was being done and emergency family applications could arrive at any time.

I was much more upset about what happened to the judge with whom I shared a room for many years at County Hall, Kingston, "Bertie" Wakley. He really was a family specialist after starting off by doing some criminal work as well. Whenever I was in the divorce courts, he seemed to be there and was a long serving member of one of the best sets of divorce chambers, as they were called, in the Temple. One day, he told me that he had received a letter from Mr Justice Cazelet who was many years his junior. He was clearly upset and it was in similar terms to the one I had received from Mrs Justice Bracewell. Perhaps, the task was divided alphabetically. I can only hope that "Bertie" was thanked for the outstanding service that he had given but he did not mention that he had been. He was nearing retirement, which makes the way it was done more unpalatable.

As far as I was concerned, I never wanted to be entirely a criminal lawyer. I do not know whether it was a coincidence but, just at this time, I received a letter from Mr Justice Alliott asking me to sit in the Queen's Bench Division of the High Court for half a term.

In the Queen's Bench Division, I was conscious of going up a gear. By and large, the cases were more weighty than in the county court and I found that the quality of counsel was obviously higher. The work was varied. I seemed to be given quite a number of personal injury cases but the range was wide. When a case was settled — as a number were — on the hearing day, the judge would be asked to wait while enquiries were made at room 100 (not room 101 which would have pleased George Orwell and perhaps Paul Merton).[3] This was the power house of the Law Courts from where all the cases were allocated. Sometimes there was nothing further to do and one could get and read the papers for the next day which was helpful. At other times anything could come alonjg, usually with a message like, "Mr Justice Blank presents his compliments and says that his present case is going very slowly and could you please take his next case". It would be difficult to decline! I once got involved in a libel case which concerned questions of what one side should disclose to the other. I was glad to have specialist and experienced counsel in front of me. I was also glad to recall, though it was some years ago, some of the things I had learned when I

---

[3] A reference to the futuristic novel *1984* in which Orwell described the room at party headquarters that contained the most hated or feared object for each person who entered; later borrowed by the TV presenter Paul Merton as the place to which guests consigned their most hated items.

was a solicitor with Goodman, Derrick and Co. It is surprising what comes back when one has done something oneself.

Some kind friends asked if I was being tried out as a High Court Judge but I knew this was not so. I had not taken silk and I did not have a civil practice of any quality. In fact, I was happy to be a circuit judge and not having to be away from home for long periods in different parts of the country and staying in the judges' lodgings. I shall always remember a High Court Judge coming up to me as I was going to a reception in Gray's Inn. He had been a circuit judge. I did not know him very well but he was always congenial and friendly. Out of the blue, and I do not know what prompted it, he said, "John, of course, it may never happen, but if you are asked to be a High Court Judge, my advice to you is to refuse". He then briefly compared the two lives. I know that some people like the status and the automatic knighthood and some wives like being a "Lady", but Joy has made it clear that it has never troubled her! She is not that sort of person. To be missing her own home in Richmond and the musical life of London are just two far important things than a "K".

We once had strong confirmation of our view when we were at a dinner and Lord Denning was in a group chatting away as he so often did and finding out about people. He turned to me and said, "Where are you sitting now?" I replied, "Kingston".

"And where do you live?"

"Richmond".

He then turned to the group, pointed to me and said in a loud voice, "He's got the best job. He's got the best job. " I was very flattered and a bit embarrassed because he did not explain what it was and speculation could have been very wide of the mark. It was a comfort, however, to know the great man's reaction.

So I was increasingly at Kingston Crown Court, though I enjoyed the challenge and stimulus of the High Court civil work which came to an end in an unexpected way. After I retired and was sitting part-time, I got a letter pointing out that my appointment to sit in the High Court had ended. This was because the legislation that permitted Circuit Judges to sit as High Court Judges did not refer to deputy judges, which was now my status when I was asked to sit. I thought this was rather a literal interpretation and I wondered what Lord Denning would have thought of it. I can hear him saying, "Does he do a good job? If so, let him sit." Alas! He had died by then and the matter was not one for the Master of the Rolls.

● ● ●

So for the last two years I only did cases in the Crown Court. This had been my main diet throughout my time as a judge. I have already referred to some unusual cases but I would like to mention a few more to show the extent of the work and the knowledge of different worlds that I experienced.

Nobody should enjoy sending anybody to prison but occasionally there are people who have behaved so badly that they deserve it—appalling violence, for example, upon helpless victims such as young children. Some cases did affect me emotionally and great care must be taken when sentencing not to get wound up.

In really terrible cases, I was minded to say that many people would think that the defendant ought to be flogged and receive a small amount of the suffering he had caused to others. Of course, there would have been a great outcry and it would not have been helpful, least of all to me!

In certain cases, the judge sentences with a heavy heart — the serious isolated lapse, perhaps due to drink, by an otherwise decent citizen, for example, causing death by dangerous driving — but others, with a feeling that it is thoroughly deserved. One of my earliest cases concerned unlawful harassment of tenants by a landlord who was the defendant. He had acquired two houses and both were occupied in flats by elderly ladies who had been in them for many years and were protected by the Rent Acts. If he could get vacant possession, he could either sell them or let them at greatly increased rents. His conduct included removing built-in cupboards, blocking lavatory drains, moving a gas cooker and refrigerator into the garden, coming and shouting abuse and so on. There were three charges. Each had a maximum of two years. I sentenced him to a total of two years with payments of compensation to each victim and payment of costs. Apart from one minor conviction, many years previously, he was a man of good character and I treated him as such, otherwise the penalty would have been more. I wish I could have done something about the fact that once he got rid of the tenants the properties were worth five times more than what he paid for them. I am glad that Parliament has since extended the law with regard to benefits and proceeds resulting from crime with a Proceeds of Crime Act 2002. The case went to the Court of Appeal and as this was my first one, I was glad to be upheld especially, as the Lord Chief Justice, Lord Widgery presided.

My usher, Stan Salmon, was very moved by this case and he often talked about it. He lived not far away. He was an old newspaper man and looked through the papers with a trained eye. Some years later, he spotted reports about the defendant who was stepping into his car when a bomb exploded. He was not seriously hurt but what interested us was that in one report he was described as a wealthy property dealer who had had disputes with his tenants and this was thought to be a revenge attack.

Stan Salmon was an interesting character. He had served in the Navy, including being a writer in the aircraft carrier *Illustriou,s* though he never revealed what he wrote! After the war he went to South Africa and joined the *Cape Times*, which was very courageous and outspoken in its opposition to apartheid. I think Stan was a compositor, but whatever he did he always retained his British passport. He was in South Africa for some ten years and then a dispute occurred at Johannesburg airport where I had the incident with customs that I referred to in *Chapter 4* about my passport. Stan refused to become a South African citizen and left the country. When he returned to England, he was getting on a bit. He was a bachelor and decided he would not go into Fleet Street so he joined the court Service. He was rather a special usher and took great pride in running the library. He liked everything to be "ship shape". I think we were some fifteen years together. I was pleased that he got the British Empire Medal when he retired.

His aim to do everything properly was illustrated one Monday morning when I arrived in my room. He got my things out, it seemed in the usual way, but he came in and said, "Your Honour, I have not put out your deaf aid this morning because you are in the middle of your summing up and you do not need it to listen to yourself"!

A category of person for whom I had no sympathy was the dishonest postman. He or she is in a position of trust to deliver the mail. Some thefts were very mean such as children's birthday cards which might contain money. There could be quite serious repercussions if any important document or payment was not received. It is a good thing that other ways of communication and transfer of such items are increasingly being used.

Technology too, though, can create its own misuses. I did one of the first computer fraud trials. It would not be right to set out the time details especially as I have got no report of the case to look at and would have to rely on my memory. Briefly, it concerned one of the big banks and it had to have a team of people in it. A customer was invented and given a name. I recall that it was "Jones"; although the branch concerned was not in Wales, there were a number of Jones holding accounts in the branch. Everything was set up with false entries for phantom payments in exceeding the actual withdrawals, so that the manager did not have to chase any overdraft or unsatisfactory balance. When cash was withdrawn, it was divided among the participants. This fraud went undetected for some time and it came to an end through complete chance. The auditors in a spot check selected this account to look at and the whole set up was revealed!

CHAPTER 8

A Sporting Chance

I think it is important that a judge's diet of cases is varied and the computer fraud case is totally different from harassment of tenants. If a judge is given a succession of similar cases, especially of a violent or sexual nature, his emotions and revulsion can lead to a lack of balance and judgement. I remember appearing for a defendant in a rape case at The Old Bailey. He was one of a gang, I think of three or perhaps four lads, in a car with a girl going home after a night out. My client, on any view, was not as involved as the others. When I started to say something on his behalf and mentioned that while all matters of rape were obviously serious, this case was by no means one of the most serious, the judge exploded and said, "This is the seventh consecutive rape case I have tried ..." and went on to deliver a general attack on the morals and behaviour of young people. Fortunately, including for him, the sentence was one that was not severe and there could be no grounds of appeal.

I would have had no hesitation in making a very strong attack on the observations of the judge who, in my view, showed that he was not in a proper state of mind to sentence anybody. However, the fault really lies with the system that allowed him to spend his time dealing with only one class of sensitive case. It is a difficult task to try and grade types of human behaviour. I have already mentioned in the previous chapter some instances where the victims were vulnerable—as in the harassment case—but one of the worst cases I had concerned three people who ran two homes for the severely handicapped and mentally disordered. They were prosecuted under the Mental Health Act 1983.

The charges were either of ill-treatment or neglect. There were appalling allegations of humiliation and degradation as well as violence. I will not go into details, but the maximum sentence I could pass was two years imprisonment or a fine or both. At the end of the case I repeated something which I and many other judges had said previously, "There is an urgent need for Parliament to provide a comprehensive review of the courts' sentencing powers". I am glad to say that this was reported in the national press but the need for action remains. The case went to appeal. Complaints were made that I had not stressed sufficiently to the jury the time gaps between the events, the interviews and the evidence and also, that I had not dealt fully enough or explained the significance of telling lies. The complaints were rejected and the appeals against the sentences I passed also failed.

Knowing the wide press and public interest in the case, I thought carefully about what I should say when I passed sentence. I have never wanted to sound pompous but I had to show that I was aware of the sufferings of the victims but appreciated the difficulties of those running homes for the handicapped. I was very pleased that my remarks were approved by the Court of Appeal in quite a lengthy extract which I will set out because I hope it illustrates the way I think judges have from time-to-time explained their decisions to the public. This is what I said:

> Those who are concerned with and have the responsibility for running homes which look after persons who are mentally handicapped or deprived in some way, have to show great patience and understanding to cope with people who, through no fault of their own, can be extremely difficult and sometimes they have to be physically restrained and, perhaps, for a time, removed from the company of others. I understand, I hope fully, the difficulties, but the primary aim of those who have and take on such responsibility must be to see, as far as possible, that the residents lead as happy and contented life as they can within their limitations. Physical contact must be limited in either helping the resident or restraining him or her when necessary. Physical punishment and any form of humiliation or degradation cannot be allowed. I can understand how people in charge of such homes can become frustrated, exasperated and indeed, provoked, however, what has happened in this case goes far beyond acceptable conduct.

It is sometimes good to have a case which provides humour, at any rate for part of the time, but care must be taken to see that the proceedings do not degenerate into a music-hall in which various performers try and make the best jokes. Sometimes, the situation itself provides welcome light relief. Once, I had to adjourn a case at the Old Bailey for eight minutes because the jury, understandably, were laughing so much. The *Daily Mirror* and the *Sun* both reported that I was also laughing and chuckling. What happened was that an officer from the vice squad was giving evidence about visiting three addresses which were said to be brothels. He went altogether five times. The alluring advertisements were answered and he then went into the premises. When it was clear what was going to happen, he made an excuse and left. Once, after some playing about, he got up and said, 'NO!" and walked to the other side of the room. The girl then said, "F— me, I've never had a bloke refuse that before!" Other times he pretended to be very shy. When a girl produced a vibrator, he asked what it was! I did wonder whether public money was being best spent in this police operation but I thought it prudent to leave any comments to others.

I have press cuttings of a variety of cases. One I am going to mention because it is an exception to a general rule about which I have remained very keen. That is, never to represent oneself unless it is something very straightforward indeed, such as giving an explanation for not having a TV licence. It is sometimes expressed in this way, "A man who acts for himself, has a fool for a client".

So, always, I tried to persuade people to be represented by a barrister and if I could, I would grant legal aid on the spot. Often, the case would then start later in the day and sometimes would turn into a plea of guilty because the defendant had accepted legal advice that he had no defence. In a criminal trial particularly, the reason is that a defendant in person is at a disadvantage. First, in being able to frame and ask questions of prosecution witnesses and secondly he or she has to "put his or her own case", as it is called, to witnesses. In other words, he or she has to challenge the evidence that is disputed and put it to them. This is not easy. Many defendants in person make long statements. A judge must help as much as he can, say by rephrasing a question so that it is clear to the witness, but he cannot conduct the case for the defendant. Secondly, if there is something good to be said about the defendant, it is not easy to do it oneself without giving the impression of bragging. Thirdly, if the defendant calls witnesses on his or her own behalf, he or she has to question them in a certain way. He cannot "lead" them by putting words into their mouths.

The exception was the one time notorious criminal John McVicar who came before me in June 1996 on a charge of assaulting his neighbour. His last appearance in court had been eighteen years previously. Since that time he had been helping to run a youth club in the East End and written extensively, having studied sociology and taken a degree. The case I had was not a complicated one. McVicar went around to a neighbour to complain about the neighbour's dog which had bitten him. According to McVicar, he wanted to show his neighbour his bitten hand—and so he raised it. He was probably somewhat angry and the neighbour mistook the gesture, thinking he was about to be attacked. A scuffle broke out and the neighbour got the worst of it. The neighbour's account was simply that McVicar came to the door, said something and went for him. So McVicar's case was self-defence. He cross-examined the prosecution witnesses very well. I allowed him to sit in the well of the court, so that he could have his papers conveniently by him. It would have been awkward in several ways, if he had remained in the dock, especially as he had a solicitor acting for him. From time to time, they spoke and although I could not hear what they were saying I believe that the solicitor played a crucial part in the case by prompting McVicar, but not excessively, so that he did not leave anything out. Of course, the solicitor could not help when McVicar gave evidence himself or in the way he made his final speech but I expect he put the points together. Anyway, McVicar did it very well with a nice touch of irony when he told one of the police officers that he ought to be out catching armed robbers! The jury were out for just over two hours and then returned a verdict of "Not guilty". I thought it right to say that he had presented his case "sucessfully, with great skill and ability". After that, he was quite exhausted. He did not want to make any comment or see the press. He declined to go on TV that evening. We had to get him out by a back door and he was whisked away.

One little consequence was that a day or two later, the court received a card for McVicar. It was from a prison and when it was held up, you could see the words, "We are sorry not to be able to welcome you back!"

As a judge, I had to be quite removed from party politics but I was the same person who had been very active in the Liberal Party and I was proud of my basic liberal principles. It was never suggested that I had acted in anything other than an independent way but now I have retired I think I can reveal that I did get undisclosed pleasure when I could find that an official or government department had exceeded their authority and I could uphold the claim of an injured individual or company.

One such case occurred in 1978. It concerned Radio Jackie, which was a local community station which had been broadcasting in south-west London since 1969. As far as I knew, I had never listened to it and therefore, had no view about its programmes so I could not be criticised on that score. It was called a "pirate station" and was campaigning for them to be legalised. It had a transmitter in a field at Malden Manor, Surrey. I do not know how long it had been there but the Post Office raided the site and tried to grab the transmitter during a broadcast. What the *Daily Telegraph* described as a "running battle" took place and a Post Office employee was convicted by magistrates of assaulting a Radio Jackie engineer. His appeal to the Crown Court was dismissed because I had no difficulty in holding that under the Wireless Telegraphy Act 1949 the Post Office had to get a court order before it could seize equipment. There was no such order in this case.

Sometimes, cases are remembered years later by chance. It was in 1989 that an old friend of mine from Oxford days, Edward Grayson, was at Kingston Crown Court. He was making a rather special and successful niche for himself in the realm of sport and the law. He was a keen sportsman but while at Exeter College had sustained an injury during a football match that ended his playing days. He therefore became a spectator and writer about sport and in particular its relationship to the law. He became enthusiastic and knowledgeable about the days of the amateur gentleman. His hero is C. B. Fry who excelled at cricket, athletics and soccer. If he had not been injured, he would also have got a rugby blue. Edward never tires of telling me that C. B. Fry went to Wadham College as I did.

Edward told me that he was preparing an article for a forthcoming publication called *Medicine, Sport and the Law*. I told him that, a little time back, I had dealt with a case in the Epsom County Court for damages claimed as a trespass to the person, for injuries caused in a football match. Edward, with his customary zeal, got the case from the court archives from which it emerged that I had dealt with it in 1983. It concerned a head butt which caused a broken nose and black eyes. I awarded the plaintiff £400. I expect it would be much more to-day. Digging up the case enabled it to be put in the article and compared with others that Edward got hold of.

Kingston is not only near Twickenham but also near other places where first class rugby is played and as a result I had to deal with two cases of violence on the rugby field which got considerable publicity and they are interesting because they produced different results. I wrote quite fully about them in 2001 in the *Sport and Law Journal*, which is published by the British Association for Sport and Law. Here, I will deal with them much more briefly and from a more general view of how I dealt with them in court. I knew about rugby although I had not played since my time at Wellington School. However, I had watched at Richmond where I was a member and had also been regularly to the Old Deer Park in the 1970s during the hey-day of London Welsh.

The first case concerned a well known player, Gary Rees, the captain of Nottingham, who had played for England, the Barbarians and a World Team. He had never been sent off or even cautioned. He was accused of inflicting grievous bodily harm on Stefan Walter Marty. It should be noted that it was not alleged that he did this with intent which is a much more serious offence.

After Gary Rees had entered a plea of "Not guilty", I had a meeting in my room with him and the barristers and solicitors in the case to see what was the best agreed procedure that we could adopt. We had to bear in mind that on any jury, as nearly always selected at random, it is likely that the majority would not know much, if anything, about the rules of rugby which are complicated and have been changed over the years, especially the line out. Rather than go in for anything hi-tech, we decided that the simplest course was to have an old fashioned large blackboard and easel. Fortunately, a lot of the facts, especially those that led up to the incident, were not in dispute and prosecuting counsel used noughts for one team and crosses for the other. I was much helped by both counsel, Messrs Jeremy and Giret. The game was a so-called "friendly" as all rugby games were before leagues and professionals were established, between Nottingham and London Irish. It is not surprising that there were no video or photographs. For what happened and the issues, I can briefly quote from my article:

> There was a line out on the side of the pitch where the stand and almost all the spectators were. The other side was open with just a handful of people along the touch line. The London Irish won the ball which went to their scrum half. He did not on this occasion pass the ball to his fly half as he had been doing during the match but kept it himself and started to go up the blind or narrow side in front of the stand. What happened to him does not matter because meanwhile, to put it neutrally, Rees who was at or towards the back of the line out, became entangled with Marty. Both were back row forwards known as "flankers". How this arose was the crux of the case. Marty's solicitors put it as a "deliberate violent act" while Rees said it was an accident that occurred during lawful play. Marty was a schoolteacher and his injuries were summarised as: "Broken jaw; one wisdom tooth removed; jaw plated, teeth wired, broken nerve in jaw".

It was helpfully admitted by the defence that these injuries, in law, amounted to grievous bodily harm. The court was full of blazers and rugby ties. I had to create the right atmosphere. It was a serious occasion, especially for Gary Rees. I did not want the proceedings to become either acrimonious on the one hand or flippant on the other. I had to avoid such expressions as "blowing the whistle". I did have to intervene when Gary Rees during his evidence, made some comments about the All Blacks and stop him because the New Zealanders were not in court to defend themselves. The defence called an impressive number of character witnesses from the world of rugby and I expect they much helped the jury to return a verdict of "Not guilty". I thought it was a very evenly balanced case that could have gone either way.

One consequence about which I was uneasy was that statements were issued by Gary Rees and also, I believe, by his solicitors to the effect that the case should not have been brought and the courts were not the place to deal with such matters. I thought that this was somewhat unfortunate and, perhaps, unfair on Stefan Marty. There was no offer of compensation and no disciplinary hearing by the Rugby Football Union (RFU). In his evidence, Marty said he thought negotiations were taking place, but when nothing happened he thought he had no alternative but to go to the police and launch a prosecution.

I would like to say a bit more about this when I deal with the second case which concerned a Gloucester player, Simon Devereux, who was playing in a second fifteen game against Rosslyn Park in 1995. Again, the case concerned a single punch causing, this time, a double fracture of the jaw resulting in the victim spending five days in hospital. The dentists had some difficulty in getting a successful alignment of the jaws which made eating difficult. Again, the defendant was free from any disciplinary trouble in the game and called a number of impressive character witnesses.

However, the cases had important differences. Simon Devereux was charged with inflicting grievous bodily harm with intent together with the lesser charge, omitting the intent, which Gary Rees had faced. The proceedings began with an application by defence counsel, Heaton-Armstrong, to remove the case from Kingston to what he called a "neutral" court. The game was played in Richmond Park. I refused that as the Kingston jurors came from a wide area in south-west London and Surrey, but I allowed Heaton-Armstrong to look, in confidence, at the addresses of the panel of jurors. He did not take the matter further.

This time, the facts were hotly disputed. The prosecution version was that after a bit of a fracas which the referee stopped and then awarded a penalty, the Rosslyn Park captain, James Cowie, was walking back when he sensed someone behind him — so he turned his face and felt a tremendous punch to the jaw. He left the ground in a wheelchair. The defence was that Cowie was acting aggressively swinging his arms around. Devereux felt threatened and punched him in self-defence. There was thus, no question of accident. The jury came back in less than two hours with a verdict of "Guilty" on the much more serious charge which has a maximum penalty of life imprisonment. The punishment is usually quite a lengthy term inside. The blow was not an act done in the heat of the moment during a violent flare up in the game itself. It was a deliberate act after the whistle had gone on somebody who was quite unprepared for it, the jury having rejected the defendant's case.

I felt that there was no proper alternative to a period of imprisonment which would be far less than normal for this offence. I thought it should be nine months, appreciating that, in the normal course, one half would actually be served. I believed I had been quite lenient. I therefore did not expect the reaction that came from the rugby world and some of the press. The *Daily Mail* headline was, "Outrage as Devereux goes to Jail". Mike Burton, a former international, talked of his "shock and amazement' and a "Travesty of Justice". The *Daily Mail* said it was "the longest imposed for an on-field violence". This was corrected by Edward Grayson who in a letter to *The Times* referred to an eighteen month sentence. The Gloucester chairman, Alan Brinn, was quoted as saying, "This is the severest sentence I have ever known in such a situation. Never in my wildest dreams did I think it would end like this'. The correspondent Simon Barnes, was quoted as saying that Devereux's place was in the scrum and not in gaol.

I knew an appeal would be made but when it came it was against conviction and not just sentence. However, in giving his judgment, Lord Justice Hobhouse, who later became a Law Lord, said it was "far from being a heavy sentence, particularly after a trial". It was argued by Heaton-Armstrong that I had not directed the jury properly on the question of intent. I was, as always, relieved that the Court of Appeal thought I had got it right.

I want to return to the reaction in both cases about the proceedings. There is a body of opinion that the courts should not be involved in sports cases but that matters should be left to internal investigations and disciplinary tribunals.

However, if they do not operate either at all or inadequately or ineffectively, in my view, the courts, both civil and criminal, must be open to a victim of unlawful violence. In one of the cases I said — to use the phrase which was widely quoted — "The law of the land does not stop at the touch line". It is because other ways should be explored first that I support the work of the Sports Dispute Resolution Panel under its able director, Jon Siddall. It has rules for arbitration, a mediation procedure and rules for an advisory opinion. It began in March 2000 and in its first two years it had forty-eight referrals from fifteen sports. I am sure this is the way forward but the courts must remain available to enforce the law when called upon. The Government later launched an initiative to encourage this.

One other matter about the Devereux case is that, after the appeal failed, as far as I know there was no report about it in the press apart from a mention by Edward Grayson in the *New Law Journal*. I have sometimes wondered what would have been the reaction of the press if the appeal had been allowed and the sentence of imprisonment quashed. However, what they did report extensively and to their credit was that I did say when passing sentence, "Warnings have been given to all sportsmen, where there is physical contact, particularly in rugby football, that unlawful punching cannot be tolerated".

As so often, not least in the law, one thing leads to another, and after these cases I made contact with Roy Manock, a solicitor from Yorkshire who was the disciplinary officer of the RFU and was later to become President. He asked me if I would look at the disciplinary procedures of the RFU. I was pleased to do this and make some comments and suggestions. Next, I was asked to hear an appeal by Dean Ryan of Newcastle and England against an order of suspension for violence. I heard it in the East India and Sports Club and was able to reduce the suspension to twenty-eight days. I wanted to have a look at the video which I saw twice. It was quite short. When I asked what happened to the punch that I saw Dean Ryan throw, I was told that it missed!

I was then asked to deal with an appeal by a number of officials of Oswestry Rugby Football Club who had been fined and banned for various periods from rugby administration. Oswestry was in a league and most anxious to get promotion. Amongst other things, it would help sponsorship. Naturally, they wanted to put out the best team they could. They had a registered player, call him Bloggs, who went to Paris and then, unexpectedly, returned to New Zealand. Some of the Oswestry officials knew of a very talented player, call him Snooks, who had been banned by the Welsh Rugby Union for three years so it must have been for something quite serious. So Oswestry played Snooks and called him Bloggs. I would have thought there was quite a risk in doing this and indeed there was, because in one game somebody recognised Snooks and wondered how he came to be playing for Oswestry! I looked into the parts played by the various officials and made some adjustments to the penalties.

One rather sour note was that an objection was made in writing at the beginning of the hearing that I should not hear the case as I was appointed by the RFU and had spoken to Mr Manock before the hearing and that I was not impartial and had "pre-determined it". I really did get on my high horse. By then, I had been a judge for twenty-five years and my integrity had never before been questioned. It was obvious that I had to speak to Mr Manock, if only for him to find out whether I was prepared to do the case and, if so, where it was to be held, what papers were available and so on. I am glad to say that I did get an apology.

When Roy Manock ended his time at the RFU, I did not do anything further for them. Much depends on personal contact and I was by that time aged seventy-three so I truly was one of what Will Carling, the former England captain, called the "Old Farts"!

I joined the British Association for Sport and Law and have found their meetings and conferences extremely interesting. The topic is growing fast and attracting a considerable number of talented people in the legal profession. I have come to appreciate how much sport and leisure plays in the life of the UK and what enormous sums of money are involved in many ways, not just the funding of such big occasions as the Olympics and the Commonwealth Games but in the marketing of both people and materials. Tiger Woods, the golfer, his Nike baseball cap gives many hours of TV time to advertising that firm. Where to pay the tax of a soccer star playing around the world occupies the time of distinguished firms of accountants. Combatting drugs and bribery are extensive operations, as drugs are often very difficult to detect.

• • •

Since retirement I have continued to be the president of the Law Department of the Kingston College for Further Education. This came about through its Director, David Finch, who asked to stage mock trials in the Kingston Crown court and I agreed to preside. I enjoyed doing this. It was done for real as far as possible. The students got wigs and gowns and played all the parts. The standard of advocacy was high. The age range was wide. Some were mature students trying to become qualified as a legal executive. Others were police officers but mostly they were young. On these occasions I was helped by the chief clerk, Ray Foster and David Finch was helped by his partner, Mary Martin. She taught English at the college and other places and—as "Mia Martin", had been on the stage and in films. Among other things, she was in Miss Marple films and Benny Hill shows. She was able to help the students, many of whom were nervous of being in court, and assist with their elocution so as to be heard properly in a large room without amplification.

I gave the occasional lecture at the College and have interested them in having a course on "Sport and Law". This is done at the Anglia Polytechnic University, Chelmsford; King's College, London and the Manchester Metropolitan University School of Law. I hope it will get off the ground at Kingston and we will be able to involve officials at Twickenham, Crystal Palace and Wimbledon as well as other sports including golf and rowing.

After I was appointed the resident judge, I had to take on a number of extra duties, but when I wanted help I found it was not forthcoming from some of the other judges. They worked hard at their judicial work and that was it. No doubt there were reasons. Some, for example, unlike me, lived a considerable distance away.

I got to know a lot of magistrates and went to their functions both social and training. I thought it was important to have a good relationship with them. They were volunteers from many walks of life who gave up a considerable amount of their time and also they sometimes sat at the Crown Court with a judge, hearing appeals from magistrates' courts. It was particularly important to get on well with the justice's clerks who provided the professional continuity. A lay magistrate would sit, on average, once every ten days in the Greater London area. Returns of sittings had to be sent to the former Lord Chancellor's Department (LCD)[1] and I remember one occasion when I was able to intervene and, I hope, save some ruffled feathers. The LCD had noticed that a Richmond magistrate who was a well-known and respected figure in the town had been sitting rather more than the recommended maximum. He was rather upset because he had told the clerk that he was willing to sit on Saturdays when there were sometimes emergency matters to be dealt with. After all, crime does not stop at the weekend, quite the reverse. I believe I was helpful and I know I spoke with some emphasis!

The same thing happened with a recorder, Frank Whitworth QC, who lived at Westcott near Dorking. He had a distinguished war record and reached the rank of Group Captain in the RAF. He had retired from the Bar and devoted a good deal of his time to looking after his wife who was not in good health. However, he would always help out and sit at Kingston Crown Court at short notice. He and the court were told that he was sitting too often and had exceeded the maximum of fifty days. I saw Tom Legg, the Lord Chancellor's permanent secretary and explained that emergencies did arise. A judge could be taken ill or we needed an extra judge to deal with a case that had been long outstanding. When he started talking about the undesirability of creating a precedent, I got pretty uptight and asked whether it was in the public interest to send everybody in a case away from court, paying fees and expenses or whether it was better to wait a short time before Frank Whitworth arrived.

Before turning to another aspect of my somewhat unsmooth relationship with the LCD, I would like to mention some other matters. The first is that after I became the resident judge, I chaired the Court Users' Committee. I attached considerable importance to this. Its members included representatives of the LCD, the staff, probation, police, HM Prison Service, justices' clerks, the Bar, solicitors and the Citizens' Advice Bureau. The urgent needs were to reduce the backlog of cases and the time that people spent waiting about for cases to come on. I got Ray Foster to present the latest position. I tried to create a good atmosphere of cooperation but I also tried to stop buck passing. I also would explain the difficulties of listing cases. There were always problems when under-estimates of time had been given and other cases were not able to be reached. On the other hand, there were pleas of guilty on the hearing day, a last minute change of mind and witnesses who may have come a long distance were not required. However, many witnesses were relieved when they were told that they did not have to give evidence. I tried to get the Kingston judges to make it clear

---

[1] As noted earlier, the LCD has now become the Department for Constitutional Affairs; but the title Lord Chancellor remains.

to defendants that the earlier they admitted their guilt, the more the sentence would be reduced. Sometimes, it takes a lot of courage to own up to a crime.

I was conscious of the ordeals that witnesses, especially victims of crime, had to go through when they came to court and relived unpleasant and sometimes harrowing experiences. I therefore, gave all the help I could to two organizations, Witness Support and Victim Support. The volunteer workers, as well as their small staffs, really do a valuable and important job.

Having been fascinated by the law from quite an early age, I have been particularly keen that school children and school leavers should know about the courts and how they work. At Kingston, I tried to get groups of youngsters to come to the Crown Court. Some schools responded more than others. I used to ask them to arrive before the court started and I would explain what was going to happen. They would stay for a while and I hoped there would be time afterwards for a question and answer session. I was especially interested in visits from the German school at Petersham which were quite regular. I would start by giving them a short speech in German which I had carefully rehearsed as the court situation was different each time – but I would have the question and answer sessions translated as I did not want there to be any misunderstandings.

This process extended to visits from the "People to People Ambassador Programme". This was an American project founded by President Eisenhower. In 1995, the Honorary Chair was Bill Clinton. It was part of the Educational Cultural Exchange (International) Ltd which was run from nearby Teddington and was concerned with groups of German school leavers who were visiting England to see how it worked. Their visits to Kingston were often on their way to seeing Hampton Court. These and other groups would vary in their level of interest. Some were very lively at question time, others were more negative, perhaps to some extent, due to shyness. I used to tip off the adult in charge to ask the first question and this, very often, set the ball rolling. I was once asked by quite a youngster what I thought of the differences between the German and English systems and to state my preferences! Unfortunately, after some years, these visits stopped and I was told that there were financial difficulties. I do not know if they extended to other European countries but I was sad about this as I thought they were very worth while.

Once, I had to hand over to judge Michael Hucker. He was well able to cope as he had served for some time with the Royal Engineers as a regular soldier. He has had a very successful career in the law. He was called to the Bar when he was aged 37 and after being a judge advocate, assistant recorder and recorder, he was appointed a Circuit Judge. He came to Kingston straightaway and I was glad to have him. I understood the military mind though some, including defendants and barristers, were less enthusiastic! . He quite liked doing long cases which is not everyone's cup of tea but it was useful when we began at Kingston to take more cases from the Old Bailey. I know that, since I retired, he has had some that have lasted for several months. My longest was six weeks which I thought was enough!

I can here conveniently insert a view about jury service which I know is controversial. To serve as a juror is a great interruption of normal life. It is a valuable service at the heart of our system of criminal justice. I believe very strongly that it is of vital importance that a considerable number of people from all walks of life are involved with the courts. That is why I am a strong supporter of lay magistrates. However, I do not think it is right or desirable to ask people to do this, day in and day out, for more than say six weeks or two months. I know that in cases lasting longer than that the courts ask jurors as they are about to take the oath or affirm if they have any representations to make. The self-employed, for example, can be hard hit, but a wife with children and a home to run can have considerable difficulties as well.

I think that the correct balance is for cases that are going to last several months to be tried by a judge accompanied — where there are technical matters — by two people, such as accountants, engineers, doctors or stockbrokers, depending on the nature of the case and the evidence that is going to be called. As now, the judge would deal with legal matters but on the facts the court would have to be unanimous before it could convict.

I have already mentioned the difficulties of the Kingston Crown Court sitting in different locations and it was clearly desirable to have one building. This was on the list of the Lord Chancellor's Department. The difficulty was to find a site that was large enough and in a suitable location for reasonable transport facilities. The Department came up with a building at Tolworth which had been used by the Ordinance Survey where one of our clerks, Joan Prince, had worked. It was opposite the station which had a half hourly service. So one morning I went there with my chief clerk who was either David Beaumont or Barry Macbeth. In one year, I had three but I was very glad when Ray Foster was appointed in 1978. We got on very well and he lasted until he retired in March 2003. He said on my retirement in 1998 that we had been associated for twenty-two years. However, back to Tolworth station, where it had become apparent that the circuit administrator, John Heritage, had missed the train! After a while, I left for court. It was clear that the site was unsuitable and that is not with the benefit of hindsight. I thought it was a waste of time to go there.

A short while later, Harry Woolf visited Kingston for one day in his capacity as one of the High Court Presiding Judges of the South Eastern circuit. He announced my appointment as resident judge. A day or so later, I was walking in the road adjoining County Hall when I saw an official-looking notice attached to a tree. Out of curiosity, I went to read it and it contained a notice of a planning application for office development of the open car park alongside, which was used by those who worked at County Hall. It was fronted by houses. I wrote to Harry urgently as the last day for making representations was Wednesday of the following week. Harry, thank goodness, acted at once and the LCD made an application for a court to be built there. At first, this was for a combined Crown Court and county court with fourteen courtrooms. The county court was not far away and due for renovation. There were objections led by Arthur Figgis, the senior regular judge there. I do not think he liked the prospect of his respectable type of work being contaminated by criminals!

The opposition succeeded and the new proposal was for a Crown Court only, consisting of twelve courtrooms. As things turned out, the renovation of the county court was much more costly than had been estimated owing to the discovery of asbestos. I did not have strong feelings but with the benefit of hindsight it may have been better to have combined the Kingston magistrates' court with the Crown Court. I knew this was explored, certainly to the extent that the magistrates would use some of the Crown Courtrooms but keep their existing building and administration. Unusually, the magistrates' courts were not owned either by the Home Office or by the Lord Chancellor' Department but were leased from the borough and formed the lower part of the Guildhall.

Politically, Kingston was having a ding-dong battle between the Conservatives and the Liberal Democrats. The council changed hands three times. When the planning application for the Crown court was heard, it was opposed by the Liberal Democrats on the ground that the site should be used for some more pressing social need in education or health. Such was the fine balance of the council that a crucial vote was carried by the casting vote of the Conservative mayor. Of course, I kept well out of this, especially with my Liberal past in neighbouring Richmond. The approval was subject to some conditions relating to adjoining houses, and also, that on the site a multi-storey car park had to be built to compensate for the removal of cars from the site where there was room for 700. With some opposition, the houses facing the main road were allowed to be demolished.

I was hugely relieved that it had gone through. The Lord Chancellor's Department was required to contribute to the cost of the new car park. It came to seven million pounds. I clearly understood, and I know that this recollection is shared by others, that the department was going to reserve a number of spaces for the users of the courts. I was quite astonished to learn at a later stage that they had not done so. This caused a number of problems because the car park under the new building was quite small and hardly accommodated the needs of the staff. I know that some magistrates got pretty annoyed, especially as there was some problem with the recovery of their expenses in going to the multi-storey!

The car park had to be built first and it soon became clear that there was trouble with the height of the water level. The only beneficiaries from that were a family of ducks who preferred it to the River Thames! One day, when I was sitting at the High court in The Strand, Barry Macbeth phoned and told me about a meeting that had been arranged about the plans for the new court. When he inquired about my attending, he was rebuffed and told it was not thought to be appropriate. My reaction was one of disappointment and anger. He offered to go back and make further representations. I may have made a mistake because I suggested that he need not take the matter further. I had hoped that the court users would be taken on hoard at the earliest stage and make a useful contribution from their experience. I did appreciate, however, that my enforced presence might create a bad atmosphere. This attitude continued and when the senior presiding judge, Lord Justice Auld, visited Kingston about a year before the courts opened, his request to see the new building was refused on the ground that it would interfere with the construction work. Strong representations were made behind the scenes and the visit took place.

I had sat in many courts and I was helped by being invited to Maidstone Crown Court which had recently been opened by the Queen who came up the River Medway in a special barge, something that Kingston was not able to repeat. The resident judge was Felix Waley QC who was also judge Advocate of the Fleet. He just missed being a senior circuit judge as Maidstone only had eleven courts and the qualifying number is twelve. He died in harness in 1995 , far too young at the age of sixty-eight. The Temple Church was crowded for his memorial service,

I went to Maidstone with the courts administrator for the group that included Kingston. He was Peter Thomas who had many years of service in the department and apart from Ray Foster and the staff and judges at Kingston he was my greatest help and supporter. I am sorry to say that the further up the line I tried to go, the less help I got. In fact, I never met the architect, who I understand had not designed a courthouse before. It is not an easy thing to do. Various groups of people have to be kept separate such as jurors and witnesses and there have to be effective security provisions for defendants, especially those who are in custody, some of whom may represent a high risk of escape.

I tried to get the message across that I did not like the design at Canbury Park, which was repeated at Maidstone, of having internal courtrooms with only artificial light. In this, I succeeded to the extent that the majority of the Kingston courts have an outlook. At first one could see both in and out but this was changed. However, it is not wise to open the windows as this interferes with the air conditioning. When plans did appear, Judge Ken Macrae and the Chief Clerk in particular were very helpful in going through them in detail and putting a number of points to me. One thing that stood out was that there were courtrooms on each of three floors but all the judges' rooms were at the top of the building. This was quite daft. If a judge on the ground floor had to adjourn for a few minutes he had nowhere to go and if he wanted a book from his room, it would take a long time to get. I half-succeeded in getting this put right. In the revised plans, six of the twelve courtroms each had a smaller room attached to it for the judge—while the other six had recesses with some basic furniture which was at least some improvement.

The courts had no galleries and I thought the facilities for the public and the press were inadequate. A number of rooms had to be relocated so that defence witnesses did not have to pass by the police rooms, while more rooms had to be provided for interviews by the probation service as well as the lawyers. I was very disappointed at the proposals for the Bar and I tried to improve them. I will not go into more details except that it really was quite a battle and in trying to get my suggestions considered at headquarters level, I did feel that the Lord Chancellor's Department was not on our side. They had their plans and were reluctant to make any changes. I will, however, refer to one other incident.

It occurred when the building was quite far advanced. I was invited to go to Court 1 and sit in the judge's chair. When I did, I could only see ten of the jurors! I said that this would have to be altered. I was told that the design complied with "Teddington Standards". Apparently, there was a mock up court at Teddington. I knew nothing about it and said that no judge could sit in a Crown court without being able to see all the jury. I was not going to give way. I would have refused to sit in that court. I do not know what happened after I left the meeting but I am sure that Ray Foster knew what was at stake. Anyway, the necessary alterations were made and the matter put right.

The next significant development was at a later stage when I made enquiries about a Foundation Stone. I remembered going to the ceremony when this was laid by the mayor at Guildford. It was a way of linking the town officially and permanently with the court. It was a worthwhile public relations exercise that created goodwill. However, I was told that at Kingston there was no provision for this and that it was too late to incorporate one. I failed to understand how it was not possible to incorporate a stone in a suitable place whether inside or on the outside of the building. I did what I could but the brick wall of opposition would not come down.

So we decided ourselves to have a Time Capsule and bury a number of items on 26th March, 1995 to be opened in sixty years time. I hope that the clear instructions where it is will be safely kept! It is buried outside the front entrance and probably trodden on by a hundred or so people each working day. Barry Macbeth and Ray Foster thoroughly enjoyed doing this which provided some light relief from their arduous and sometimes worrying duties. I have got a copy of the schedule of contents. I am not going to set out all the details, but they include photos of the judiciary and staff with identifications and pen pictures; a note of pay scales for each staff grade, various court papers, diaries, minutes, copies of magazines, the Charter for Court Users and best practice guide for CREST computer system. I do hope that when all this is opened up, it will be well preserved and provide some interesting material for a legal historian.

At one time, it was thought that the building would open in 1985. This proved to be wildly optimistic. There were still some difficulties in 1990 about the acquisition of the site. Work began in 1994 and there were, I suppose inevitably, a number of snags, some of which I have mentioned. One which went on for a long time concerned jurors and the risk of "contamination", namely being in the vicinity of others and chance remarks being overheard. There was also the risk of intimidation. This was still an issue in 1996 when Ray Foster, with my agreement, put forward a proposal of a corridor for the use of jurors from their reception area. By this time, the framework of the building had been completed and I performed the Topping Out Ceremony on 12th May, 1995. I was presented with a trowel which I used and, more important, I had an opportunity of meeting a number of the workforce of the main contractor, Kyle Stewart. I did want to show that I was interested in what they had done and that I was not just a remote figure living in his own ivory tower. I was glad that the chair of the Surrey County Council, Cecilia Gerrard, came along from County Hall next door and also the mayor of Kingston. I felt it was important to retain good relations with them.

When the building was nearing completion, the judges were consulted about the furnishing of their rooms which was not too difficult except that there did not seem to be an awareness to provide anything like enough shelf-space for books. The law reports and textbooks take up a lot of room. I know that I provided some book cases myself, one of which I left behind when I retired!

I was also concerned with a number of practical matters in the courtrooms themselves. For example, in none of them was there any amplification. When I raised this, I was told that with modern design and materials there was a degree of resonance that did not need amplification. The courts were of three different sizes. I did some tests myself. It was obvious that a lot of volume was lost owing to the size of the rooms, even the smallest, and the distances between the speakers. I was particularly interested in what could be heard by the back row of the jury from the witness box. I explained how people tend to lower their voices when speaking of some unfortunate experience. I did not want the judges to have to keep on interrupting and telling witnesses they had to speak louder. Again, a compromise was achieved. There would be hand microphones available when required. This needed working out in advance and with some tact. On the whole, it worked well but a permanent system would have been preferable and I doubt whether it would have been very costly in proportion to what was being spent. The courts were finally opened in April, 1997. It was a big operation. Canbury Park Road, County Hall and Surbiton, all had to close and then, the new courts would open with the minimum of delay. The staff were magnificent and had to learn how to get round the building which was complicated, as various parts were self-contained. The clerks had most legwork to do, going from their rooms to the courts. There were various lifts but they did not go to all the floors.

I think it took a week before we restarted court business proper. One of the clerks who sat with me quite regularly, Pippa Westing (now Lindley), had a pedometer for one day and walked over three miles!

Just before the move, the Surrey County council and the court, gave a Farewell Dinner in County Hall. The chair of the council was Baroness Thomas of Wallisford whom I had known as an active Liberal in Richmond. At that time, the council did not have a party government but all three parties held different offices and I believe it worked quite well. It did not last long as the Conservatives regained their majority, rather against the national trend.

The Lord Chancellor, Lord Mackay, came and he, like others, much enjoyed the tour of the new building before the dinner. He had been to Kingston before. He came for the centenary of the courts at County Hall in 1993. He was extremely good on both occasions at meeting a lot of people especially the staff, and asking them about their work. At the farewell dinner, I had one unexpected experience. I understood that Lord Mackay was reputed to be a staunch teetotaller so I asked the catering manager to put a bottle of Highland Spring water in front of him. He comes from Sutherland in the Highlands of Scotland. When we sat down after grace, I explained what I had done and to my astonishment, he turned to me and said, "I think I'll have a glass of white wine!" So much for tactful gestures! It was a good occasion as the new building is really very impressive and everybody was in a cheerful mood at dinner, despite the ending of the long association with County Hall and the council. I had done my best to foster good relations and I was pleased when, in 1986, I was made a Deputy Lieutenant of the county. The Deputy is sometimes required to attend a function in place of the Lord Lieutenant but I was not called on at first as I was working and after that because I was too old!

Two things happened before the royal opening in November 1997 which I thought were very curious. I am not sure whether it was Ray Foster or I who found out that the royal arms were not going to be displayed on the outside of the building but only inside the court building itself. I thought this was quite unheard of. I therefore wrote to Lord Mackay and was told that the decision was made because the building was not built by the government but by using an agency, so it was not a government building! I was just not content with this so after the General Election in 1997 with its overwhelming New Labour majority, I wrote to the new Lord Chancellor, Lord Irvine of Lairg. He was then an unknown quantity and I am glad to say that in a letter to me of 5th June, he reversed the decision. A great effort was made to find what was required and I am glad to say it was done fairly quickly and the arms look very impressive above the front entrance.

So that was one victory but on the other, I failed completely. I found out that there was not going to be any flagpole. This time, no Lord Chancellor was involved but every suggestion that was made was blocked. If it were put on the roof, there was a danger of it falling down from the strength of the wind (not inside the building!); if it were to hang at an angle over the front, it might fall down and was therefore, a potential danger to passers-by; if a pole were to be erected at the front, it would affect the aspect of the building and as it was listed this would require the approval of the Fine Arts Commission. This all took time and in the end, no flagpole was ever erected. In my retirement speech I did ask that, if ever a flagpole did arrive, I might raise the flag for the first time!

During the summer of 1997, three evenings were available for the public to view the courts. A good number of people came along and we particularly tried to go beyond those who would be using the courts professionally. There were of course, a number of lawyers. I was very glad that Harry Woolf was among them. One thing we did want to show were the facilities for hi-tech presentation, with screens for presenting evidence – and also to give out information about court proceedings and our ability to take evidence from abroad by satellite. With all this and more, we did feel we were on the modern map. Including the original amount of seven million pounds for the car park and other building matters, the total cost was thirty-six million pounds which I remember as being three million pounds per courtroom.

Gradually, things began to settle down. I had already thought about an official Royal opening, Kingston being a royal borough. I hoped that the Queen herself would come as she had done at Maidstone. I asked about the proper procedure and after a number of enquiries it seemed to be down to me to make the initial approach – although the official request would have to come from the Lord Chancellor's Department. So, I corresponded with the Secretary at Buckingham Palace, Sir Robert Fellowes, now a life peer. He was very courteous and in view of the Queen's heavy programme in June and July the invitation was put by until the autumn. However, it could not be fitted in, but we were extremely lucky in getting the Princess Royal on the 10th November, 1997. She was with us in between other engagements for the day for exactly an hour and a quarter.

The preparations, though, took many hours of careful and detailed planning by a committee which I chaired. The whole programme had to be worked out so that everybody knew exactly what to do. The first problem was the order in which distinguished guests had to be greeted. Research had to be done on whether, as was claimed, the first citizen of the royal borough, i.e. the mayor, preceded the High Sheriff of Greater London. She did not and was very nice about it!

There was no doubt that the Princess was to be received by the Kingston Representative Deputy Lieutenant for Greater London, who was the broadcaster, David Jacobs. He was helpful throughout on the day itself. He made some introduction to HRH who then came to me. I had to explain that I would be making some more introductions and she, being very well briefed, said, "This is your patch". She was presented with a bouquet and I then asked her to unveil a plaque. She gave quite a tug and all went well. I then had to take her down the building to Court Two. The others had to go to Court One alongside and get to their allotted places. The two of us were led by an usher, Sheilah Dee—and here the press missed a story. Sheilah walked in a very correct and dignified way, though not overdoing it. She had been on the stage and had been a dancer in the Black and White Minstrel Show which ran for a long time at the Victoria Palace. It was very popular on television, not least when Leslie Crowther was in it. It would probably not be considered politically correct now. Before that Sheilah had been a dancer and a Windmill Girl but she was fully and correctly dressed on this occasion!

When Her Royal Highness and I got to Court Two, I explained that all the screens were because a case concerning a child was being heard. The child would give evidence by video link from another room with only one other person present who would be looking after him or her and was trained for this class of work. Before I knew what was happening, the Princess had got up into the judge's chair and asked me how it worked. It is a bit complicated—who can see what and who on the various screens—but I did my best and she picked it up very quickly. In a way, I was glad of the interlude because I knew it would take a bit longer before everybody sorted themselves out in Court One. I explained that I had to put the child at ease so that he or she could give evidence clearly. I said that it was my practice and that of many other judges, to remove their wigs and counsel, their gowns also. I explained that this does not always work as I once dealt with a child aged eight and when I saw the person looking after him afterwards, and mentioned that he had seemed very coherent and confident, she told me that when it was all over he had asked if I was "a proper judge". He then explained that I did not look like the ones he had seen on TV. The Princess enjoyed this and laughingly said that one could never win with children!

We then went into Court One and. after I had asked the Vicar of Kingston Parish Church, Jim Bates, to offer a prayer, we all sat down and Michael Lawson QC, the leader of the South Eastern Circuit and now a circuit judge, made a first-class speech, striking the right note of welcome balanced by tributes to those who had done the work in creating the court. The Princess Royal replied and was not in the least outshone. She had a few notes on a small piece of paper. I cannot say it was the back of an envelope but it could have been. I watched closely and I do not think she referred to it once. She showed her knowledge of the work of the courts and her own work with charities such as the Butler Trust which helps families of prisoners. She was very practical and straightforward. After that, the court rose. She walked down the corridor and talked easily to a large number of people, mostly the staff. When she got to the end, she said goodbye to David

Jacobs and myself, threw the bouquet into the back of the car and drove herself off to her next engagement in Westminster.

The rest of us went upstairs for a party. I cut a cake and David Jacobs very generously proposed my health coupled with the success of the new building. It was a memorable day.

• • •

My last official day came on 3rd April, 1998. I had quite a short list of cases. My last was to sentence a paedophile. I am not going into the circumstances for the sake of the relatives but I had to pass the longest sentence in my career which was fifteen years plus being put on the sex offenders register for life. This was upheld by the Court of Appeal. I then adjourned in a rather emotional state.

I was then told that there was another matter in my list. I think that my clerk, Pippa Westing, said this with a wry smile. One of the presiding judges of the circuit, Mr Justice Gage (now Lord Justice), arrived and when we went into court it was crowded. Joy and my daughter, Jenny, were there together with Desmond de Silva QC and Herendra de Silva QC from my old chambers and the clerk, Robin Driscoll and very many others. Mr Justice Gage was very kind about me as were Georges Khayat QC who spoke on behalf of the Bar in the absence of the circuit leader, Michael Lawson QC who took the trouble to send a message. Ray Foster spoke on behalf of the staff with many amusing cricket illusions. I replied in the spirit of the late and much loved Harry Secombe who once said, "The old look backward; the young look forward and the middle aged look round". I was able to do all three, especially the latter, as the new building with which I had been so much involved had been open almost exactly a year. We had a good party afterwards and I was presented with a telephone-cum-fax machine so as to be able to keep in touch!

I did not want to retire but I had gone on to the end, namely, the anniversary of my appointment after I had reached the age of seventy-two. When an official of the Lord Chancellor's Department came to see me shortly before I retired, I asked about sitting part-time as I knew this had been done for some judges. I appreciated that it was a matter of discretion and not entitlement. I was told that this would be against policy as the retiring age had been reduced to seventy for Circuit Judges. Incidentally, at the same time, the pensions provisions were altered so that to qualify for a full pension, a judge had to serve for twenty years and not fifteen. It was not retrospective but the resident judges of the South Eastern circuit at a meeting at which I was present, expressed a strong view against this, as did the other circuits. The Lord Chief Justice, Peter Taylor, saw the Lord Chancellor, Lord Mackay, speeches were made in the House of Lords, but nothing changed. The practical effect was to have judges appointed five years earlier which robbed them of their maximum earning years at the Bar or as solicitors.

However, the door could not be shut on me so I applied direct to Lord Irvine to sit part-time for another year. I was pleased that he agreed to this. He has not exactly been the most popular of Lord Chancellors, but he did show over this, that he was his own man. In due course, he extended me for another year and I sat in court on the last working day before I was seventy-five at which time, I knew, I was senile by Act of Parliament!

During the two years that I was sitting part-time, I had two very different assignments which I am glad I undertook. The first of these began in March 1999 when I got a letter from the chief executive of the Surrey County Council, Paul Coen, asking if I would chair an independent panel to report to the council on members' allowances and to make recommendations. Quite properly, the members thought they should not do this themselves especially if they proposed and voted for significant increases!

I agreed to do this and had two colleagues, Liz Hewitt, a director of 3i and a former vice-chair of the Surrey Police Authority, and Colin Harris who was the regulator for the Mortgage Code of Practice and had held a number of appointments concerning financial services. We got on well together and were most competently served by John Quinton, the committee services manager and Peter Edwards, head of committees and member services of Surrey County Council. They provided us with a lot of background material and the results of inquiries by other authorities. The legislative background was that in 1995, new regulations removed the limit on the overall amount that authorities could spend on their allowances scheme The political background was that the county authorities as well as metropolitan ones were large organizations that were responsible for a wide range of public services. Surrey had a budget of over six hundred and fifty million pounds and a staff of some twenty-four thousand. It had seventy-six councillors and it was not easy—and many would say, not desirable–to find and rely on people who had the time and the money to come forward and serve the community in this way without payment.

The second assignment started in December, 1999 with a letter from Mr A. Wallace, the head of the International Division of the Lord Chancellor's Department which said that the High Commissioner in Guyana was looking for retired judges to sit in that country. There was a serious backlog of cases and it was suggested that there should be a review of High Court Procedure, and the production of a training manual. I was asked if I was interested. It was also suggested that at least one judge should sit from the beginning of 2000 to the end of the legal year in June. No fees would be payable but air fares would be met "and generous sums for living and accommodation costs are available including a one-week holiday in Miami".

I replied expressing surprise that no fees were offered and added, "In my experience, especially, if I may say so, with the LCD, expenses allowed, leave one out of pocket". I asked if a shorter period could be envisaged and some payment made, "perhaps on the basis of what would be paid to a part-time judge in Guyana". So, negotiations began and I got a call from Georgetown from the High Commissioner's wife, Audrey Glover, from whom I learned a lot. She was pretty high-powered. A member of Gray's Inn, since 1998, she had been the Leader of the UK delegation to the UN Human Rights Commission in Geneva with the rank of ambassador. This call was followed by an informative letter from the High Commissioner, Edward Glover, who had been in Guyana since 1998. It was his last post and he retired in 2002. It was clear that he was devoted to the concept of human rights and was keen to act as the link with the UK in helping

Guyana to build up politically and economically. In addition to judicial reform, he had introduced inquiries into police and prison reform which were ongoing. He had been successful in getting some funding. The judicial reform project was supported by the Foreign and Commonwealth Office (FCO) under the Human Rights Project Fund.

I was somewhat hesitant to sit in court or even to act as a mediator or arbitrator in a country I did not know. I appreciate that the legal system was English in origin but no country is a carbon copy of another and in my view, as perhaps has already become apparent, judges are part of a team that has to work together.

I was then asked to go with Esyr Lewis QC to the FCO to meet Edward Glover and others in the South American section. I knew Esyr. He was a bencher of Gray's Inn and Treasurer in 1997. He had been the senior Official Referee (OR) from 1994 to 1998. The title has been abolished. It is not easy to understand but basically, the ORs, as they were called, dealt with building work. Their new name is the Technology and Construction Court. Esyr had fought Llanelli as a Liberal in the General Election of 1964 but I found him to be very much a lawyers' lawyer which was his great interest in life. When we went to the FCO, we thought we could best help by examining the legal system in Guyana and making recommendations for changes based on our combined experience and also by producing the training manual that had been asked for. I felt I could make a useful contribution as a result of what I had done as the resident judge at Kingston which did include, as I have already mentioned, trying to tackle a serious backlog of cases. I also felt that I could help with the family work. This would leave Esyr to concentrate on the civil side which he knew well, especially court procedure and the way that our system worked.

There was quite an argument about payment, but with Edward Glover helpfully mediating and understanding our point of view, we were able to agree satisfactory terms. At one time, there was rather an undignified squabble about if we were to be paid a daily fee whether this would include Saturdays and Sundays. I only wished my old clerk, Walter Butler, could have taken this over, It is not always easy to speak up for oneself without, perhaps, giving an exaggerated view of one's importance.

One interesting thing was that the FCO seemed reluctant for Esyr and I to visit the Guyanan High Commissioner in London. We were keen to do this and find out something more about the country, its leading personalities and the workings of their legal system. Anyway, we made an appointment to see him and he and a barrister who also attended, were most helpful.

The main conclusion of our meetings was that Esyr and I were not going to be attached to the Guyana judiciary. So we set off. The plane went to Barbados where we had to check out and then come in again immediately. There did not seem to be any procedure to cope with those in transit. I missed a trick here although it would have meant disturbing the arrangements, which is never easy. I had a former pupil, David Patrick, who I know would have liked to see me but I did not get in touch with him.

When Esyr and I arrived in Georgetown, we were taken to the Cara Lodge Hotel. It was an interesting building dating from the eighteen-forties with rooms on two storeys that had long verandahs. It had been the home of the mayor and then a cultural centre. With the restaurant downstairs, to which people regularly came and with a friendly and helpful staff, we were made comfortable. After we arrived and settled in, Esyr and I went for a short walk up to the seawall. I was disappointed as there was rather a lot of mud and no Atlantic breakers. Anyway we felt better for it but when we met Edward Glover later in the day he was horrified at what we had done. He asked us not to go out alone again as there was a real risk of getting mugged. Like a number of cities, especially where there is poverty, Georgetown had an unlawful, violent element.

Edward and Audrey Glover were extremely good, not just inviting us to their home and letting us use the swimming pool but arranging dinner parties, receptions and meetings. We soon met the judges, the High Court Registrar, some of the magistrates, the Bar and indeed the Prime Minister and a number of other political figures. There was a lot of interest in us and what we had come to do. On the judicial side, we had most to do with the Chief Justice, Désirée Bernard and Mr Justice Carl Singh. Désirée was quite exceptional. She was not of Indian origin like many of the other judges and there were not many other women who made it to the bench. Carl was also dedicated to the job and got to understand and use modern technology (at the time the judges took down all the evidence in longhand). He kindly took us out into the country over a weekend where, amongst other things, we went to a sugar factory. Our assessment of these two judges proved correct because after we left, Désirée became the Chancellor, who is the head of the judiciary and Carl succeeded her as Chief Justice.

It soon became apparent that there was an acute shortage of judges. They were below complement by three or four and the shortage of magistrates was far worse, at just over a half of the establishment. One thing that disturbed us was the ease with which the judiciary could return to private practice. Generally speaking this does not occur in England. Guyana, which is the only English speaking country in South America, then had a total estimated population of 835,000 of whom 250,000 lived in Georgetown. The next largest town, Linden, had 35,000 inhabitants so it is not surprising that a large proportion of the legal profession knew each other.

We were much helped, throughout our visit and indeed, afterwards by Sandra Seenan, the Press and Public Affairs Officer at the British High Commission, who was described as our "resource person". In a letter to me before we left England, she explained that the legal profession in Guyana was "fused" in 1980 and all legal practitioners were known as "Attorneys-at-Law". We were also helped by Miles Fitzpatrick, a recent president of what was still called the Bar Association. He had been a judge for a short time and was dismissed by then President Cheddi Jagan for not giving decisions conforming to the socialist principles of the country. Miles had a considerable practice and appeared in a number of cases when Esyr and I went to court. He entertained us at his house and had another house in England. He was a lover of classical music and used to like to visit England during the summer and go to the Albert Hall for the Promenade Concerts. One day, I hope to see him there!

It was when we went to the Registry that we began to appreciate more of the practical problems. The registrar, called Sita, saw us a number of times although she was grossly overworked. She had no deputy though one was required by the High Court Act. She was also the accounting officer for the courts and oversaw the work of the Marshal regarding the levying of execution for debt. We were dismayed to learn that the pay of the staff was well below that of office workers generally. It was not surprising that there were vacancies and a high turnover. There were suggestions of corruption regarding missing files, but there was no evidence to support them.

It was a better picture when we went to the divorce court. I do not know what Esyr's experience was, but for me it was a trip down memory lane. There seemed to have been no reforms of law and practice since Guyana became independent in 1966. There was a long list of undefended petitions and evidence was heard orally, exactly as I had known it done. The court was run with considerable efficiency and petitioners were sympathetically listened to by Mr Justice Roy. From what we could tell, there did not seem to be any undue delay in the hearing of cases. It would be a major step to modernise the procedure along English lines but there are more urgent things to do.

I was particularly saddened to learn of the extraordinary lengths of time that some people had been on remand in custody awaiting trial, sometimes for several years, far longer than the sentences they were likely to receive. We saw the co-director of the Human Rights Association and got a list of those who had been in custody for more than three years. I got it circulated and spoke very strongly about it in a television interview. I think that Esyr thought I was not being judicial but I do feel that there are times when one has to speak out.

Esyr and I worked in different ways. He got a computer, I think from the hotel but, wherever he got it from, it used to play up and his progress was slow. Also, in the civil procedure, he had to examine quite complicated matters which meant a good deal of painstaking detail. I had a broader brush. I would take notes and go through them when back in the hotel. I did not have access to a typewriter and am not computer literate in any case so I would write up my notes and then show them to Esyr. Fortunately, we worked well together and when we had finalised a draft it would be typed up through Sandra Seenan. I wanted to do this quickly while my impressions were fresh. Esyr would then show me his work. Again we got on well but it was obvious that my task was going to be completed before his. So I then got down to writing a draft of the training manual. I pitched it high because of the important role of any judge to maintain the rule of law. While I made references to what happens in England, I did say, "One has to stand back and consider what is suitable for Guyana. We are not here just to advocate a reproduction of what happens in England." I dealt with a number of matters including initial training before appointment, refresher courses, keeping up to date individually, keeping order in court and the relationships between the judges, the attorneys and the court staff. This is not the place to go into detail but I hope that this and the whole report which, thanks to Esyr, was very comprehensive, was of some practical help.

I left after five weeks. Esyr and I agreed the report and he stayed behind to do the hard job of putting it into a coherent shape.

The difficulty was that a number of the proposals required money. I have not mentioned the court buildings, for example. A general election was going to take place in the following year. The report was not released-for fourteen months which was subject to a very strong editorial in a local newspaper that pointed out that there were some things that could have been implemented without any extra cost.

I believe that the report was well received. I met Désirée Bernard when she visited London in 2002. Esyr kindly, arranged a lunch in Gray's Inn and clearly, she and Carl Singh are doing all they can to improve things. Some judges are going to come to England for a training course and I have tried to help in getting some more books for the law libraries. They are in great need of restocking. So, I was glad I went and saw something of what went on in a Third World country which has a determination to improve its quality of life. There were some diversions including a two-and-a-half day Test Match between the West Indies and Pakistan which was drawn owing to rain—as frequently happens in Georgetown.

I enjoyed the extra two years. I was told how many days in the year I was eligible to sit and if I exceeded that number I would not be paid! I waited to see what would happen. I did not put any restriction on where I would sit except that I thought it was right not to sit at Kingston except in a real emergency. My successor as resident judge was Charles Tilling QC who came from Croydon. He might want to make some changes and would not want me breathing down his neck though he was very kind and said I was always welcome. In any event, I thought I would like some changes of scenery.

What was revealed was a considerable shortage in several parts of the country. My phone was very busy. I was in the garden when Joy came out and said it was Lucy from Stoke. I said what any chap would say in such circumstances, "I do not know any Lucy from Stoke". It turned out that she was the courts' administrator and wanted me to sit urgently in various places. I settled for Worcester where Joy and I had good friends, Betty and Jack Travers, so we went there for a fortnight and Joy was well looked after, being taken to several trips in glorious countryside. I was sorry it was not the cricket season as the county ground below the cathedral always looks so attractive—except when it is flooded!

I went quite a lot to Isleworth—known as "Terminal 5" as it does so many drugs and other cases from Heathrow. Sentences had to be severe for those acting as drugs couriers, although some of the people doing it were poor and acting out of desperation to get some money and sometimes acting under pressure. Often, they used dangerous methods such as swallowing contraceptives containing drugs. They knew what they were doing and the high risks they were taking if they were caught.

HM Customs obviously acted on tip offs—and also on suspicion. Some flights were subject to particularly detailed searches and questioning of passengers. It is difficult to know the percentage of success and Customs have a difficult job of detection to do. I once asked a couple of customs officers why they had stopped two men at Heathrow whom they, quite properly, believed to be involved in smuggling heroin instead of following them to see where they went which would enable them to discover and break the next link in the chain. They told me that they had tried that with some others, the previous week, believing them to be going to a certain hotel which they were watching. Unfortunately, they lost the men in the traffic to London so they escaped and no arrests were made. I suppose it has to be the old story of "the bird in the hand".

I went back to my home town of Plymouth and also visited Exeter where I enjoyed going to evensong in the cathedral and where I completed my last case. This concerned a man who I will call Hyde. It is such a remarkable story that it deserves a book in itself, but here,I can only give a summary.

Hyde was highly intelligent and a one time high flyer in local government. At about thirty, he became the youngest chief executive in the country. Unfortunately, he got involved in no fewer than sixteen civil actions up and down the country. They concerned a variety of matters: disputes with neighbours, the running of a school and planning applications were among them. His activities were unsuccessful to the extent that he was adjudicated bankrupt. In 1996, he was first interviewed about matters that led to his trial on charges of making false representations to insurance companies arising from alleged thefts and burglaries of which Hyde was the victim. He made a number of applications about documents held by the Official Receiver.

Once the trial was fixed for 20th July, 1998, there was a succession of applications to adjourn, on various grounds, by which time, Hyde had had four counsel acting for him in succession. The applications included matters of documentation and the state of the defendant's health. One way and another, the defendant succeeded in getting the matter put back until December, 1998 but this was adjourned as a result of a letter from a cardiologist. The case was put back further until March, 1999 and then, until September.

Hyde had appeared before many judges who sat at Exeter but in 1999 he was due to appear before me which I think was appropriate in that I had had nothing to do with the case previously. The prosecution case was that the alleged thefts and burglaries had never taken place. Police suspicions were confirmed when the Trustee in Bankruptcy carried out a thorough search of his house. When they came to a desk, they found a diamond and sapphire ring valued at about £10,000 which had featured in one of the claims. There was another charge of making false representations to obtain a mortgage from a building society. In this, a man called Warren was on the face of it involved, but the prosecution case was that he never existed and was invented by Hyde. One of the grounds for an adjournment had been that there was difficulty in contacting Warren and that he had gone to New Zealand.

On the day of the trial, Hyde who had been on bail, arrived at court but complained of chest pains so he got in a waiting taxi and went off to the local hospital. One difficulty was that the doctors there did not know anything about him so they had to be careful and conduct an examination though in all probability they did not know what a litigant Hyde had been. In view of the history of repeated adjournments, I granted a warrant for his arrest to be executed on his discharge from hospital. He was to remain in custody until he could be brought to court. He was discharged the next day but a most unfortunate development occurred which I inquired into as I was dissatisfied with what had happened. A police officer with warrant was at the hospital or at least on call, but when Hyde was discharged he was not told about it. Hyde was met by a car which he got into and then disappeared. He kept in touch with his solicitors and wrote a letter to me after the first hearing day questioning some of the points that had been made. I believe that members of his family were in court throughout the proceedings.

When Hyde did not appear later in September, I allowed an application by the prosecutor to proceed in his absence. I thought the nettle had to be grasped and I had no difficulty in finding that the absence of the defendant was wilful. I knew that it was inevitable that my decision would be challenged in the Court of Appeal and so it turned out, but I will touch on that in a moment. The defendant was represented by Stanley Best, a very experienced counsel who, like me, had been a solicitor before going to the Bar. He writes frequently on legal matters, not least in letters to *The Times*. He defended with great skill and I paid tribute to him but that was not the view of the defendant. He made a complaint about him to the Bar Council and also complained to the Law Society about his instructing solicitors. In fact, at an early stage of the trial Hyde tried to sack them — but very properly they continued to act for him in the public interest. I, also, did not want an absent defendent to be unrepresented. The defence did call a witness but it was not Mr Warren. In fact, staff of a building society said that when money was collected from them by Mr Warren, the man was the defendant. I had to give the jury a careful direction about identification evidence and the possibilities of mistake.

Despite all the efforts of Stanley Best, he faced what the court of Appeal described as "overwhelming lay and expert evidence" on the crucial issue of the existence of Mr Warren. The jury convicted on all five counts. I adjourned the case until October in the hope that the defendant would either be arrested or give himself up, but neither happened. So I sentenced him to a total of three years imprisonment. The search for him continued and it became quite a big operation. There were a number of reported sightings. He was reported in the press as having been known to wear women's clothing which, if he did, presumably made detection more difficult. He was caught on camera in Bournemouth when he walked into the Bristol and West Building Society to withdraw money and the staff became suspicious but he walked out and got in a car.

He was not traced until December, 1999. He was in hospital in Bristol under an assumed name and was recognised by a very keen-eyed nurse from a press photograph. He had a triple by-pass heart operation. The police were called and, subject to his medical condition, he began to serve his sentence.

When he went to the Court of Appeal, a number of matters were argued on his behalf, not by Stanley Best but by John Davis. He suggested that Stanley Best should have withdrawn from the trial when he was sacked and that his failure to do so was detrimental to the defendant. A more interesting point and as far as I know, a novel one, was that there had been a breach of Article 6(3) (d) of the European Convention of Human Rights, now incorporated into our law. This states:

Everyone charged with a criminal offence has the following minimum rights:
(d) to examine and have examined witnesses against him and to obtain the attendance
and examination on his behalf under the same conditions as witnesses against him.

Both these submissions failed and the Court of Appeal emphasised that the
defendant's solicitors were in daily contact with the defendant and "he
continued to provide instructions".

There were other complaints about photographic evidence and pre-trial
publicity which were also rejected and his application for leave to appeal against
sentence was also dismissed.

I heaved quite a sigh of relief at this because it is a very unusual thing to try
and sentence a man in his absence. The judges at Exeter and other places were
also relieved as they had had a number of difficult experiences with Hyde over a
number of years. But it was not the end for me. I eventually saw him for the first
time at the Plymouth Crown Court in March 2000. He had been brought from
prison. He was not represented and I had quite a tussle with him in trying to
explain that he would have to come before me to show whether he had any
reasonable cause for not appearing at his trial. There were continued health
problems and he did not appear again until November 2000, at Exeter. He had
yet another counsel, David Osbourne, who had been briefed at the last moment.
Hyde wished to challenge the accuracy of the police records—I think the ones
about the alleged sightings of him—and also to raise again the question of
documents and other matters on why he would not get a fair trial. I could have
taken a stern view and said that I could not see, whatever complaints he thought
he had, how this could justify him not turning up at his trial. I believe this would
have led to an immediate appeal.

I adjourned the court and the prosecution took the view after some
consideration that enough time and money had been spent on this and in view of
the sentence that was being served, did not wish to press the matter further. With
some reluctance, I agreed and so the matter finally ended as far as I was
concerned. It was also the end of my career on the bench, somewhat of an anti-
climax, though I did enjoy going to Exeter again.

Just previously, I had my very last sitting at Kingston which caused some
amusement as I had officially retired from there over two years previously. I was
given a final, final farewell and Ray Foster again made a very amusing speech.

So I was a circuit judge from March 1973 to November 2000. I have often
been asked if I miss it and of course I do as it has been a significant part of my
life. I have also been asked if I enjoyed it and the answer is again "Yes"—in the
sense that it gave me great satisfaction and a sense of fulfilment, not just the
hours in court but the work that went with it. Though there were anxious
moments, especially about sentencing, I felt that I could do the job.

I was lucky to be at Kingston for so long and to see what is a splendid
building up and working, and also to have a most loyal staff. I think I can go
along with Lord Denning and say, "He's got the best job". So, I am going to end
with 'Baker's last case'. I could say something about retirement and some of the
things I have done but that is another story!

Index